Richard Flood   Notes from the Playground

Richard Flood
Notes from the Playground

Ridinghouse

This book is dedicated to Kynaston McShine

Foreword by Philippe Vergne

One of Us

If I were to tell you the story of a man who fell off a kayak in the Boundary Waters of Minnesota, minutes before he set his friend's cabin on fire, with his own belongings in the middle of it all, you might plausibly think that I was overly elaborating on some incidents in this man's life. This is too much of a Keatonesque or Coen Brothers–like series of events. Or, you might tell me that I have spent too much time with Richard Prince's joke:

> *Fireman pulling drunk out of a burning bed*: You darned fool, that'll teach you to smoke in bed.
> *Drunk*: I wasn't smoking in bed, it was on fire when I laid down.

Thankfully for my friend, the lake was not on fire ... but thankfully for the story, the rest is all true.

Life, at times, can be better than fiction, if your attitude toward life is aimed at crystallizing, in a Stendhalian move, the beauty, the serendipity, the horror, the conflicts, the elegy of your everyday stumbles. It is a fair and charming paradox that my friend who fell into the open waters is named Richard Flood. Mr. Flood survived both the water and the fire and lived to tell the story; he lived to share many stories.

When not swimming toward a fire, Mr. Flood is known for his peculiarities. He hates adjectives and is the inventor of the word "gravitas." He invented a time zone named Fooly Time—a no-man's-time in a work day that unleashed irrational streams of consciousness informed by bad television, the fashion police, word play, and salon jousts.

Mr. Flood has the ability to bring into the same sentence Antonin Artaud and a Ralph Lauren advertising campaign while singing Snoop Dogg's lyrics "With my mind on my money and my money on my mind."

Mr. Flood can teach you about B movies and make an argument for Hans Jürgen Syberberg and Wagner. With his hands flipping through the pages, he can find Visconti in a *House & Garden* magazine. He has the agility to bend all of Leni Riefenstahl's contradictions and to pinpoint Manny Farber's centrality. Like all Catholics, he loves Silvana Mangano, and he could cast the late eighteenth-century writer Claire de Duras in a Coen Brothers film. Mr. Flood does not like it when art is interested in being his friend. He has higher and deeper expectations. And, very important, Richard Flood blames everything on Mel Gibson. As we all should.

More than twenty years ago I was deeply affected by an essay (published in this volume) that Richard Flood wrote for the catalogue of the Paul Thek retrospective organized by the Witte de With in Rotterdam. At first the essay rubbed me the wrong way; it was too autobiographical, too emotional for my need of theoretical reassurance. It took several readings and time to truly appreciate that it was a privilege to have such direct access to this artist, whose work cannot be grasped without allowing the power of emotions to guide your gaze and your understanding of the times during which Thek elected to be an intensely emotional artist and being. Between the lines of that essay, in the space between the words, not only the closeness and the friendship but also the sadness of what was a true relationship are naked without ever overshadowing the power of Thek's art. Ultimately, Richard's words gave me the audacity to use and assume the "I."

Richard Flood has a singular way with words and with narrative. As this volume shows, he is not an academic and he does not write like a curator. What transpires through this collection of texts is a genuine and rigorous attachment to the world of ideas and beauty, as long as they are relevant to the understanding and the critical and aesthetic experience of our times.

Whether he is writing on Matthew Barney, Robert Gober, or Curzio Malaparte, he often starts from a subjective point of view fed and transcended by an uncanny knowledge of history, cinema, literature and poetry, design, architecture, and vernacular culture. Nothing is off limits to the constellation of signs, the necklace of digressions that he invites to our understanding of the arts. As he has written about Thek, Richard Flood, too, is animated by *the knowledge that you could wrest beauty out of absolutely anything—for a moment.*

His prose follows the volutes and the loops of Baroque or Victorian embroidery, and in the folds of a sentence lie the muses of quiet but sharp disruption. At times his words are harsh and rightfully demonstrate no patience for mediocrity. Throughout all his successive lives in the arts—as an editor, a gallerist, a curator, a mentor, and a teacher— Richard Flood has committed and submitted himself to exacting standards that he has shared generously but no less exactingly with several generations of artists, students, and younger curators.

This book is a reminder of the integrity of the art we signed up for, and the integrity of a life, of a working life, in the arts. A life of defiance against compromises and easy self-indulgence. His choices are radical without being ideological. His subversiveness resides in his commitment to knowledge and education. At a time when we often feel that our world has been abducted by an increasingly vulgar consumerism and, to paraphrase him, by *wave after wave of flatulent, instantly commodified art*, his work is a reminder that we have a duty to do better, to reach deeper, and to continue to trust the arts more than we trust ourselves.

Under his pen, knowledge and connoisseurship are political and ethical weapons of resistance, attempting to warn us that the bed we are about to lie down in is on fire. Ultimately, he might be, despite his own denials, a Baudelairean character, a conflicted modernist wandering within *L'époque, la mode, la morale, la passion.*

A few years ago, Richard Flood wrote, "Gober's sculpture accompanies me throughout my America." So it is that Richard's words and world have accompanied me, and many others, throughout our lives in art, and they will continue to invite us to wrest beauty and meaning out of everything that captures our fancy.

Something though is missing from this book. A book cannot capture or contain it. It is the spirit of Richard, standing at the threshold of his Walker Art Center office and about to step into Fooly Time, screaming from the top of his lungs the anthem from Tod Browning's *Freaks*: "One of Us, One of Us, One of Us..." It was his way of paying tribute to the dysfunctional family of the art community, where one can belong without conforming.

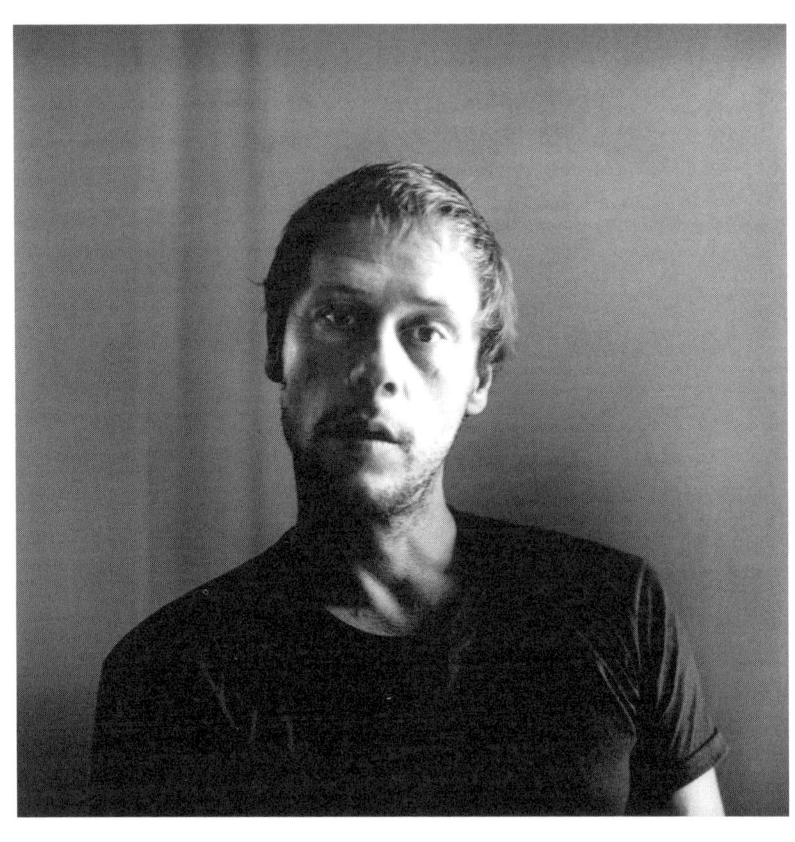

Peter Hujar, *Paul Thek II*, 1975
Vintage gelatin silver print, 37.5 × 37.5 cm (14¾ × 14¾ in.)

Paul Thek: Real Misunderstanding

Regardless of my own beliefs and my own doubts ... it is my opinion that art lost its basic creative drive the moment it was separated from worship. It severed an umbilical cord and now lives its own sterile life, generating and degenerating itself. In former days the artist remained unknown and his work was to the glory of God. He lived and died without being more or less important than other artisans; "eternal values," "immortality" and "masterpiece" were terms not applicable in his case. The ability to create was a gift. In such a world flourished invulnerable assurance and natural humility.

INGMAR BERGMAN[1]

In the context of mainstream American art, Paul Thek is an outsider. Except for three years in the late 1960s, his work has, almost exclusively, been created and chronicled in Europe. While he is well represented abroad, not one painting or sculpture by him has found a home in an American public collection.

One can speculate endlessly as to why Thek has been so ignored in his own country. The adamant secularism of contemporary American art has certainly not helped to advance an artist so deeply responsive to Catholicism, scholasticism, current events, folk ritual, legend, and literature in his creative expression. But the simplest reason for his exclusion may well be expressed by a qualified saw from that most irascible of American thinkers, H. L. Mencken: "It is almost as safe to assume that an artist of any dignity is against his country, i.e., against the environment in which God hath placed him, as it is to assume that his country is against the artist."[2] Thek's acceptance in Europe, where the emergence of Arte Povera provided a nurturing climate for his maverick, melting-pot aesthetic, makes sense.

From 1968 to the present, Thek has traveled through Western Europe with a small band of collaborators constructing enormous, complex environments that, whenever possible, coincide with seasonal and/or religious celebrations. These environments, referred to by Thek as "Processions" (a pun on process art), often involve improvisational events occasioned by the construction and maintenance of their environment, and always celebrate regional custom, national myth, and universal aspirations. Once incorporated, objects and artifacts tend to be carried from one Procession to another. These "props," like members of a repertory company, advance and retreat in importance according to the demands of the occasion; of consistent importance, however, is the mise-en-scène, which is structured to absorb and activate the spectator. As with Artaud's unrealized dream of theater, Thek's Processions aspire "to make space speak, to feed and furnish it, like mines laid in a wall of rock which all of a sudden turns into geysers and bouquets of stone."[3] Thek's environments are inevitably exercises in spatial choreography, but they are also occasions for the dramatization of the spectator/participant—a theater designed to ennoble and stimulate a poetically conceived common man.

In addition to the environments, Thek has produced a remarkably varied body of paintings and sculpture. The paintings, executed on canvas and newspaper, are unique in their bravura virtuosity, racing expertly through those styles and subjects that the artist feels a need to exorcise or advance. Thek's sculpture is a curious combination of the intensely self-analytic and the ingenuously dogmatic. From the melodramatic wax pieces of the late 1960s through the clunky, homely bronzes of the mid-1970s, Thek's sculpture provides an odd artistic outline that backtracks from a Yeatsian Byzantium to Altamira. And, lest any of it become too precious, Thek has often literally heaped his paintings and sculpture into the democratic maws of the Processional environments, where every actor is an extra. It is an unfashionable, intoxicatingly humane aesthetic that resists the co-optation of the artist through the alternatives of service to the public and achievement through simplicity of means.

It is convenient to return again to Mencken for an appropriate caution: "The special quality which makes an artist of him might almost be defined, indeed, as an extraordinary capacity for irritation, a pathological sensitiveness to environmental pricks and stings. He differs from the rest of us mainly because he reacts sharply and in an uncommon manner to phenomena which leave the rest of us unmoved, or, at most, merely annoy us vaguely."[4]

Paul Thek's first New York show took place in 1964 at Eleanor Ward's Stable Gallery when the artist was thirty-one. In the words of Suzanne Delehanty, the work emerged as "a protest against pop art's ready acceptance of mass production and minimalism's idealization of technology."[5] Yet Thek's "protest" was curiously complicit with the work that occasioned it. For four years, his pieces involved the fabrication of wax facsimiles of raw meat embedded in increasingly luxurious Plexiglas cases. Looking back, the pieces are temptingly analogous to the America of that period, when the lid was still firmly clamped on the disaffection that would eventually boil up over Vietnam. All that putrefied flesh in those glitzy cases now seems horribly, presciently accurate. What follows is one side of an annotated conversation with Paul Thek conducted last May.

⋆   ⋆   ⋆

The Artist rejects painting, embraces wax, sculpts faux meat, finds a gallery, changes galleries, and reflects on the nature of his role: I went to see a Jasper Johns show and I saw that he was working in wax and I started to work in wax. Then the meat pieces happened. Very clearly I saw this meat on a wall, almost crucified, hanging on a wall like a painting. The first sculpture was just a piece of meat in a strange case. After I'd done that two or three times, the pieces became squares on squares—puns on the Albers of the period. I did meat in just about every conceivable way, always enclosed in a cage or a box or a frame. About as far as I got into baroque humor at that time was a birthday cake that grew out of an homage to Albers, although I never indicated that in the title. I took a piece to Eleanor Ward at Stable and she liked it and kept it overnight and was very imperial—something like no, I never make decisions while the artist is here—and then she called me the next day and asked how quickly I could have a show ready. I think she may have called me in June or July and the show opened her fall season. That's how quick it was. After that, some of the pieces became less mathematically square, more gouged, like large portions of the limbs of monsters.... By then I'd moved to a gallery on Fifty-Seventh Street and the cases became very ornate and very expensive. I was much influenced by people like Larry Bell and the incredible—I keep wanting to say '50s but it was actually '60s; it feels '50s to me—pristine construction of the period.... It didn't seem to hurt my work, which just got stranger because that chunk of whatever it was that I was presenting was still such a gripper. Though, toward the end, I think that the cases got out of line. I was through with them anyway.

I was amused with the idea of meat under Plexiglas because I thought it made fun of the scene—where the name of the game seemed to be "how cool can you be" and "how refined." Nobody ever mentioned anything that seemed real. The world was falling apart, anyone could see it. I was a wreck, the block was a wreck, the city was a wreck; and I'd go to a gallery and there would be a lot of fancy people looking at a lot of stuff that didn't say anything about anything to anyone. Not that I will in any way negate the value of beauty and patience and dedication and the work of the contemplative. Of course not, how absurd of me. But still, I thought there was a lack and that it was my job to say so.

The Artist combines meat and Plexiglas to address a conspiracy: Sylvia Kraus was a wonderful lady of the period. She was always very nicely dressed in a kind of Schrafft's, middle-aged-matron way, and gave out mimeographed papers on Fifty-Seventh Street. She would mount attacks on communism and pesticides and all that sort of thing. The attacks were worded in a really fanatic, assertive way so that it seemed that she was bananas, but frequently her causes were right, and, if not right, were just slightly to the crazy side of what was right. She had a kind of poetic misunderstanding of reality in a very beautiful way. And the *Hippopotamus Poison* piece was taken from one of her tracts. ["I Sylvia Kraus, before God, do hereby allege that a protracted desolating weapon HIPPOPOTAMUS POISON is being used to insidiously annihilate men, women and children. This poison is being blended into food, beverages and tobacco to simulate heart attack, cancer, stroke, etc. Lest we perish from within … STOP THIS MASSACRE."] I think I only changed one word and put in "Hippopotamus" for something else. I wanted to throw it away from the simply anecdotal. I wanted to blow the logic of that particular understanding and, at the same time, enlarge it beyond the anecdotal.

The Artist addresses the meaning of meat sculpture and moves on: I don't know that there was that much to understand. For me, it was absolutely obvious. Inside the glittery, swanky cases—the "Modern Art" materials that were all the rage at the time, Formica and glass and plastic—was something very unpleasant, very frightening, and looking absolutely real. It seemed to me that nobody noticed the fact that I was dealing with a frightening subject with absolute patience and control so that it became serene. Nobody noticed that I was working with the hottest subject known to man—the human body—and doing it in a totally

controlled way, which, I thought, was the required distancing....
I remember going to a party and having someone say, "Oh, there's
the meat man." And I thought, "Well, that's enough of that."

Thek's final, American-produced sculpture of the period, The Tomb—Death
of a Hippie *(on which Neil Jenney worked as his assistant), was a* succès de
scandale *that has both dogged and cemented his career. His gallery at the time
did not want to exhibit the piece and, in 1967, Thek returned to Stable Gallery.
Accompanying* The Tomb *was work that had, rather poetically, evolved from
the meat pieces. Here, instead of chunks of flesh, were the severed limbs of heroes.
The Plexiglas cases remained, but they now held arms and legs sheathed in
fantastic, occasionally whimsical (an armlet covered in butterfly wings) armor.
The focus, however, was a virulent-pink pyramid containing a beeswax effigy of
Thek attired in a pink suit, adorned with delicate jewelry of gold and woven
hair, surrounded by pink goblets, a funerary bowl, and private letters. Near the
entrance was tacked a put-down of minimalism, which began: "Welcome: You
are in a replica of the tomb. It has been prefabricated at a cost of $950.00."
At the time, Robert Pincus-Witten described* The Tomb *as "a monument which
may easily prove to be one of the unanticipated yet representative masterworks of
American sculpture of the sixties. There are many indications in this piece that,
like Duchamp's* Large Glass, *the work represents a summation and an adieu."[6]
He was right on both counts.* The Tomb—Death of a Hippie *definitively
wrapped up a decade of "flower power." Within a year came the violence in
Chicago during the Democratic Convention; for Thek, the end had already come.
The week that* The Tomb *opened in New York, he was on his way to Europe,
where, with only an occasional trip home, he would remain through the 1970s.*

*The Artist experiments with body parts, creates a body, and ponders the impor-
tance of technique*: The body pieces were elements in the show [*The
Tomb*]. They were laid out on the floor in their cases and roped off
with red cord, placed in a way so that they looked like finds from a
tomb or an archaeological site.

But they were also totally nonarchaeological-looking because they were all glittering and plastic and terribly refined. And in another room was this absolutely simple pink thing. [*The Tomb* itself.] I was making jewelry from hair and gold, which was too fragile to ever be worn, but it was really beautiful, so I thought there must be something to put it on. [The *Hippie* in *The Tomb*.] The body pieces began appearing because I was trying to figure out how to make a full body cast. I'd never done molds or anything like that before. I was working with dentists' moulage, which is used for open wounds and is extremely quick-setting. I had a studio filled with imperfect limbs covered with different-colored wax, to test the tinting, so it was an easy, natural thing to make use of them. If I have an aesthetic, it's rooted to some extent in pragmatism. If you have something around, you might as well try and make something out of it. I knew technique was of no importance. In one of the reviews of that period, somebody [Pincus-Witten] called me a master technician ["consummate technician" was the actual phrase] and I thought, "That's absolute nonsense and an insult; you don't call an artist a master technician—that's somebody else."

In Europe, Thek created another doppelgänger, Fishman *(1968), a life-size latex body cast strategically attired in a school of gray fish. Thek's former apologist, Pincus-Witten, saw* Fishman *as a "noxious bit of self-parading"*[7] *and there is certainly something piously creepy in the piece's Christian-martyr complex. Nonetheless, it didn't take Thek long to put* Fishman *in its place. Once reverentially/purgatively displayed on its own,* Fishman *entered the Processions as just one more member of the corps de ballet. (Removed from* The Tomb *the same fate was later to overtake the* Hippie, *a piece Thek appears to regard with something between avuncular affection and sibling antagonism.)*

Fishman's first ensemble appearance was in Thek's Processional The Artist's Co-op *(1969), at the Stedelijk Museum in Amsterdam. Here,* Fishman *was somewhat cavalierly strapped under the worktable on which it had been made and situated in the center of a chicken coop (with, naturally, real chickens).*

The Co-op, *which wandered through two galleries, was a densely populated but essentially linear installation that, while significantly altering the museum space, did not deny it. The sum effect was a kind of Beuysian baroque. But where Beuys was already undeniably icy, Thek was courting an intellectual and emotional thaw. Among the elements swirling through the* Co-op *were, in no particular order, a stuffed dog with applied Mama Roma teats, a deluge of suspended tissues, an assortment of decorated eggs sprouting shoestring umbilical cords, a selection of Van Gogh paintings from the Stedelijk's storehouse, and a latex dwarf ("Assurbanipal"), which simultaneously evoked every awful lawn ornament you've ever seen, one of Santa's elves, Rumpelstiltskin, and a goofy Nibelung. With* The Artist's Co-op, *the ultimately dead-ended solipsism of* Hippie *and* Fishman *was irrevocably reversed.*

The Artist criticizes the critics and discovers process: Reading reviews from the New York show [*The Tomb*], a lot of critics seemed outraged that I had strayed from the path of "true art" and had actually dared to involve myself, warning me of the consequences. And I thought, "I'm well aware," but also thought that I'd had no alternative at the time. I didn't think it was up to the critics or anyone else—speaking aesthetically, stylistically, or therapeutically—to tell me what to do. And if art has any validity, or my original action any purpose, I had to do it again.... The show that I did in Germany in 1968 [*A Procession in Honor of Aesthetic Progress: Objects Theoretically to Wear, Carry, Pull, or Wave,* Galerie M. E. Thelen, Essen, West Germany] changed from day to day by necessity because the pieces had all arrived broken. That taught me how important process was; there was no point at which you could logically say, "Now, it's finished."

Apropos of *Fishman*, an Italian craftsman who was struggling to keep alive in Amsterdam was hoping to get a contract from the city to produce trash cans around this latex dwarf with a big receptacle mouth. But the city fathers didn't buy it.... Every time I'd go to the man's studio, I saw this big dwarf there unused and I fell in love with the hopelessness of the situation. A Dutch friend of mine said, "Oh, Assurbanipal the dwarf," because the treatment of the beard looked kind of Assyrian. So from then on, I tried to squeeze him into the shows, and he became indispensable.

The Artist encounters and adapts Beuys: Beuys was someone I worked off. He certainly had a great impact on me. I saw his work for the first time—I'd never heard of him before—in the summer of 1968 in Munich. I walked into the museum and I thought I was in the wrong building. I was totally thrown off. Above that, it seemed to be incredibly moving— but ponderous, really ponderous. The work seemed totally devoid of wit or humor or grace, and was didactic to the point of extinction. But I thought there was a visual presentation I could work off. It seemed to me that all it needed was glamour and worth and charm and a woman's touch. It needed some softness. It was all hard edge and nasty; no relationship to the spirit.

The Artist establishes Van Gogh as a forefather of funk and gets to handle some masterpieces: At that point [spring of 1969], I was very much into funk. I don't know what funk is, but if it means "earthy," and "down home at the farm," and "folks," then I liked that. Those Van Goghs are so beautiful and that particular man is the personification of the artist for that time. The paintings were available—they were in the store- house of the museum—and it seemed silly that they weren't being seen. The work [*The Artist's Co-op*] was about country, in addition to being about myth and ideas. Everything in the show was rough, stained, literally lived-in; not shiny, not new, very handmade. It was a revenge against the wax and plastic pieces, a rebellion against those years which were totally inhuman. That stuff was so fragile and the cases so delicate; after years of that, I thought, "This is insanity." From then on, as much as possible, the work was easy to deal with—hard to break and not especially valuable, not especially important. It was the cult of funk, really. And those Van Goghs seemed to fit in perfectly because they were about country. They were the early ones, which have always seemed to me to be some of the most beautiful because they're not bananas like the ones at Arles…. It seemed natural to relate the earthiness of my piece to the earthiness of those paintings…. Besides, that way I could actually get to touch them.

The Artist distinguishes between himself and another artist with funk associations: I don't feel related to Edward Kienholz at all, but he is certainly a current-events person. He's certainly of the world and he's not lost in abstraction or aesthetics—for yea or nay—but I don't feel related to him visually or aesthetically. I think he's very good at presenting the pain, but he doesn't present any solution. And the solution would have to be in execution and beauty. When I think of execution, I think of the pain—the discipline—of doing those things.

The first of Thek's all-over environments was Pyramid/A Work in Progress *(1971–72), at Stockholm's Moderna Museet. With* Pyramid, *Thek managed to totally reinvent the space in which he was working. Sand and planking formed walkways; theatrical lighting and candles provided dim illumination; structures of newspaper and screening, buttressed with saplings, created bowers of disposable information. For museumgoers, it was a free fall into Western culture. References were so abundant that an old fishing barge became a vessel capable of Protean metamorphoses—a Viking longboat, Noah's ark, Huck's raft, Kon Tiki, the raft of the Medusa, the Flying Dutchman, the Ship of Fools, the Ark of the Covenant. Visual juxtapositions came and went like colors in an oil slick. Much of the encyclopedic layering was due to the myriad details provided by Thek's collaborators, who were given creative autonomy within areas of the overall environment. As, over the years, the Processions moved from Essen to Amsterdam to Stockholm to Kassel (1972) to Lucerne (1973) to Duisburg (1973) to Philadelphia (1977) to Venice (1980) to London (1981), the collaborators (most notably and consistently Franz Deckwitz and Ann Wilson)*[8] *developed an increasingly*

sophisticated visual language that fed off of and into Thek's ecumenical plural-
ism. With his Processions, Thek managed to create a transitory equivalent to the
collective effort occasioned by the medieval cathedral.

The Artist gives a tour of his Swedish Procession: They wanted me to do
The Tomb in the Moderna Museet in Sweden. [*The Tomb* had been recon-
structed several times for what Thek refers to as "soul jerker" shows à
la *Human Concern/Personal Torment: The Grotesque in American Art* at the
Whitney in 1969.] By then I was more than tired of doing the thing,
but they were insisting that they wanted to see it, so I consented to let
the "corpse" come but decided to leave it in its packing crate and do
something else with it entirely. I made it look like it was in a boat.

When we were in Sweden, we saw images of Viking chieftains on
funeral boats that were floated down the rivers to the sea in flames.
And I put something like that together, with tables and chairs. So a
part of the show had the "corpse" in it, but by then I put a beautiful
fresh blue blanket on it with a sheet and a pillow. And I filled the crate
with tulip bulbs and onion bulbs which, during the two months that
the show was up, sprouted.

That was the show where I first did the pyramid. The *Hippie* was
simply placed in the choreography of the movement of the public
through the space. One had to come through a twisting, almost-pink
newspaper tunnel, and walk up some steps onto a wharf, which is in a
truncated pyramid. On the inside are blue newspaper walls held up by
trees from which I had not stripped the branches or leaves so it feels
like a forest. So you are in a forest in a pyramid at the end of a tunnel,
and it is painted blue like the sea and lit by candles. And then the
wharf is set as a dining room. There's some bread on the table and some
wine and newspaper clippings and books and prayers. In a corner are
a little light and a chair and a flute. There is also a piano and a bathtub
with oars. And then you leave the pyramid and there's a large room
to wander through with all sorts of things [notably *The Artist's Co-op*,

Fishman, and "Assurbanipal"] and it's all lit by candles and filled with waves of sand. And at the very end, just before you exit, is the *Hippie* as a Viking chieftain in a kind of boat. But you almost don't see it. There's no light on it; it's a total throwaway at that point.

The Artist clarifies his environmental goals: I want to present an atmosphere—an ambience—which is so peaceful and so beautiful that you're shattered when you leave. My feeling is that the only way you can make things better is by showing how good things can be.

I like to work in a way that people mis-see. I like people to mis-see. I like puns. I like them to mis-hear. I think Arthur Koestler said something about mistakes being the route to creativity. I notice that in myself. I make a mistake—I mis-see or I mis-hear—and it's much more creative than had I understood it correctly. If I can possibly provoke an instance for people where that can happen spontaneously, I want it to happen.

Thek has never been willing to censor himself out of his work. The result is a kind of visual roman à clef in which the artist assumes and describes those personae that, for him, are emotionally expedient. An etching, Artist's Proof *(1975), was a position statement and introduced a new alter ego, based on the legendary black minstrel Bill "Bojangles" Robinson. The etching's secular adaptation of the Stations of the Cross reads like a post-Watergate exorcism, and along with a number of Thek's paintings on newspaper, provocatively addresses the erosion of the American spirit in the aftermath of Vietnam. Included in* Artist's Proof *is a depiction of a tar baby, another artist surrogate, which Thek later executed in bronze. Interestingly, Thek's mid-1970s bronzes are totally antithetical to the earlier wax and Plexiglas pieces. Exhibited in 1976 under the umbrella title* The Personal Effects of the Pied Piper, *the bronzes are assertively ugly little things with a rustic finish. They are also disarmingly amusing and in keeping with the whimsical, postmortem title. Included among the "effects" are several families of mice, the remains of a campfire, a bowl of*

The Artist reveals the origin of three alter egos: *The Pied Piper* came into
being of necessity and as self-defense. I had to get rid of the cancer
fodder in my emotional system. I hope that I turned it into something
very beautiful. I'm just sorry the pieces never came to their final
fruition, but I'm sure I'll put them together at some point. Also, by
then I wanted to stretch out of that Christ image that *Fishman* and
Hippie had put me into and to broaden it.

I was by then, unwittingly, a kind of mystic showman and, of
course, a fraud. It was just me. I was continually getting people who
were furious with me for having tampered with the mythology or
iconography of something. I thought, "What are they talking about,
it's my job." The Bo Jangles etchings are my attempt to update the
Stations of the Cross a little bit and slide them sideways. I was hoping
to do things like "Bo Jangles falls the second time." Bo Jangles is a
poor clownish collaborator—as we all are—in a hopelessly lethal,
totally inhuman system. All I wanted to say was that you can do the
Jesus Christ routine if you want to—we can all pretend to be noble—
but we're still enriching a vicious system and passing on one sick
family after another as we continue to overpopulate the planet.
And I thought in just a couple of images—pithy images, you would
say—I could, if the beholder would but be aware, connect a couple of
ideas. I had Jerry Jeff Walker's song in mind. I did the etchings in Paris
so the "Bo" had been misspelled into "Beau," which is kind of nice.
I wanted to be Tar Baby. I wanted people to become stuck in my ideas,
so you couldn't get away from them. That's all there is to it.

Thek began as a painter, and painting is a medium to which he constantly returns. His paintings on canvas are filled with a gestural exuberance and icon-oclastic sassiness that block easy categorization. Thek's unwillingness to settle down, dig in, and get tagged hasn't done much to solidify his reputation as a painter. (Stylistic and thematic virtuosity fly in the face of the American art market's passion for genrefication.) In a climate that encourages absolute critical nomenclature to advance careers predicated on visual and/or thematic consistency, Thek's high-spirited disregard for aesthetic conformation appears wantonly subversive.

*Another factor that tends to isolate Thek's work is a humorous irreverence, characterized by titles (frequently included in the composition) and subject matter satirically undercutting and commenting on paint handling and com-position (or the reverse). Whether he is picking up where Johns's number series left off (Thek's series begins with 11), suggesting profanely tender religious conjunctions (*Jesus in the Arms of Krishna *[1980]), celebrating childhood media memories (*Bambi Growing, Bambi's Father Upon His Bluff *[1979]), or honoring prosaic still-life conventions (*Tomato *[1974]), Thek always brings a highly charged expressiveness to his canvases.*

The paintings on newspaper are cooler, not so impacted, more impatient asides than emphatic declaratives. In their graphic economy and limited palette, they offer an experiential immediacy that Thek's other work forestalls. In their casual, notational elegance, the newspaper paintings have as unmannered and direct a feel as a firm handshake.

For a recent show (1980), A Lot of Little Paintings, *Thek turned down the gallery lights, spotlit an extravagant orchid plant ringed by delicate gilt chairs, attached goose-necked museum lamps to the paintings, and stuck punch-tape labels on sham gold frames. The effect was as glamorously artificial as Marlene Dietrich's platinum Afro in* Blonde Venus, *and almost as outrageous. But it was also a delicately sensual reminder that paintings do not have to be lit as if they are about to be combed for microbes, that they unfold by degrees rather than in the white light of an instant. As is usual with Thek, the message was a massage—at once invulnerably assured and naturally humble.*

The Artist elaborates on his exhibition strategy and the limitations of self-evaluation: I wanted the room to look good for people. I was tired of going into galleries and feeling like I was in a lineup. They're all so brightly lit and there's no place to sit down, and the gallery people are all peering through their windows—what a hostile environment. So it seemed the first thing to do was to humanize the environment; then you can look at a work of art. And, of course, you do that by turning down the lights, giving people some chairs to sit on, and not having the art restricted in any way.

Bambi [the subject of one of the "Little Paintings"] has always been one of my favorite movies, especially because of the voice of Bambi's mother: so mature and so resonant and so patient; no shrillness, none of the virago, no bitchiness—just a wonderful woman's voice, restful and soothing. And Bambi's wonderment at his first rainstorm, do you remember, when the rain drops from leaf to leaf? It's absolutely glorious; it's better than the infant Jesus in a way. It certainly has hit a lot of people. Billions of people have seen it and are in love with him.

The paintings [in the *Little Paintings* show] were about theology, psychology, philosophy, art, and, hopefully in all of them, humor. Though, in some, I got caught in beauty. I thought, "Let's just make this one be beautiful, not have anything to do with anything else!" I frequently get up on a stupid high horse of fright and say, "Only the perfection of the stuff I do in Ponza, where I have the time and patience and peace of mind to devote myself to a certain 'finish' is really valid." But it's not true, because one little line or humorous sketch on newspaper may be more valuable. How hard or how well I painted is not important. I sometimes think of technique as one more brick in the wall. You know, Pink Floyd. And that, in fact, is what it is, so you'd have to be a fool to be limited by that.

The Artist declares his preferences and prejudices: My favorite art is regional art. One of the things that drives me crazy is the "international style";

I find that so boring. I'd hate going to Sicily and finding the local kids doing stuff out of Nancy Hoffman or Pace. What's happening in America now is just a lot of slapdash, tomfoolery chic. Just because, traditionally speaking, an artist is frequently the contemplative, removed from the world and devoting himself to an idealized and perfected image, doesn't mean that art can't be very much from the world as well. So, I believe in regional art. You do what has to be done when you're there.

The Artist states his position: A lot of people say that I give them too much, that the cake I come up with is simply too rich. There are a lot of people, especially in this country, who are totally dedicated to art as sensory training—which I do not disagree with at all—but I think that myth and literature can also improve the senses. A lot of people get very angry if you're this most verboten of all things—literary; God forbid you should be intelligent. I don't think they understand how much they limit and how much they cut out. From what my knowledge of history and people in my culture has told me, the sensual life to which they are aspiring is a bore and doomed. Now, that may be old-fashioned Catholicism, but it sounds like what every religion tells me, or what the voice of reason tells me.

Artforum 20, no. 2 (October 1981): 48–53.

Wagner's Head

For a moment, it appeared that an enormous, sixty-five-foot-long facsimile of Richard Wagner's death mask, which had provided the craggy landscape for Hans Jürgen Syberberg's film *Parsifal* (1982), might be trucked into Kassel and installed on the grounds of Documenta. For a moment, Syberberg enthusiastically investigated the possibility of shipping it. In the end, the tentative offer from Documenta 7 was withdrawn and the head remained on a back lot in Munich. It is, perhaps, foolish to speculate on the implications of something that was only, for a moment, a possibility, but I think not. Nor is it possible to ignore the role assigned to Caspar David Friedrich (a precursor of Wagner in his loathing of the French, his intractable nationalism, and his wild Northern Romanticism), whose *Sea of Ice* (1823–24) is reproduced in the catalogue adjacent to Rudi Fuchs's introductory preface, as the illustration for a metaphor of Fuchs's own devising wherein "The river [the practice of art/culture as we know it] is gradually freezing over; it is time for a new departure" (navigated, one assumes, by Fuchs).

In "The Case of Wagner," a witty, acidic purge of his onetime idol, Friedrich Nietzsche states: "Wagner is *the modern artist par excellence*, the Cagliostro of modernity. In his art all that the modern world requires most urgently is mixed in the most seductive manner: the three great *stimulantia* of the exhausted—the *brutal*, the *artificial*, and the *innocent* (idiotic)." So, too, in the *Gesamtkunstwerk* of Documenta were Wagner's *stimulantia* enshrined. The *brutal* was exalted by Hermann Nitsch, the *artificial* by Syberberg, the *innocent* by Joseph Beuys.

Not inconsequentially, each of these artists is also pursuing his vision of *Gesamtkunstwerk*, his Grail.

Through the intervention of Nitsch, Documenta 7 went careering back to the origin of it all. Nitsch's art epitomizes the primal hysteria of bloodied hands beating away the terrifying, silent onrush of thought. When, in the early 1960s, Nitsch climbed up on his cross, the act could be read as political, brazenly in opposition to bourgeois reconstructionism. Claiming for himself the "negative, unsavoury, perverse, obscene, the passion and the hysteria of the act of sacrifice so that YOU are spared the sullying, shaming descent into the extreme," Nitsch appeared as a proletarian Siegfried bathing in the blood of a new, polemical dragon. Only as the hypotheses surrounding his orgies-mysteries (o.m.) theater were institutionalized was it understood that, under the guise of Bacchic therapy, Nitsch had allied himself with the reign of Wotan, had become lost in the realm of the *brutal*.

In the survey of work accorded him by Documenta, Nitsch was represented by a combination of photographic documentation and performance artifacts. The photographs (mostly in color) show o.m. initiates spread-eagled under eviscerated sheep, sheathed in animal entrails, crucified upside down, and anointed with incarnadine bladders. Interspersed with the photographs are the relics of Nitsch's *Aktionen*: here a row of litters, there an arrangement of soiled ecclesiastical vestments—all stained a rusty red. In his catalogue essay Nitsch claims that "The concentrated aesthetic liturgy of the o.m. theatre can spread and extend itself to the whole life and can transform the course of life into a being-and-life-affirming, aesthetic ritual." It is through the o.m. theater that Nitsch is pursuing his dream of *Gesamtkunstwerk* in the Austrian countryside. There, in the role of hieratic facilitator, he conducts six-day "feasts of existence" in which flesh and blood and music are orchestrated to transport adepts to heights of visceral ecstasy. This is a domain that Wagner knew only too well and in which he believed enough to sow therein the seeds for Siegfried's destruction, and, later, to tempt Parsifal to the edge of the abyss.

Enter Documenta's Parsifal, Joseph Beuys. Enter the *innocent*. Beuys was present in Kassel ostensibly as the dean of the Free International University for Creativity and Interdisciplinary Research. Not unpredictably, the dean found the time to act as a master of ceremonies, a *droit de seigneur* autocrat, and, for the pictures for posterity, "the holy fool." Early on in Documenta—at the opening press conference, in fact—Beuys deflected questions addressed to the exhibition's organizers in a pantomimic exercise that smacked of a publicity stunt. (Such is Beuys's power that his right to disruption was given official sanction even at the risk of making those who had given the sanction look ridiculous.) Although his pride of place was publicly exercised at the press conference, it did not protect him from an antic act of subterfuge directed against the materialization of his Documenta-sponsored project, *7,000 Oaks*—a long pile of rough-hewn stones on the lawn in front of the Fridericianum. The mechanics were as follows: for 500 Deutschmarks one could provide for the purchase of one oak, its planting in Kassel, the installation of one of these basalt stones next to the tree, and maintenance of both. In return, the donor would "receive a receipt acknowledging their donation and also a TREE DIPLOMA, stamped by the FREE INTERNATIONAL UNIVERSITY, and bearing Joseph Beuys' personal signature." The mechanics of the subterfuge were even simpler: a guerrilla attack on the dignity of the stelae whereby, under the cover of darkness, much of the mound was painted a hot, punk pink by a few young "troublemakers." Only in the young of Kassel does one see signs of friction, hints that living in a cozy, geranium-bordered Alphaville may take a toll. In the children, one can see the kind of cultural degeneracy that expresses its need for anarchy in stance and costume. The Götterdämmerung experienced by their seniors—the humiliation and, after it, the steely will for a persuasive new order—means nothing to the international army of children who have come of age since the media revolution. In his press materials for Documenta, Beuys quotes Goethe: "Germany? But where is it? I do not know how to find this country." On the walls of their city's pedestrian underpasses, the children of Kassel scrawl "Where is punk?" The dean was not amused by the attack, and, well before nightfall on the day of discovery, the rocks were power-hosed back to their original stoneness.

In a letter of support included in the project's promotional package, artist Otto Muehl lent his voice to the troubling poetics of nationalism: "You rinse the roots—of Wotan, through to Wagner, Hitler and the crusaders with their oak leaves and diamond filth—out of the branches of this innocent tree. I already hear the murmur of a new oak wood…. I admire your courage for having dug this tree out of the ideological swamp." Thus blessed, Beuys marches forward. Or, and this is the fear, backward—right into that ideological swamp. Let us not forget that Germany has been methodically reforesting since the Franco-Prussian War and, ritually, since time immemorial. (As late as 1819 Caspar Friedrich's adherent Carl Gustav Carus, on a visit to northern Germany, "noted the persistence of an ancient custom whereby every male, upon the arrival at maturity, was required to plant an oak tree.") It also bears remembering how, in Leni Riefenstahl's *Triumph of the Will*, forestry rangers parade past Hitler with shovels (not guns) on their shoulders, setting out for the greening of the Reich.

Beuys is out to forge a new construct—a "SOCIAL SCULPTURE"— that will forever alter that which is to follow. Still, he is incapable of taking one step forward without the accumulated baggage of centuries trailing along in his wake. In a revisionist assessment of Beuys (in *Artforum*, January 1980), Benjamin Buchloh states:

> In the work and public myth of Joseph Beuys the German spirit of the postwar period finds its new identity by pardoning and reconciling itself prematurely with its own reminiscences of a

responsibility for one of the most cruel and devastating forms of collective political madness that history has known. As much as Richard Wagner's work anticipated and celebrated these collective regressions into Germanic mythology and Teutonic stupor in the realm of music, before they became the actual reality and the nightmare that set out to destroy Europe ... it would be possible to see in Beuys' work the absurd aftermath of that nightmare.

In his four-page manifesto in the Documenta 7 catalogue, Beuys advances along the "Alternative of the Third Path" on his way to the Grail of a "postcapitalist and postcommunist NEW SOCIETY OF TRUE SOCIALISM." Given the realities of Germany's last embrace with socialism this exercise by the *innocent*, filled with "CONSTRUCTIVE INITIATIVE ACTION," "SOCIAL SCULPTURE," and "UNITY IN PLURALITY," requires a cautious critical eye. It is easy to be romanced by Beuys's utopian desire for a new order (old orders are inevitably non-sympathetic), and it is far more gratifying to align oneself with the path of the *innocent* than that of the *brutal*. (Parsifal's quest was, after all, sanctified by his naïveté, by his ignorance of the rules.) Yet, the *innocent*, in its generic transcendence of conscience, poses problems of affiliation that are more intricate than ever were those encountered in identification with the *brutal*. Each generation needs its Parsifals—they satisfy our need for romance—but they are not citizens above investigation. Beuys has become one of our leading visionary artists. Once that is acknowledged, his program must be assessed as part of the world it aspires to change.

In the remarkable exultation "Syberberg's Hitler," published in 1980 in the *New York Review of Books*, Susan Sontag wrote:

Syberberg is a great Wagnerian, the greatest since Thomas Mann, but his attitude to Wagner and the treasures of German Romanticism is not only pious. It contains more than a bit of malice, the touch of the cultural vandal. To evoke the grandeur and the failure of Wagnerianism, *Hitler, a Film from Germany* uses, recycles, parodies elements of Wagner. Syberberg means his film to be an anti-*Parsifal*, and hostility to Wagner is one of its leitmotifs: the spiritual filiation of Wagner and Hitler. The whole film could be considered a profaning of Wagner, undertaken with a full sense of the gesture's ambiguity, for Syberberg is attempting to be both inside and outside his own deepest sources as an artist.

Sontag's analysis might well stand as a description of Syberberg's contribution to Documenta, which is, in every way, the continuation of an old feud-cum-love-affair. From *Ludwig: Requiem for a Virgin King* (1972), through *The Confessions of Winifred Wagner* (1975), and *Hitler, a Film from Germany* (1977), to *Parsifal*, Syberberg has manifested an abiding fascination with his heritage. To a great extent, each of the films preceding *Parsifal* explores its title character through their appropriation of and identification with Wagner. Now, with his adaptation of *Parsifal*, Syberberg draws perilously close to those he had previously autopsied. He moves from the role of inquisitor to that of interpreter and, in so doing, arrives at the shores of the Sea of Ice.

Although it occupies a suite of six rooms in the basement of the Fridericianum, Syberberg's installation goes unacknowledged in the catalogue. Asked to do an installation of props from his film *Parsifal*, Syberberg was given two weeks to arrive at a strategy that would both fill the allotted space and act as a complementary element in the *Gesamtkunstwerk* of Documenta. Possibly, the organizers should have guessed that the artist who took nearly three hours of film to deal with Ludwig of Bavaria and over seven to ponder Hitler would take up a lot of philosophical room, but they didn't and the piece cast a very long shadow, which, unanticipated as it was, threw the issue of art-as-a-manifestation-of-conscience into high relief.

Manipulating his grottoed chambers like a fractured narrative, Syberberg used his props to set up an impacted walking tour through the ruins of German history. The subject is, of course, Wagner: Wagner, the thought of whom caused Gabriele D'Annunzio's mind to go blank when commissioned to write the composer's epitaph; Wagner, whose rhythmic machinery Sergei Diaghilev referred to as "saliva." Again, as in all of Syberberg's work, the Parsifal suite acts as both an homage and an exorcism. Carpeted with leaves and studded with incongruous ruins (an enormous fragment of a sculptural rendering of Delacroix's *Liberté*; an engorged stone penis rising cobra-like from the floor and capped with a German helmet of a foreskin; the base of the fountain that appears in Van Eyck's Ghent altarpiece), the rooms unfold like visions in a dream. Everywhere are reminders and representations of an undigested past. In the final chamber the spirit of the thing becomes provocatively clear. There, in the center of the floor, is a litter, draped with a blood-stained shroud, bearing the death mask of Wagner. All around the room, meditating as it were, are representations of Aeschylus, Charlemagne, Ludwig, Nietzsche, Marx, and—boy sized, a puppet dressed in lederhosen—Hitler. All of it is extravagantly and unrepentantly *artificial*. One could almost hear Nietzsche declaiming from the grave: "Ah, this old magician, how much he imposed upon us! The first thing his art offers us is a magnifying glass: one look through it, and one does not trust one's eyes—everything looks big, *even Wagner*." Even, I might add, Syberberg.

The Parsifal suite is, ultimately, an extended reverie on the awful toll of hubris—on the metamorphosis of art into weapon. It is a theme that Syberberg will not, cannot let go (one wonders if he clings to it with such tenacity as a guard against the sins of ambition); and one which, with its aura of high-strung vigilance, contributed an intellectual nervousness to an exhibition that Fuchs was determined should not be about nervousness ("We did everything to avoid a nervous exhibition...").

So, in a way Wagner's head did finally come to Kassel. Instead of the original plan, it was brought by Nitsch, Beuys, and Syberberg. And as was originally feared, it provided an uncomfortable moment. It would be convenient to see Wagner's legacy as belonging only to a specific time and place. But that's wrong. It belongs to the West and he is all of ours. Our artists, Nitsch and Beuys and Syberberg, also refuse to fit gracefully into a structure. Their projects not only encourage followers, they demand them—that is the point. Without followers, they would simply have an audience and the world that they want would be left as an idea. Like Wagner, their aesthetic requires first reevaluation, then appreciation. Their effect, or potential effect, is what elevates their art to life—to our lives, to our collective society, which is no less exhausted than the one that longed to cry out "Brother ... master" to Wagner when he took his bows at Bayreuth.

Artforum 21, no. 1 (September 1982): 68–70.

Sugar and Vice and ...
Balthus: A Retrospective

I saw the polka dots dancing, so to speak, on the ruffled jumpers of the two smaller girls seated side by side in the warm grass and holding hands, blowing chubby laughter in my direction as if they had never seen me before. And the peace, the warmth, the stasis, the smell of it—in such circumstances how could I help but enjoy my own immensity of size or the range of my interests, how help but appreciate the adaptability of certain natural scenes which, like this one, allow for the play of children one minute and the seclusion of adults the next? I felt a coolness between my porous thin white shirt and the skin of my chest. In linen slacks and alligator belt and hard low-cut shoes the color of amber, I sensed the consciousness of someone carefully dressed for taking care of children.

JOHN HAWKES, *THE BLOOD ORANGES*

The Metropolitan Museum of Art's installation of *Balthus* began with *The Window* (1933), in which a young model—her blouse ripped back to expose one breast, her hand raised to ward off something melodramatic—teeters precariously toward an open window. The emotional mood of the painting is unattractively underscored in Sabine Rewald's catalogue comments concerning its genesis:

When the young model Elsa Henriquez first arrived at Balthus's studio in the Rue de Furstenberg, he opened the door dressed in his old army uniform, a dagger in his hand and a scowl on his face. He grabbed her blouse and tried to pull it open. Elsa recoiled in horror, just as Balthus had intended. Now she looked like the frightened Sarah from the Tobias Legend, a subject planned for another painting.[1]

The anxious sexual terror of Elsa relaxed in the exhibition's next gallery, which concentrated primarily on the early portraits and street scenes and concluded with that huge kitschy iceberg of a painting, *The Mountain* (1937). Then, looming around the corner, installed like an altarpiece, hung *The Room* (1952–54). It is one of Balthus's best-known paintings (the virtually unseen but oft-reproduced *The Guitar Lesson* [1934] being probably the most "notorious") and it was the fulcrum of the exhibition. It is also, again according to Rewald, the painting that portrays "the most erotic and self-abandoned of Balthus's narcissistic adolescent girls." As if to accelerate the confirmation of that judgment, the rest of the core gallery was all aquiver with pedophilic tremors.

Why was the Metropolitan unfurling one of its football-field Fifth Avenue banners in honor of Balthus as if he were a contender? The bulk of Balthus's work occupies essentially the same aesthetic tier as that of Fernando Botero or Tamara de Lempicka. Both stylistically and technically, it is often difficult to differentiate among the *faux naïf*, the clumsy, the fashionable, and the facile. To be sure, there are the occasional lovely landscape, competent still life, and *dramatique* portrait. There are also a few paintings that could be taken seriously (*Joan Miró and His Daughter Dolores* [1937–38], *The Children* [1937]), and there's always Balthus's chef d'oeuvre, the suite of drawings illustrating *Wuthering Heights* (1934–35). The problem is that there really isn't a lot about this work to differentiate it from the output of thousands of other perfectly okay painters. What makes the problem worth noting is that Balthus's specialty, his gimmick, is eroticism. Take it away and you've got a series of compositional exercises. Propped up on the twin crutches of academic acceptability—classicism and mannerism— this is heroicized bourgeois naughtiness being saluted for being the right kind of pornography.

In the confines of *The Room* there is a whiff of something in the air. It is as if the much-remarked-upon light that suffuses Balthus's canvases carries in it the moist, sickly texture of sirocco. As if awaiting the rustle of dustcovers, exquisitely denuded rooms gasp for the particled light that hesitantly reveals fungal walls and luxe draperies. Accessories—a cascade of fabric, a weathered prayer rug, the "simplest" of wash basins, a soigné arrangement of overripe fruit—heighten the artful austerity of the rooms and suggest that they have less to do with life than with interior decoration. These chambers are backdrops for ritual, and what props they possess—chair, chaise, or table—are altars for choreographed communions.

Inhabiting these breathless sacristies are Balthus's dewy postulants. Posed in attitudes of embryonic abandon, the girls are supposed to occupy a world of precognitive sensuality. Curtain after curtain is drawn back to reveal yet another pair of precocious thighs awaiting the lazy attention of the tiny hand that, only a sunbeam before, caressed the kitten by the window. In the inviolate privacy of their deserted rooms, the children's hands—oddly, consistently reminiscent of forks and spoons—resolve themselves into utensils for sleepy sexual banqueting. Their heavy, classically modeled heads recall ancient *kouroi* and have that same tentative expression of smugness that once, nobly, whispered the tender union of god and man. Unlike the *kouroi*, however, Balthus's children tend to lounge.

Often accompanying Balthus's girls are boys, maids, and cats. The boys are, for the most part, adenoidal Nibelungs retained to repetitively lose at cards or stoke the occasional fire. The maids are merely compositional elements, usually placed in close proximity to a window. Then there are the cats. In almost every sense, the cats act as the girls' privileged familiars. Treated with an anthropomorphic flourish, they come from an illustrative tradition that includes such inspired moments as Gustave Doré's Puss in Boots and John Tenniel's Cheshire Cat. But in Balthus's hands, the cats are cast as pimps, sometimes hopelessly vulgar, sometimes smugly discreet. At best, they are insinuating. At worst, they are punch lines for dirty jokes. Either way, they set the mood for Balthus's sinister operettas.

The girls themselves are demimonde poppets. Here Colette's darling Gigi, there Zola's feral Satin. A description of the spoiled Pauline Bonaparte languishing on a Haitian plantation in the fiery heat of revolution comes very close to capturing the quintessential Balthus girl:

> She was in a room darkened by Venetian blinds, lying on her sofa ... and amused General Boyer, who sat at her feet, by letting her slipper fall continually, which he respectfully put on as often as it fell. She is small, fair, with blue eyes and flaxen hair. Her face is expressive of sweetness but without spirit. She has a voluptuous mouth and is rendered interesting by an air of languor which spreads itself over her whole frame.... She hates reading, and though passionately fond of music plays no instrument.... She can do nothing but dance.[2]

While Balthus is presumably painting children, there is little of the child left in his girls' faces. Long gone is that expression "as surprised and ecstatic as a young girl who has discovered her puberty" that Zola ascribed to his marvelous whore, Nana. Habitual sensualists, these children are bored with self-discovery; they are posturing for the delectation of familial voyeurs. Balthus drains these children of innocence and replaces it with something dark and cunning. And in that transfusion lies the corrupt seductiveness of his art.

In his classicist compositions, decorator palette, and eccentrically stylized line, the objectification of children has become acceptable, even chic. These masturbatory paintings attain a serpentine refinement similar to that assumed by Elsa de' Giorgi literally waltzing her way through a monologue on shit and subjugation in Pier Paolo Pasolini's *Salò, or The 120 Days of Sodom* (1975). Nowhere is there the touch of bittersweetness, of first feelings; everywhere is debasement. Every point of view, including the children's to each other, is one of adult libidinousness. Yet this is not admitted within the work as it is in, say, Baron Wilhelm von Gloeden's work, where the interest is so up-front, so apparent, that the issue of morality is gratuitous. No situation is being presented or confronted; no attempt is being made to elucidate a truth. The hook is the girls. By situating them in a narcissistic purdah of their own devising, Balthus is, one senses, scrambling to avoid the liability of his vision. Giovanni Carandente, in the Spoleto catalogue for an exhibition of the artist's drawings and watercolors, spouts what has by now become the party line for the artist's apologists: "Balthus considers the eroticism in his work to be sacred and for this reason he likes it to be neither publicized nor commented on."[3] Period. Carandente then obediently wanders into a compositional discussion of *The Guitar Lesson* without ever alluding to its subject matter. Obviously, clitoral spiritualism mitigates against any hyperventilated discussions of subject matter.

Too much Balthus leaves one longing for something akin to the honest, albeit faux-Ferlinghetti, articulation of Larry Clark in his description of the adolescent hustlers he photographed on Forty-Second Street:

It's what the kid is offering, that's what I'm getting. The picture of what the kid is offering. The kid is offering himself. He's selling something. It's more a look than anything. It's a look, right? It's an entire attitude. It's a way of seeing things, but it's all polished up. It's point of sale.[4]

Well, it's "point of sale" in Balthus as well and, for sure, it's "all polished up." However, Balthus substitutes the eye of a jaded connoisseur for the lens of an artist. And the result is as chilly and artificial as Lautréamont's Maldoror, who "whenever he hugged a rosy-cheeked young child ... was longing to hack off those cheeks with a razor and would have done so often had not the idea of Justice and her long cortège of punishments restrained him on every occasion."[5] (Every occasion, that is, except *The Guitar Lesson*.) Clearly Balthus strains toward the dark, self-conscious surrealism of Lautréamont and its "sweet atmosphere" of evil. Still, for all his efforting, he emerges as a poseur caught in an onanistic web of artifice. In the end, a drop of semen on a silk handkerchief is not really the stuff of great art.

Artforum 22, no. 1 (June 1984): 84–85.

Cumulus from America

She stands on a river of prayer rugs. At her feet, a filigreed brazier purrs its fumes into the envelope of fabric that she holds above her head. Her face, with kohl-smeared eyes and pouty crescent mouth, is soft-focus in shadow. Her naked arms rise from cascading sleeves to tenderly support the fabric that snares the incense. Her gown is a languid series of hieratic transitions, rippling from wimple to bib to paneled alb. Her only adornment—a manta-shaped silver clasp—slithers across her bosom toward her shoulder. The room in which she stands is almost coagulent with milky light. Its one architectural detail—a simple column that turns into a horizontally fluted arch—could just as easily evoke Wilhelm von Gloeden's Taormina as Ingres's Morocco. Suffice to say, the indolent artificial ambience of it all is staggering.

The woman, the gown, the room—all are elements in John Singer Sargent's *Fumée d'Ambre Gris* (1880), which resides in the collection of the Sterling and Francine Clark Institute, Williamstown, Massachusetts. It is, in fact, one of twelve Sargent paintings in the Institute's collection. And, to be fair, not one of the best in a selection that includes such wonderful representative portraits as *Mademoiselle Jourdain* (1889) and that of Sargent's teacher *Carolus Duran* (1879). However, in *Fumée*, Sargent's staggering addiction to soigné chic reaches some kind of awful (old sense of the word) apogee. It would take no suspension of disbelief to move this Pasoliniesque Arabian Nights tableau onto a couturier's runway. (Claude Montana would be a perfect interpreter.) This is fantasy as fashion as art, and its aesthetic is highly debatable. But—and the qualification is enormous—*Fumée* is a beautiful painting.

The liquescence of its dairy light alone demands attention. The luscious transitions from white to cream to pearl to gray are a technical tour de force. Then, too, there is the priestess/hetaera ambiguity of the woman. The passive formality of her ecstasy is so curiously poised between that of connoisseur and initiate that, regardless of one's editorial reading, she emerges psychologically inviolate. One does not truly need this painting to understand either Sargent or his age, but it is a gorgeously decadent evocation of both. And—mea culpa—I love it.

I am obsessing about *Fumée* because its presence in the Institute's jewel box of a collection both delighted and provoked (best sense of the word) me. Robert Sterling Clark (1877–1956) was a very American kind of collector who, as the heir to a vast nineteenth-century fortune, wandered into the twentieth searching for a kind of truth-in-beauty that was dying even as he pursued it. Clark began, like most would-be aesthetes of his generation, rifling through the Renaissance in search of contemporary cachet. Here a Piero della Francesca, there a Signorelli. Here a Botticelli, there a Mantegna. Along with these bona fides came the more available masters (like he of the "Female Half-Lengths" or he of the "Embroidered Foliage"). Finally, out of high-priced rummaging came the kind of focus that differentiates a collection from an accumulation. Clark got obsessive in depth. Like his eccentric contemporary in Philadelphia, Dr. Alfred Barnes, Clark discovered impressionism. Works by Degas, Monet, Pissarro, and—most conspicuously—Renoir poured into the collection. And, from the sun-dappled heights of impressionism, the collection spread through the latter part of the 1800s in an intriguingly horizontal posture. Working with two dealers (M. Knoedler and Durand-Ruel, who supplied nearly three-quarters of the collection), Clark began to seriously define his aesthetic. And, what he was after—with a few notable exceptions—was a pretty picture, usually one with a well-turned ankle.

One of the Institute's great rewards is the portrait it offers of an age. Here is the ripe, shiny apple of Europe before World War I. Glorious skies and gorgeous women are everywhere. If there is a worm in Clark's apple, it is the eloquently melancholic vision of Winslow Homer. Indeed, Homer's idiosyncratic chef d'oeuvre *Undertow* (1886) is probably the single most unsettling painting in the collection because of its gothic congruencies of necrophilia and narcissism. Elsewhere, rubbing shoulders with the impressionists, are Alma Tadema's swooning maenads, Bouguereau's frolicking nymphs, Gérôme's undulant "Orientals," and Boldini's haute-couture soubrettes.

The collection's most glaring and endearing excess is its abundance of work by the Belgian Alfred Stevens (1823–1906). Stevens doesn't exactly have to be seen to be believed but it certainly helps. His entire oeuvre is devoted to the notion of woman as bonbon. In painting after painting, the overdressed lounges on the overstuffed. What is amazing is that Stevens was certainly one of the most successful artists of his day, friend and competitor with the likes of Degas and Manet. A catalogue to the Institute's *Highlights* half-heartedly calls attention to Stevens's "understanding of the paint medium" and, discussing his bathetic *Memories and Regrets* (1875), didactically continues: "Note the diaphanous sleeve of the model's dress, the softly lit items on her dressing table and the sensitive way the curls in her coiffure are recorded. The delicate lighting of her face is especially effective." Why do I suspect the selling point of the painting was the unremarked, vibrantly pink aureole of the model's nipple, which winks at us from atop her baby-blue corset?

Still, I am glad there is a place for Stevens in an important American collection. Certainly—aesthetically and sociologically—his pre-eminence in the Clark collection is riveting. Oddly, it is Stevens, more than anyone else, who gives us a dose of reality beyond the hopefully self-correcting mechanism of art history. His paintings make us conspirationally privy to the siren call of the moment, which, occasionally, diverted Clark on his way to claiming a piece of the rock. Back then, Stevens was a viable alternative to Whistler, whom Clark really didn't like and, fortunately for America, Henry Frick did. Clearly, these are no longer "important" paintings; yet, in their way, they are necessary paintings. Because, in the end, Stevens reflected the haute bourgeois denominator better than most. His importance lies in his accessibility. His promise of a world filled with palpitant, easily dominated, beautifully gowned ruminants is also the promise of a world in which order is as easily maintained as a hairdo. Next to Stevens's dewy bouquets, Sargent's opiated postulant almost suggests a subversive metaphor for a narcotized Third World that, once the smoke clears, could just as easily wield a scimitar as don another bracelet. Seeing Sargent and Stevens as pieces in the same puzzle, a theme of submissive passivity begins to surface as the Institute's aggressive leitmotif in Clark's collection. Like all good private collections, the stamp of the collector informs and expands the nature of the collection. The satisfaction imparted is that of a stimulating, intimate conversation—a retinal dialogue that is ultimately much larger than the sum of its parts.

As a codicil to my musings on the Clark Collection, I would like to mention an issue of *Artforum* that appeared in February 1982, which broke the magazine's tradition of reproducing works of art on its cover. That particular cover featured a photograph of an occidental model wearing an unwearable ensemble by an Asian designer, Issey Miyake, that was dubbed "a paraphrase of light Samurai practice armor." A lengthy editorial by Ingrid Sischy and Germano Celant explained the cover, in part, as follows:

This issue is born out of the tradition of "Modernism as a convergence of languages" where boundaries disintegrate, allowing limitless permutations and commutations of signs, independent of any concept of territory. These signs are indeterminate; they alternate crazily and without finality, having a relationship only to the velocity of consumption and of information, which is altered or negated from season to season, like fashion. This is why we chose fashion for the cover.

This statement was, as I remember, the first of what has since become a torrent of cautions concerning the art world's increasing resemblance to Seventh Avenue, where an endless parade of disposable merchandise is heralded with enough trumpeting to usher in the Second Coming. It is a phenomenon that, thus far, has characterized the 1980s, where the thirst for the moment produces ersatz movements and schools as if they were being spewed out by competing fast-food franchises. *Artforum* had itself already taken a spin around the marketplace with "energism" while the Berlin painters and Manhattan graffiti artists were in the process of being replaced by Italy's alphabetically alluring "three C's" and the symbiotically attached trans-avant-garde. Yet to come—or just out of the paddock—were the British sculptors, the Cologne painters, the Spanish, the East Villagers, the appropriators, the Lacanians, the neo-surrealists, the geometric abstractionists, and the reemergent minimalists.

I bring all this up one more time because I see it as a major impediment to the creation of contemporary collections built with the special connoisseurship of a Sterling Clark. The current vaudevillian rapidity with which art and artists enter and exit threatens the whole notion of in-depth collecting. Instead of a banquet, we are ending up with a badly catered buffet that satisfies no one's appetite. I must assume that, eventually, something like real time, as opposed to coke time, will return. I can only hope that the Alfred Stevens of the 1980s, whoever he or she may be, survives long enough to find his or her Sterling Clark. Obviously, the good artists will endure and prevail, but I would hate to lose the fashionable artists simply because fashion forgot how to tell time.

Parkett, no. 8 (1986): 141–43.

Romance Language

I love good adjectives. They give a noun the same gloriously contradictory odors as those emanating from a well-kept baby. Unfortunately, more often than not, adjectives (particularly in the arts) tend toward impotence as a result of promiscuous usage. Adjectives too easily bestowed (whether laudatory or pejorative) do little more than extend the length of a sentence. I, for example, have developed a love/hate relationship with one particular adjective—Fabulous. There have been days when I've tossed it around with the studied abandon of a starlet tossing her mane for the paparazzi. What did it matter that everyone else was tossing it around too—that art openings developed a nightmarish soundtrack of escalating fabulousness? Then, feeling like Ray Miland in *The Lost Weekend*, I ran amok. Standing in front of a painting that looked like the doormat to Hrothgar's mead hall after Beowulf finished wiping Grendel off his feet, I gratuitously mumbled, "Fabulous." That did it. I was off to the Betty Ford Clinic for Adjectival Abuse. Never again, I swore. But, as the fates conspired, Fabulous wasn't through with me yet. And it was Richard Wagner who indirectly provided me with the occasion for my undoing. Let me explain.

New York's Metropolitan Opera gave its first performance of Wagner's *Tannhauser* in 1884. It gave its 306th in 1987. My guess is that little has changed. The set design from 1977 (Günther Schneider-Siemssen) is a dogged homage to the banal romanticism of William-Adolphe Bouguereau (1825–1905). The road-company costumes (Patricia Zipprodt) and esprit-d'Isadora choreography (Norbert Vesak) were already passé by the time of the Ballet Russe's first American engagement in 1915. What the Metropolitan is dragging along the road to the twenty-first century is a vast, dull Wagnerian lump that will never find a watering hole big enough to refresh itself. It's an epic that got hit with an aesthetic stun gun—it's still moving, but only barely.

What was right with the Met's *Tannhauser* was Jessye Norman's presence in the role of Elizabeth. When, regrettably costumed like a gravy boat, Norman erupts into song at the beginning of Act II, something that is irrefutably new enters the aged *Tannhauser*. What is new is a voice that curls up from the stage of the Met and sculpts itself into a three-dimensional entity. Until Norman's appearance, one could go mad repeating Antonin Artaud's modernist mantra: "Masterpieces of the past are good for the past; they are not good for us." Then, out of Jessye Norman, comes a manifesto predicated purely on sound. She is, again in the words of Artaud, assuming "the right to say what has been said and even what has not been said in a way that belongs to us, a way that is immediate and direct, corresponding to present modes of feeling and understandable to everyone." When, in Act III, Norman directs "Allmächt'ge Jungfrau" straight up to an existential heaven, the result is nothing short of ... gulp ... *fabulous*!

Now, in Jessye Norman's case, "fabulous" comments on her ability to wrest something breathtakingly new out of something grown palsied with age. Fabulous fits her achievement perfectly—such an operatically generous word overleaps normative criteria and bounds right into the realm of myth. Fabulous sounds hyperbolic but, in truth, aims at something well beyond hyperbole—something unrepeatable, priceless, resistant to qualification. It is as without fixed boundaries as a fata morgana. Because it defies the notion of limit, it's also a boom-town kind of word as appropriate for Brecht's Mahagonny as Koch's Manhattan. It is in this context that fabulous undoubtedly gained its art world ubiquity. It spread rapidly through the early 1980s at the height of New York's postmodern party when there was an almost innocent, anything-can-happen magic in the air.

Around 1984, however, fabulous developed a nasty little cough and, when it took to its chaise, an understudy—Major—rushed to the fore. (It was a semantic version of *All about Eve*.) The reason for the substitution was, I suspect, a need for stratification. A lot of what had been fabulous was getting flushed, and maybe painting was actually having a crisis of sorts. Major became a convenient adjective for consumer differentiation. So, anything could still be fabulous but, god knows, that didn't mean it was major. Major also developed a companion adjective—Important—and together they marched forward, often in the same sentence, as in "The art advisor placed a major work in an important collection." It was also around this time that people started talking about investing in "the art market" and, for sure, they wanted to know what they were getting for their buck. Major and important became conveniently discreet indicators of worth. They had just enough phallic bluntness to signify that possession of a major and/or important work also included a transferal of power from the possessed to the possessor. Just as significantly, they implied that other things were not major, were not important. This need for oppositional value played a large part in the ultimate emergence of two more intensely calibrated adjectives: Smart and Intelligent.

Late in 1985, as major works were getting harder to come by and important collections were getting swollen with a surfeit of fabulous work by a shrinking number of major and/or important artists, something unexpected (but not unpredictable) happened. A seeming generation of young American artists rose up almost as one and were embraced (also almost as one) and in no way whatsoever did the old adjectives fit. The work, in the broadest possible terms, was media-evolved and commodity-oriented and called for heightened adjectival sobriety, for a Quaker restraint suggesting theoretical (not marketing) rigor. Moreover, one needed IQ-adjectives like Smart and Intelligent to feel at home with the increased critical dominance of structuralist thought. With what might be termed undue haste, any number of artists who had been slathering away on their important canvases were sacrificed to the beast of the postmodern labyrinth and, when that beast staggered forth covered in expressionist gore, its name was Simulacrum and it was speaking French. Now the Freeway was clear for the Smart Inheritors and they cruised forward in their glistening convertibles with the brute, hypnotic arrogance of rubberneckers looking back over their shoulders at a nightmare on the side of the road.

My feeling is that it's only seconds before the Freeway Cruisers get escalated to Major and Important and all that goes with those signifiers. And I think it is probably their due. However, just before that happens, I would like to offer a cautionary proposal. If we are to truly participate in a definition of the art of our time, we need more than five adjectives. Here's my suggestion. Call a moratorium on the use of Major, Important, Smart, and Intelligent. Flail around for other modifiers until you find one that personalizes rather than neutralizes. And, finally, when you feel Fabulous coming on, if it doesn't bubble up from deep inside like a giggle or a scream, you've got the wrong adjective.

Parkett, no. 13 (1987): 129–31.

Down the Airshaft

Isn't this the sofa on which your father bled to death?
ALBAN BERG, *LULU*, 1936

The cheap originality which finds expression in putting things to uses for which they were not intended is often confounded with individuality; whereas the latter consists not in an attempt to be different from other people at the cost of comfort, but in the desire to be comfortable in one's own way, even though it be the way of a monotonously large majority.
EDITH WHARTON AND OGDEN CODMAN JR.,
THE DECORATION OF HOUSES, 1897[1]

Let's play a game! Quick, pick a work of art—one you truly love. Now, think of a setting that would seriously compromise that art. Hurry up, be specific. How big is the room? Are the walls papered or painted? Is the floor carpeted or bare? What style of furniture? What kind of bibelots? When you see it, freeze it. Let your eyes wander. What element is most damaging to the art? Is it the paisley wallpaper, or the zebra-covered wing chairs, or the Navajo throw rugs, or the arrangement of gladiolas next to all those Toby mugs? Don't waffle; be firm. As soon as you've identified the biggest problem, think about the art. Would a great something else pale quite so definitively if it were proximate to that wallpaper or those mugs? Well, would it? If, in your mind's eye, that something else isn't experiencing nearly as many problems as your first choice, you're playing the game. Congratulations!

I started playing the game a couple of years ago in a dentist's waiting room while leafing through an issue of the magazine *House & Garden*. There, in the middle of a glossy living room layout, hung a painting by an artist whose work I particularly admired. Yet, clinging to a wall of aubergine silk from Scalamandré and overlooking a settee in chintz from Colefax and Fowler, the painting looked mindlessly decorative— just one more cupbearer at a catamites' convention. I found myself thinking of what exactly (and by whom) might have a fighting chance in the middle of all that texture, and the game was born. Since then, I've floated Gerhard Richter landscapes between Venetian sconces, hefted Richard Serra sculptures into faux-marbled foyers, and propped Francesco Clemente watercolors over gold-fauceted bidets. I've also become addicted to interior design publications; their pages were my playing field. Month after month, I devoured an assortment of magazines (*Architectural Digest*, *Metropolitan Home*, *Vogue Interiors*, etc.), uncovering ever more startling aesthetic abuses, finding that there was no concept too vile for some decorator to perpetrate on a guileless work of art. Or, conversely, that there was no work of art too vile to elaborate on the endless arabesque of decor. Through it all, my favorite magazine remained the first I had seen, *House & Garden*. But that was then and this is now and everything has changed. Sadly, my playing field has run to weed.

The *House & Garden* I discovered at the dentist's was an endearing, capricious vamp. I felt my interest in it to be not unlike that expressed by the narrator for Henry James's most exasperating of heroines, the Princess Casamassima (née Christina Light):

He was not in love with her; he disapproved of her; he distrusted her; and yet he felt it a kind of privilege to watch her.... The background of her nature, as he would have called it, was large and mysterious, and it emitted strange, fantastic gleams and flashes. Watching for these rather quickened one's pulses.[2]

Or as the Princess said of herself: "In plain English, I am odiously frivolous."

What, you may ask, had so effectively baited my attention? Well, initially, it was the pictures—pictures of rooms, rooms that were organized into thematic narratives where the theater of their invisible inhabitants was played out. Only infrequently were the inhabitants named; more often than not, they were referred to by vague appellations like "young professionals" or "art collectors" or, more picaresquely, an "enchanting Persian couple." So, anyway, here was this stream of rooms and some were decisively urban and some were casually country, and some were pointedly decadent and others were upstandingly traditional. The layout set a pace that moved one through a thicket of Biedermeier into a cool modernist glade at a jogger's pace. And behind the visuals was the prose, which actually seemed to be written and/or edited to a weight that complemented the accompanying pictorials. One of the first pieces I remember reading cited a "hostess" who had removed her Syrie Maugham sofa from storage "now that hyperbole is back"—an eminently quotable gesture that got me perusing the type with the same avidity as the visuals.

House & Garden's only real American competition was *Architectural Digest*, and, believe me, it didn't come close. For starters, it named names (usually "iffy" celebrities like Carrie Fisher and Tom Selleck) and featured rooms that looked as if the price tags were still stuck to the bottom of every Han dynasty vase in the mirrored bookcase. Then too there was the prose—puff pieces that tended to inflate like monstrous, atomically altered blowfish:

> The owners—he, the president of a large automotive sound and telecommunications company; she, a former film and television actress and singer—knew precisely what they wanted: a resplendent Italianate villa recalling the glamour of old Hollywood.[3]

It's the kind of grotesque gush that can stray off, as the foregoing did, into such necrophiliac visions as "a formally garbed Gable and Lombard, Hepburn and Tracy sipping apéritifs." Suffice to say, my heart remained with *House & Garden*'s hyperbolic hostess.

In all fairness, it should be noted that *House & Garden* was also capable of attempting to cash in on the cult of personality, but their choices —Dominique de Menil or Balthus—were so giddily *entre nous* that it was amusing to second-guess upcoming selections (maybe Ned Rorem or Doris Lessing). Even when the prose was at its silliest, its writers erred more toward Evelyn Waugh than Hedda Hopper:

> All his favorite pictures were there patterning the redness, illuming the gloom, and so were the lovely gold tiered console in the manner of William of Kent, beneath the painting of a shivering dog cushioned between black marble busts, the battered old cupboard with its crowning marble Laocoön agonizing among the branches of coral, and the blue Adam armchair with the subtle upholstery of seventeenth-century Mughal velvet.[4]

So, if you'd mourned the passing of Bloomsbury, you needn't have. More important, if you feared misplacing your brain, there was always something historically revelatory (mostly by in-house editor Martin Filler) that tended to advance a concisely authentic revisionist position. Share, for example, a moment in Filler's appreciation of Villa Savoye:

> Looking at the colors of this most recent repainting of the Villa Savoye, one realizes that the salmon pink, sky blue, dark blue, dark green, maroon, terra-cotta, and orange are nothing less than the very palette the Postmodern architects, and especially Michael Graves, have claimed as their own in reaction to the supposed colorlessness of the International Style. It is doubly ironic that one of the least attractive and uncalled for features of Graves' lectures proposing the

need for an alternative to Modernism has been his belittling attacks on Le Corbusier, whose style he copied earlier in his own career before moving on to more remote historical sources.[5]

Not a bad smoking gun for the Noguchi coffee table. Nonetheless, Filler aside, I eventually felt the need to justify my reckless nibbling on the awful, chichi ooze of decor by swallowing the antidote of historic precedent. For my historicist rehabilitation, I turned to *The Decoration of Houses*, by Edith Wharton and Ogden Codman Jr. Published over a century ago and recently reissued, this Brahminical tome had imperiously dictated American taste for more than several decades before lapsing into obscurity. Reading it now—getting caught up in the sacerdotal absolutism of the prose—is alternately charming and appalling. Share with me the salubrious fanaticism of the authors' thesis:

> When the rich man demands good architecture his neighbors will get it too. The vulgarity of current decoration has its source in the indifference of the wealthy to architectural fitness. Every good moulding, every carefully studied detail, exacted by those who can afford to indulge their taste, will in time find its way to the carpenter-built cottage. Once the right precedent is established, it costs less to follow than oppose it.[6]

Undeniably, the odious simplicity of this kind of premise is scary on a whole lot of levels. It is also ingenuously provocative and leads to Wharton and Codman's weirdly touching conclusion, in which sails are set for a sea of aesthetic equilibrium where:

> There is no absolute perfection, there is no communicable ideal; but much that is empiric, much that is confused and extravagant, will give way before the application of principles based on common sense and regulated by the laws of harmony and proportion.[7]

Now, who wants to pick a fight with that? Not me. And yet ... there is something more than peripherally creepy about it all. Looking for a historic placebo, I stumbled on a bunker full of live ammo. Suddenly, I was reminded of the insidiously glib fascism of Ralph Lauren's advertising campaigns as they appear month after month in upwardly scaled American magazines. In these advertisements, Lauren's marketing features pictorial constructs in which chiseled white models enact scenarios exploring the narcotizing properties of power. (If John Updike had written the screenplay for Visconti's *The Damned* and set it in Connecticut, the result would have been a Lauren promotional video.) Those Lauren models, it occurred to me, were being installed as the proud inheritors of Wharton and Codman's houses—as the "young professional" inhabitants of all those *House & Garden* interiors. Shockingly, my flight of associative fantasy was leading me straight into the dark night of an American Halloween where razor blades slide silently into luscious autumn apples intended for the baskets of credulous children like ourselves.

Let me pause for a moment. Perhaps I've gone too far. My topic has made me conflicted. I want to pull back and temper my anxiety. I want to return to *House & Garden*. I want to go back to March of 1988, when the magazine's long-standing, wonderfully named editor, Louis Oliver Gropp, was replaced by Condé Nast's smart-ass wunderkind Anna Wintour. With that transfer of power, *House & Garden* became *HG* and the battering of an institution began. What Gropp had raised to a level of charming discourse, Wintour turned into a hyperventilated hen party. Where Gropp encouraged editorial diversity, Wintour dug in with a relentlessly anal series of theme issues. (Banner headlines on her covers have gone from "Romance" to "Heat Wave" to "Into the Garden," with each issue maniacally conforming to its pastry shell of a theme.) Where Gropp molded writers and rooms into elegant little divertissements, Wintour brutally goosed the magazine with pinking shears to generate page after page of jagged-edge photo layouts in which details are scaled up for color, not content. Where Gropp cultivated the art of the essay, Wintour became the queen of the blurb. Her "Into the Garden" issue, for example, began with a double-page spread of a celebutante in a Philippe Model hat waving a garden fork; she was accompanied by the following copy:

Hail Botanica! This year's garden yields a bumper crop of surprises—hats crawling with ivy, friendly follies, torso topiary, flowers of power.[8]

Where Gropp was putting out a magazine with a four-star menu, Wintour is dishing out leftover stew. Her *HG* has been jokingly referred to as *House & Garment*, but that makes it sound more focused than it is. What Condé Nast has wrought with its new editor is just another ubiquitous Condé Nast publication dedicated to the proposition that the Siamese twins of consumerism and illiteracy are inoperably inseparable and temptingly lucrative. Most regrettably, from my point of view, Wintour has taken *House & Garden*'s rather delicate little feet and shoved them into tissue-crammed jackboots. She has aggressively politicized my innocent game and I resent it.

I also resent having to turn to a muddled hack like Ayn Rand for my conclusion, but Wintour is simply too like Dominique Francon, the operatically conflicted heroine of *The Fountainhead*, to let the similarity pass unremarked. Rather romantically, I see Wintour's destruction of Gropp's creation to be very like Francon's destruction of a sculptural antiquity—an act she justifies thusly:

I had a statue which I found in Europe—a statue of a God. I think I was in love with it, but I broke it.... I threw it down the airshaft.... So that I wouldn't have to love it. I didn't want to be tied to anything. I wanted to destroy it rather than let it be a part of a world where beauty and genius and greatness have no chance.[9]

As for me ... well, I feel badly. I never wanted to see interior decoration as another imperialist cancer that bears watching. I never wanted to play a game that was slick with the sweat of the needy. Unfortunately, when one is caught in the shadow cast by the leveling hammer of capitalism, such thoughts are inescapable. Good-bye, *House & Garden*.

Postscript:
In June of 1988, Anna Wintour's slash-and-burn reign at *HG* came to an end. The magazine had been vulgarized, ubiquitized, and given a more pluralistic advertising base. As had been rumored from the start, Wintour was named editor in chief of American *Vogue*, where she replaced the legendary Grace Mirabella. A Wintour trainee took her place at *HG* and Condé Nast's dollar-bill formula remains solidly and brutally in place. [After another design remake in 1995, the magazine published its final US issue in December 2007. RF]

Parkett, no. 17 (1988): 152–56.

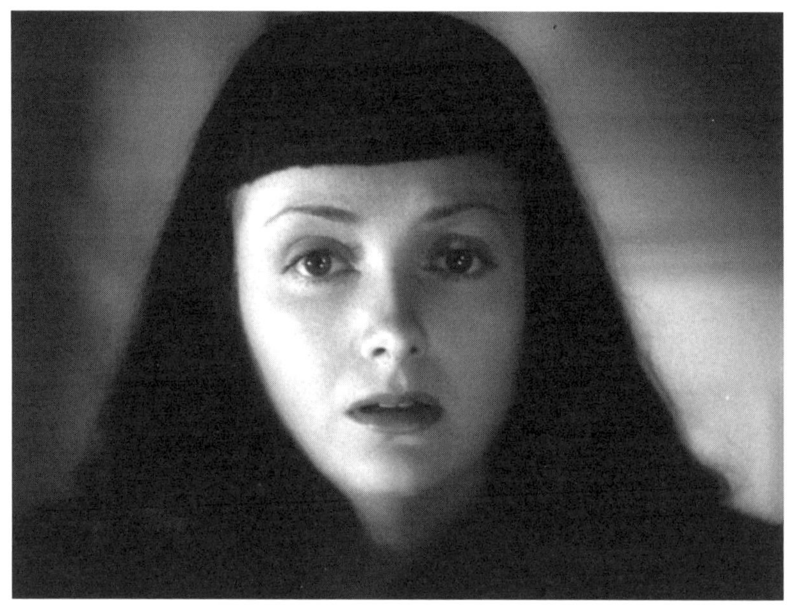

Jean Brooks as "Jacqueline Gibson" in *The Seventh Victim* (1943)

The Dog and the Suicide

On the boat to St. Sebastian, Betsy is interrupted in her contemplation of the ocean by Paul's Byronic musing. He tells her that the sea only seems beautiful because she does not understand it; that the flying fish are not leaping for joy but in terror, escaping their predators; that the glittering water "takes its gleam from millions of tiny bodies. It's the glitter of putrescence. There's no beauty here—only death and decay."

JOEL E. SIEGEL ON VAL LEWTON'S *I WALKED WITH A ZOMBIE*[1]

I like lots and lots of atmosphere and I like it damp. I'm talking about the kind of atmosphere that permeates floorboards, curls up pant legs, chills spines, and laces undulant tentacles around the brain. It's that ferocious Brontëan rot that got hold of Heathcliff and Mr. Rochester. It's the terrible percussion that danced Richard Strauss's *Salome* and Alban Berg's *Lulu* over the edge of the abyss. It can't be reasoned with, and once it's taken hold, it can't be shaken off.

My favorite master of atmosphere is Val Lewton, who, between 1942 and 1946, produced nine indelibly corrosive films. All were shot on a shoestring in two months or less by RKO Studio's cheapie unit and rushed into release. Lewton worked with three directors (Mark Robson, Jacques Tourneur, and Robert Wise), each of whom had his own distinct stylistic demeanor, but all of whom served Lewton's overwhelming unity of vision.

Superficially, Lewton made horror movies; intrinsically, they were meditations on death—always death. One of the producer's tenderest critics, Manny Farber, quite accurately described Lewton's special gift:

"He ... hid much more of his story than any other filmmaker, and forced his crew to create drama almost abstractly with symbolic sounds, textures, and the like."[2]

Lewton's images glide by almost languidly, but once experienced, they rarely depart. A terrified woman swims in a shimmering darkened pool, stalked by shifting masses of shadow that momentarily congeal into the silhouette of a stalking panther. Two women, their billowing garments caught in a sultry wind, drift through stylized cane fields, past burnt offerings and witching circles, toward an oddly decorous voodoo ritual. A chic catatonic slumps in a wing chair, surrounded by participants in a sinister cocktail party who repeatedly and seductively offer her a cut-glass tumbler of poison. An angry mother bars her home to her hysteric daughter only to hear the girl fall silent and to see a wash of blood course beneath the door.

It is Lewton's perverse genius that makes these images so insistently, troublingly beautiful. It is a beauty as innocuous and menacing as a sliver of glass cast into a streambed. His are those rare back-lot films in which the controlled elegance of the vision is so confident it renders reality quite simply irrelevant. (Albert P. Ryder, another master of atmosphere, wrote of just such a phenomenon when he rejected painting from life in favor of painting from the imagination: "It was better than nature, for it was vibrating with the thrill of new creations.")[3]

My favorite Lewton film is the humblest of them all, *The Seventh Victim* (1943). Oddly, for a Lewton production, nothing about it looks particularly good. The sets are dog-eared, the costumes makeshift, and a really bad wig almost sinks the proceedings midstream. Yet there is an exquisite melancholy suffusing everything in the film— a melancholy that ultimately becomes its raison d'être. Here Lewton assumes a transcendental posture more common to seventeenth-century poetry than to twentieth-century horror movies. And in this melancholy lies the key to my kind of atmosphere.

A taste of one scene from *The Seventh Victim* may access its strange power. Two neighbors are in the hall of their boardinghouse. One, the self-doomed Jacqueline, moves like a somnambulist and speaks in a mesmerizing, honeyed voice that drifts listlessly from one sentence to the next. Wrapped in a fur coat, dark hair cascading over her shoulders, she is sleek and expensively alien. The other character, Mimi, is a trembling, damaged Kewpie doll in an old bathrobe. Here is their conversation:

> JACQUELINE: Who are you?
> MIMI: I'm Mimi … I'm dying.
> JACQUELINE: No …
> MIMI: I've been quiet, oh, ever so quiet. I hardly move yet it keeps coming all the time … closer and closer. I rest and rest and yet I am dying.
> JACQUELINE: And you don't want to die … I've always wanted to die. Always.
> MIMI: I'm afraid. I'm tired of being afraid … of waiting.
> JACQUELINE: Why wait?
> MIMI (with sudden determination): I'm not going to wait. I'm going out … laugh … dance … do all the things I used to do.
> JACQUELINE: And then?
> MIMI (turning to return to her room): I don't know.
> JACQUELINE (very softly and almost with envy): You will die.[4]

The meeting changes nothing for either of the women; it only accelerates the inevitable. Elsewhere in the boardinghouse, Jacqueline's husband and sister, while awaiting her return, acknowledge their love for each other. Yet, for Jacqueline, their love has no more weight than a decal loosed in a riptide. Nor does Lewton care: he ends the film with Mimi descending the stairs for a night of anxious pleasure, oblivious to the sound that signals her glamorous neighbor's suicide. As Mimi departs, Jacqueline's voice on the soundtrack intones John Donne:

"I run to Death and Death meets me as fast, and all my Pleasures are like Yesterdays." That Jacqueline achieves a sort of metaphysical ecstasy in death, while her husband and sister (the film's nominal hero and heroine) seem pathetically sentimental in their fragile, mortal huddle, gives the scene a haunting irony.

Now, lest you think my sense of atmosphere smells too much of the grave, let me introduce another artist who, like Lewton, was also a master of the horror genre: Francisco Goya. I actually arrived at Goya well before I discovered Lewton, but like Jacqueline's lightweight husband, I was too nervous in the presence of an authentic obsessive and wandered off into the etiolated topiaries of El Greco. At the time (early adolescence), I preferred a soft-focused, stigmatic decor to anything really dangerous. Later I got it right. What first brought me back to Goya was the exhilarating bravura with which he celebrated his boredom. And, trust me, nobody gets bored quite the way he does, right there in the middle of a painting. When, willfully, he decides to turn a hand into a ruffled knob or a foot into a stockinged fin, he does it bluntly and without apology. When he snips and pastry-tucks yet another monarchical crotch into a sexless, avian fold, one understands how daring and careless his relationship was with his aristocratic sitters. When one sees how very close to the earth his potato-eyed peasantry is, one intuits instantly the careless ease with which the awful ecology of revolution is plotted. But this is only a fraction of Goya's art.

Always, echoing through the corridors of the Prado, are dark *saetas* leading you literally down into what remains of Goya's most terrifying, most modern moment—the frescoes from La Quinta del Sordo. Tucked away in the museum's basement, their surfaces glazed with something very like phosphorescent excrement, are the Black Paintings. Begun when the artist was seventy-three (was stone deaf, was demoralized, was madly in love, was dying), these are the paintings of a man with nothing left to prove and everything left to understand.

One painting in the gallery, only one, forms an equation the sum of which almost suggests hope: *The Head of a Dog*. Aggressively rectangular, the composition is cleft by an extreme, low diagonal that separates a shifting, strongly raked incline from an enormous, inhospitable wedge of sky. Truly, here in these two attenuated slices of archetypal "above" and "below" is the terra incognita. It is a land that bears no fruit under a sky that sheds no warmth (*"lasciate ogni speranza, voi ch'entrate"*). Silhouetted against that sky, peeking over that hill is the face of a hound. The animal's eyes are cast apprehensively up the slope; frozen in ambivalence, it could just as easily turn back as trudge ahead. The composition is so daringly close to the kind of emotive abstraction that was still centuries away that one almost resents the presence of the animal. However, it is the hound that points the way to the future, whose goofy, doggy face allows us proximity to the heart of the painting, and that is our relationship to our mortality.

The Head of a Dog works because it is preceded by a career that works but also because the artist knew an awful lot about the distillation of life and death. Here is an exercise in pigment where colors are absolutes and their application results in a moral imperative that defines the act of making art as an act of conscience. What makes it transcendent is the artist's unsentimental declension of melancholy. This is Goya's atmosphere.

My atmospheric hysteria arises from a real fear—in this moment of all too many horrors and of creeping fundamentalist fascism—that art is getting weirdly in line with the culture. I worry that people are forgetting that great art is never easy or reassuring, that it is a barb and it should make us bleed. I worry too that sentiment, not melancholy, is on the rise, and I know that sentiment is the most dangerous narcotic on the market.

I get nervous in front of the right Pollock or Rothko or Klein or Still (those midcentury giants of anxiety) and that's the way I like it. What I don't like is art that's interested in being my friend; that's way too easy. I want nothing less than the same awful choice as the B-movie heroine in her back-lot boardinghouse or the dog on the Spanish hill. I want art that tattoos skid marks on your soul. I want to stay scared.

Parkett, no. 23 (1990): 146–48.

December 1989: After the Fact

How does one track the origins of an obsession? In my case, it started with a poster publicizing a festival of Italian neo-realist films back in the early 1970s. The image—I'm looking at it as I write—is of a girl standing immersed to midcalf in the water of a rice field. Where the water stops, a pair of black cotton stockings continues up the sapling length of her legs. Garterless, the stockings cling to the flesh of her upper thighs and end a critical two or so inches before a form-fitting pair of shorts take over and lead the eye up the torso, which ripples with a second skin of a black sweater. Floating above all this fetishized agrarian voluptuousness is a head that is provocatively at odds with it. The long oval face, the scimitar eyes, the Magyar cheekbones, the full crescent lips all work beautifully with the requisite tussled mane of hair and (forgive the cliché) jutting breasts. But what's wrong is how the face is composed and here, I think, is where my obsession took off. Instead of sexual invitation, the expression on the face is much more akin to intellectual skepticism. Phew! It's really weird and it really works. What, in heaven's name, is this girl doing in a rice paddy wearing that outfit? Years later, another Italian actress, Sophia Loren, would take the same pose in much the same outfit and walk into international stardom. Loren, however, was an ebullient promise of good fleshy fun. This girl in the rice field promises nothing but trouble, and existential trouble at that.

The poster was for *Bitter Rice* (released in 1949) and the actress was Silvana Mangano. For me, the name was half of it. It was dark and throaty and, yes, sexy. Take it syllable by syllable and you'll know what

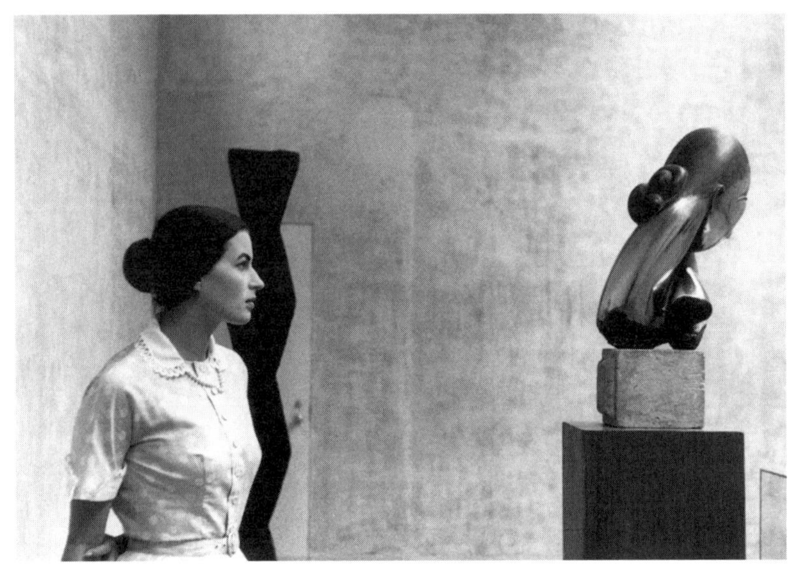

Eve Arnold, *Silvana Mangano and Brancusi at the Museum of Modern Art, New York*, 1956

I mean. Màn-ga-no. It sounds like a luscious fruit; it might even be poisonous if eaten before it's ripe. And, in that curious alchemy of name and persona that can alter a performer's career, Mangano is a name that suggests a lot more heft than a mere starlet with a good pair of legs.

Bitter Rice was for Mangano what *The Blue Angel* was for Dietrich or *Gilda* was for Hayworth: it fixed her forever in the eyes of her audience. However, it is here that a sharp irony emerges. Everyone in this country knows the names of Dietrich and Hayworth but virtually no one has heard of Mangano. Other of her countrywomen (Loren, Lollobrigida, Cardinale) have had their moments in the Hollywood steeplechase. Even the proto-ethnic Anna Magnani is more likely to jog a responsive chord than is Mangano. Why? I think that Mangano's absence from the American consciousness is due to two factors: her instinctive reserve as an actress and her nose. The former is a matter of speculation; the latter is a matter of fact. Mangano's nose was her most sensitive instrument. What the pose in the rice field didn't show was the nose. Had she posed in profile rather than front on, the remarkable equine alertness could easily have unbalanced the already precarious mix of sensuality and intellect. And, as Mangano's career developed, her profile became increasingly important. Sniffing her way through a succession of international costume epics produced by her husband, Dino De Laurentiis—films like *Ulysses* with Kirk Douglas and *Barabbas* with Anthony Quinn—Mangano was cast as goddess and whore but always, inevitably, she used her profile to buy a little distance from the inanity that surrounded her. Over time, the nose was held ever higher until the possibility of international stardom lay so far below that she simply floated away. Then, sometime in the 1960s, Mangano stylized her film persona even further by removing her eyebrows. By the time she reemerged outside Italy in the now legendary films of Pier Paolo Pasolini, she had perfected the hieratic façade of a kabuki geisha.

Two of Pasolini's greatest films, *Oedipus Rex* (1967) and *Teorema* (1968), are structured almost exclusively around the enigmatic presence of Mangano, who is also featured in a pivotal mute cameo in his *Decameron* (1971). A fascinating, biographical narrative shows Pasolini casting her in *Oedipus* as mother/lover, in *Teorema* as mother/whore, and in *Decameron* quite literally as La Madonna. *Teorema* was my first Mangano video rental after her death in December of 1989. In it, she plays the bored wife of a Milanese industrialist who, like everyone in her cinema family, succumbs to the Dionysian charm of a mysterious houseguest played by Terence Stamp. Her surrender to Stamp subsequently leads to the solicitation of her son's school friends.

In Mangano's mandarin grip, this potential cliché of a role becomes a piece of ritualized choreography. It's an extremely risky dance in which she essentially mimes the farther boundaries of desire. Sheathed in body-skimming silks, she drifts from scene to scene with an opacity that is mesmerizing; the closer she draws to the heat of fulfillment, the cooler she manifests her presence. When she drops the spaghetti strap of her chemise or strips off her pantyhose, her autoerotic abandonment is fueled by an icy calm, leading us into the awful vacuum of animal need. Watching the enormous, haunted eyes in that perfectly cosmeticized face is to witness one of the great late refinements of silent-screen acting.

Mangano's most internationally visible role was in Luchino Visconti's *Death in Venice* (1971). In this film, the dialogue simply fills in around the corners of the plot. The real propulsive language is in the voice-over monologue delivered by Dirk Bogarde as a dying composer coming to grips with a final fantasy of redemption. His internalized fantasies revolve around a young boy staying in the same hotel. Mangano plays the boy's mother. Set in fin-de-siècle Venice, Visconti's film conjures up a gorgeous dying rose of a world. Mangano has an essentially nonspeaking role. She murmurs a few motherly niceties to her children. She registers affection, consternation, and apprehension.

Occasionally, as when she is serenaded by a vulgar performer at the hotel, the nostrils of her glorious nose flare ever so slightly, as if catching a whiff of something putrid in the expensive air of the Lido. She models a succession of exquisite day-dresses, tea-dresses, and gowns. She is quite frequently veiled. Most of her perceptible activity is given over to arranging strands of creamy pearls or adjusting her veils. She's more perfume than persona. And yet, without her, the film would have no center. Somehow, Mangano's mother is at once self-absorbed and all-absorbing. The performance is as clean as a sterilized scalpel. Again, as in *Teorema*, she is detached from all that surrounds her and suffused in a dreamy melancholy. In *Death in Venice*, Mangano's extreme mannerism, which by this time was her trademark, is softened by the kind of weighted grace with which she interprets the role of mother. Visconti does not simply focus on her as a woman but as woman. It works. She provides a virtual sea of otherness for Bogarde to paddle in.

Mangano's last international film was Nikita Makalkov's *Dark Eyes* (1987), in which she plays the faithful wife to Marcello Mastroianni's philandering husband. By then she was already ill with the cancer that would take her life. She had lost a child in a plane crash and had been divorced by De Laurentiis, who subsequently married a much younger American woman. By 1987 there was something haunted in the fragility of her beauty. Her role frames what is essentially an extended anecdote about the husband's vain pursuit of the ideal mistress. She is the wife who is abandoned and reclaimed, only to be abandoned again. If just anyone had played the part it would inevitably have been about a shrew or a hysteric. Mangano has the grace to simply let it be about a wife who is more often than not conveniently forgotten about by her husband. She gives the role a delicate gravity that never tips the scales in her favor at the expense of her silly, careless husband. What she does do, however, is to strip away the makeup artist's façade. In *Dark Eyes* she discards the artifice of surface and presents the naked face.

Without the tilt of her nose or the shiver of her exquisitely penciled
eyebrows or the studied languor of her movement, she is simply a
woman of modest expectations in love with the wrong man. At no
point does she signal the need to share her character's isolation; she
inhabits it and that's that. Watching Mangano play around the periphery of this film is to understand what a great and selfless actress
she had become.

Now, I like to think of *Teorema*, *Death in Venice*, and *Dark Eyes* as
a trilogy. From the theatrically manicured façade of *Teorema* through
the gauzy transparencies of *Death in Venice* to the background presence
of *Dark Eyes*, one can watch the actress saying good-bye, removing
herself ever further from the intrusive vision of the camera. The
elegiac isolation increases from role to role until, inevitably, she must
disappear. To watch Mangano continually and incessantly pare away
and simplify what she is willing to offer as an actress is to understand
just a little better what we must all let go of to get through a life.

Parkett, no. 30 (1991): 176–78.

Interview with a Valkyrie

Review of *Leni Riefenstahl: A Memoir*

It's terribly difficult knowing what to think about Leni Riefenstahl's
Memoir. She began writing it when she was eighty, finished it at eighty-
five, and now that she's ninety-one the English-language edition
has just been issued. While the *Memoir* concludes in 1982, a new documentary (Ray Müller's *The Wonderful, Horrible Life of Leni Riefenstahl*,
1993) shows her soldiering on with enough projects to last another
lifetime. Together, the film and autobiography should meld into a
hymn to the wondrous possibilities of simply, magnificently getting
on with the job of living a life.

They don't. The epic ambiguity that has accrued around Riefenstahl is an impenetrable cloud bank resistant to all forms of conventional navigation. Caught in that vast whiteness, I keep thinking of
a line by D. H. Lawrence: "If people lived without accepting lies they
would ripen like apples, and be scented like pippins in their old age."
In February of 1932, Leni Riefenstahl forever lost the possibility of
becoming a Lawrentian apple. It was then that she heard Adolf Hitler
for the first time, and it induced a vision: "It seemed as if the earth's
surface were spreading out in front of me, like a hemisphere that
suddenly splits apart in the middle, spewing out an enormous jet of
water, so powerful that it touched the sky and shook the earth."

What makes everything such a mess with Riefenstahl is that her
greatest achievement was also her greatest offense. Between the ages
of thirty and forty, at the height of the Third Reich, she became a
legendary filmmaker; and the very authority of her accomplishment
forever compromised her reputation and her work.

It is perhaps easiest to begin with what seems most clear. Riefenstahl was a dancer and an actress of some renown in prewar Germany. In 1932 she directed and starred in *The Blue Light*, a film of great technical and aesthetic significance. Not long after, she became a highly visible supporter and sometime acquaintance of Hitler. At his behest she made two documentaries, *Day of Freedom* and *Triumph of the Will*, both commemorating the Nuremberg Party Convention of 1934. Two years later, at the invitation of the International Olympic Committee, Riefenstahl shot *Olympia*, her revolutionary documentary on the Berlin Games (released in 1938, after two years of editing). From 1941 to 1943 she produced, directed, and starred in *Tiefland*, which by the time it was released, in 1954, was a gorgeous antique.

This superficial narrative might easily lead one to believe the Riefenstahl problem is Hitler. It is not that simple. Like the architect Albert Speer's, Riefenstahl's real problem was an aesthetic vision every bit as complicated and grandiose as Hitler's political vision. In *Triumph of the Will* and *Olympia*, she created documentaries that not only enhanced reality but aggressively surpassed it. Within the stadiums of Nuremberg and Berlin, Riefenstahl choreographed a world of clockwork precision in which individuality is achieved only by its approximation of perfection. Everything feeds the spectacle; everything is consumed to fuel the final, idealized vision of the creator. And, indeed, the vision is literally ravishing. Nobody ever really caught the allure of fascism like Riefenstahl. She knew instinctively that by building from its imperially classicist underpinnings, she could harmonize its most nihilistic excesses by imposing a hypnotic rhythm that kept everything sailing forward to a Valhalla where hero and herd are as one.

Riefenstahl's relationship with the Reich appears, as she tells it, to have been one against all. I'm inclined to believe her. Simply being a woman in the midst of Hitler's all-boy fraternity must have been tricky. Her major grievances are typically directed at an obstreperous, malfunctioning bureaucracy. Hitler is portrayed as a man with his head in the clouds—a pose in which Riefenstahl frequently filmed him. That he was a bad person is concealed, attributed to a hazily defined schizophrenia. Their talk has the leaden cadence of plot filler in an operetta. She says: "If I had been born an Indian or a Jew you wouldn't even speak to me, so how can I work for someone who makes such distinctions among people?" He says: "I wish the people around me would be as uninhibited as you." Cut! Cue orchestra!

What Riefenstahl knew about the death camps is, she says, exactly nothing. (After the war she was accused of using Gypsies from one of the camps for crowd scenes in *Tiefland*; she was found innocent.) Given the amount of time she devoted to filming and editing, it is plausible. Even her sexual relations during this period were, like meals, grabbed on the run with the occasional crew member or, during *Olympia*, athlete. The biggest howl in the book is the inauguration of her affair with the American decathlon champion Glenn Morris: "The dim light prevented any filming of the ceremony, and when Glenn Morris came down the steps, he headed straight towards me. I held out my hand and congratulated him, but he grabbed me in his arms, tore off my blouse, and kissed my breasts, right in the middle of the stadium, in front of a hundred thousand spectators.... I never wanted to speak to him again, never go anywhere near him again. But then I couldn't avoid him because of the pole vault."

The *Memoir* is at its best when Riefenstahl is working—is on her way to the next metaphoric pole vault, first on her completed films, then on the films that never were (but became three books of photography). When Riefenstahl isn't working she makes herself miserable and then reaches out to make those around her miserable. That portion of the book devoted to her inability to work (initially because of her past) is brutal. Riefenstahl recounts her mile-high fall from grace with a relentless reliance on facts. You get the feeling that if, for an instant, she abandoned the neutrality of her reportage, the seams would come apart with the sound of tearing metal. Then, finally, like Melville's great whale, "bedraggled with trailing ropes, and harpoons, and lances," Riefenstahl breaks free and heads for Africa.

When, in 1956, Riefenstahl arrives in Khartoum, both she and her book come vividly back to life. She travels to the Nuba tribes of Sudan and, in their culture, finds her kind of theater of plastic exquisiteness. Central to the Nuba is the wrestling festival, which, for Riefenstahl, becomes a visceral grail. I have a suspicion Riefenstahl is in a funny way cleansed by these matches. Year in and year out, the clans gather and a man upends a man, and the people rejoice, and order is maintained, and crops are harvested, and the great stinking waste of a world war becomes smaller and smaller.

For fifteen years Riefenstahl shuttles between Europe and Africa to document the Nuba. Her mother dies, and she is beset by illnesses, lawsuits, and attacks from the media. Movie deals blow up in her face; the rights to her films are constantly in jeopardy. But Riefenstahl chugs along like the little engine that could and, against all odds, gets two remarkable books (*The Last of the Nuba* and *The Nuba of Kau*) published. Her career is rehabilitated, her films are rediscovered, and she is culturally de-Nazified.

But, because she is Leni Riefenstahl, there is yet another bomb waiting to explode. This time it is lobbed by Susan Sontag, who, after leafing through *The Last of the Nuba*, writes an essay for the *New York Times* called "Fascinating Fascism." It gets nasty very quickly: "If the photographs are examined carefully, in conjunction with the lengthy text written by Riefenstahl, it becomes clear that they are continuous with her Nazi work." The impact of Sontag's attack takes a tremendous toll, and newly opened doors begin slamming shut.

"Fascinating Fascism" was published in 1975, and I get the feeling that it killed any hope Riefenstahl might have seriously entertained about making another film in this lifetime. She takes a chapter to refute Sontag's charges and then, very quickly, the memoir moves to its conclusion. Things happen, but something has snapped. At seventy-two, she takes up scuba diving and publishes her third book of photographs, *Coral Gardens*. It's vaguely depressing, as if Riefenstahl had exiled herself to the very bottom of the sea.

The book's end is distressingly painful. "My aim was to tackle preconceived ideas and to clear up misunderstandings and I spent five years working on the manuscript. It was not an easy task since I was the only one who could write these memoirs; it did not turn out to be a happy one." I prefer the conclusion of Ray Müller's film, which shows Riefenstahl far below the surface of the water watching a giant stingray sweep silently by. As the creature passes her, she drifts up, glides over it, and then propels herself down onto its back. The need to measure herself against that which can destroy her persists. It is the troublesome heart of her art.

Artforum 32, no. 4 (December 1993): 9.

The Levelers

Let us imagine that we are the keepers of British culture. We're wearing spotless white flannels and boater hats. We're lounging on ingeniously portable campaign furniture. Our position is atop the Dover cliffs, but our membership rings the island. Idly, we chat; occasionally, we read. Beautifully trained spaniels laze awaiting our command. Every once in a listless while, a balloon drifts toward us from elsewhere, from beyond us. Some balloons are prettier than others or remind us of ones we have seen being hawked at country fairs. Those we let sail over us and inland. Others are not pretty at all. They are misshapen and occasionally garish. Those we take aim at and shoot from the sky. If the spaniels have not fully destroyed the balloons upon retrieval, we make short work of what's left. Our vigilance is infrequently compromised by the passing individual who, placing him- or herself between us and the escarpment, blocks the view and, if one puts a good face on it, inadvertently permits free passage to an alien inflatable. As we have colleagues farther inland, it is relatively safe to assume that escaping balloons will be brought efficiently to ground before reaching any densely populated urban center.

Now, let us imagine that we are the makers of British art. We cluster, easily identifiable, in a handful of towns and cities. We wait for the balloons and, as gently as possible, snare them from the sky. Often, leaking air, they come to earth willingly. Rarely are they undamaged. The original color is drained; the shape, a hypothesis. We do what we can to reimagine them and, painstakingly in our studios, we create new balloons in colors and forms reminiscent of the originals. Sometimes, we release them to the currents of air that blow away from the island. The danger in this is that, if our new balloons are caught in a lull, the culture-keepers will mistake them for foreign free-floaters and bring them plummeting back down.

At the end of the last century and the beginning of the one now drawing to a close, the culture-keepers momentarily relaxed their vigilance and three blimp-sized balloons dug craters as they crash-landed on British soil. Impressionism, cubism, and constructivism didn't fragment when they fell. Unlike the trial balloons—futurism, dada, surrealism—which followed and came to earth in tatters, these remained whole. Because of the blimps' extraordinary size, the makers of art found it necessary to camouflage them and, although the contours remained suggestively intact, the surfaces were often radically altered. While the camouflage kept the culture-keepers at bay, it also had the effect of ultimately confusing the artists, who gradually forgot everything but the general outline of the originals. Ultimately, the culture-keepers were not disheartened by this turn of events. They felt that the act of camouflaging might actually simplify their mission. Eventually, in the late 1950s, they decided to test that theory and intentionally permitted an enormous, horrifically patterned balloon to whiz toward London and into the nets of the waiting artists.

When abstract expressionism was brought to earth, the artists again went quickly to work, taking copious notes on the structure and summarily camouflaging it. The monitoring culture-keepers marveled at the artists' curious, seemingly complicitous activity. Are we all unwittingly working toward the same goal? they wondered, as they experimentally fanned a little balloon called Pop inland, where it wafted down in London. This time, the artists took no notes and devised no camouflage. They simply tossed it among themselves as it slowly deflated of its own accord. The culture-keepers were mystified until a canny newcomer posited that perhaps the artists simply thought that Pop was one of their own balloons and felt no need to disguise it.

Such a conclusion was ominous for the culture-keepers since it implied that all the balloons, regardless of their point of origin, were beginning to look the same. Anxious and depressed, the culture-keepers returned to their coastal posts where even today they keep their watch with the gnawing apprehension that their mission has been aborted.

Camouflage in British art has, for the better part of the twentieth century, been the figure and the landscape. Regardless of what impulse swept the international art world, Britain invariably clung to the measure of the man on a plot of land. Skeins of paint and toffee rolls of stone were laboriously engineered to conceal just another somebody or someplace. The subterfuge reached epic proportions but, whether the medium was oil or marble, the subject was steadfastly an Englishman on English ground. This is intended as neither a slight, nor exactly a compliment. It is simply the way it evolved. In truth, by 1987 and the "take no hostages" blockbuster *British Art in the 20th Century* at London's Royal Academy of Arts, only Bridget Riley could be seen as running defiantly against the representational current. Elsewhere, everywhere, "my body, my landscape" dominated.

The good news is that British painters and sculptors have, as a whole, kept the body more inventively and weirdly alive in art than most of their European or American peers. The landscape is another, less interesting contribution. What the entrepreneurial critic Lawrence Alloway termed "nature romanticism" simply can't compellingly compete with the "neurotic humanism" identified by Charles Harrison in his catalogue essay for *British Art in the 20th Century* and seen most aggressively in the work of Frank Auerbach, Francis Bacon, Lucian Freud, R. B. Kitaj, and Leon Kossoff. The work of these painters, when contextualized within the more wholesome volumetrics of such sculptural predecessors as Jacob Epstein, Eric Gill, Barbara Hepworth, and Henry Moore, literally sustains the body's heartbeat in Western art of this century. The irony is that as the painters of the body themselves age and die, their work may be seen as a tolling bell presaging the end of a concern that grows increasingly, pathologically funereal. Curiously, what has saved and, to a degree, internationalized the British body is the schematicized, depilated anatomy of Pop.

While the chicken or the egg debate concerning British versus American Pop will probably never be settled, what is clear is that Pop's impact was enormous and enormously liberating on both sides of the Atlantic. Its therapeutic release of previously debased subject matter and its confidence in totemic representationalism allowed artists to access a Pandora's box of historically flatlined stimuli. Suddenly, both the body and the landscape were stunningly new. Emptied of romanticism and Freudian narrative, liberated from the personal to the popular, they were able to serve a new generation with images that set them apart from the past without rupturing their connection to it. Pop's recycling of known, media-derived sources opened the door to a compelling, internationalized, culturally analytic art practice. Superficially, everything remained in place; the body still dominated the landscape. Yet, purged of emotive morbidity, the iconic Pop anatomy allowed British artists to move into a larger world unencumbered by regional costuming or coffins filled with their native soil. Seen today, the British Pop of Peter Dean and Richard Hamilton doesn't look particularly disjunctive. Nonetheless, it changed what it preceded.

What immediately preceded the artists in *"Brilliant!"* was the work of Gilbert and George and, further back and to a lesser degree, David Hockney. Gilbert and George liberated the photographic image in Britain like no artists before them. They also chronicled the wheezing end of Empire through their depiction of a numbing, postcolonial cityscape. The East London seen in their photo-constructs is a rotting piece of real estate whose inhabitants can no more escape from than they can fly. The deadpan equations with which they structured their work from the mid-1970s inevitably added up to a sum of less than zero. Monitoring the decay are Gilbert and George themselves in their dreary Orwellian ordinariness, like statisticians dispatched to a massacre to keep track of the body count. While their subject matter is determinedly British, Gilbert and George manage to suggest an apocalyptic West where the flies are buzzing around a corpse that has yet to drop.

David Hockney's world is hardly apocalyptic but its depiction of lascivious anomie is no less chilling. His London was a crucial decade earlier than that of Gilbert and George. Nonetheless, at the height of the "swinging sixties," Hockney depicted the dysfunctional narcotization of postwar society. A paralyzing boredom informs and corrupts everything he portrays but, hey, that pastel haze really deadens the pain. The people in Hockney's pretty, sybaritic sets didn't know about the dole and disease and IRA bombs that were coming to the London of Gilbert and George, but they had long lost the power to react anyway. Their poisonous passivity was symptomatic of the future they would awkwardly age into.

In 1995 London's artists are still primarily following a figurative tradition. However, the body is fractured and unlikely to mend itself. Those artists who conform most congenially to a historically recognizable tradition are, not surprisingly, best known. Damien Hirst and Rachel Whiteread have studiously avoided the human body but their work is aggressive in its referencing of it. While Hirst has repeatedly utilized animal carcasses (sheep, cattle, fish, a shark) in his work, their role has been insistently anthropomorphic. Like a poetically deluded taxonomist, he uses the beasts to address issues of human mortality and humanist despair. The theater of his work is most commonly played out in vitrines containing either the exemplary beasts or chilling, characterless tableaux. With his twinned preoccupations of mortifying flesh and transparent cages, Hirst is the natural inheritor of Bacon, to whose work he brings an additional horror—that of the actual as opposed to the illusionistic. The literalization of Bacon's inevitably suspended violence lends Hirst's work a dreadful, finished absoluteness that Bacon only implied.

Whiteread continues the British preoccupation with formalist volumes. There is a comfortable objectness about what she makes that neatly builds on a tradition of demystifying yet modern-looking sculpture very much in the arena of Moore. Her castings of mattresses, floors, and the negative spaces of rooms are resonant with the poetry of loss. Even when her work draws perilously close to that of Bruce Nauman (as in her castings of "spaces beneath"), there is an implied social agenda about who is missing as opposed to what is revealed. This is particularly true of her extraordinary accomplishment *House* (October 1993–January 1994), the hallucinatory cast of an abandoned London row house that evoked in the British public all the shame and outrage as would be engendered at the sight of a hardly known neighbor running naked down the street.

Gary Hume is a painter of brutally agreeable portraits. Using a cloying palette of insinuatingly bland pastels, he builds up almost sculptural surfaces that are reminiscent of Ben Nicholson's geometric abstractions but rendered in the *gelati* hues of Hockney. Drained of any essential identity, his portraits still manage to signify cultural attitudes and authorial ambivalences toward the subject matter. Even the teeth-itchingly luscious surfaces conspire to enhance the neutered imaging. Glenn Brown, on the other hand, relies on the loaded recognizability of his subject matter, which is, by and large, the work of such revered modern painters as Auerbach and Kossoff. He reduces the hysterically paint-laden surfaces of these artists' portraits to a surface that looks like nothing so much as a color photograph suffering from generational loss. The luxuriant angst of their paint handling is translated by Brown into meticulous technique whereby the toil of his process both satirizes and neutralizes the opera of their existentially evolved hubris. For Brown, the privilege of engagement has been replaced by the need for analysis; he is a doctor performing heroic surgery on a mannequin.

Alessandro Raho's program is essentially simpler than that of Hume or Brown. What he shares with them is an obsession with portraiture.

Superficially, his work might be seen as an odd amalgam of Hockney and Alex Katz. Again, there are the awful pastels and the blandly inexpressive sitters. Yet the narcissistic vapidity of his models is oddly telling of a generation for whom the mirror is quite simply an acknowledgment of existence. Unlike Hume's, Raho's subjects would be instantly recognizable but there is no alignment between them and the viewer. Neither adolescent nor adult, they are caught in a state of suspended animation. Like Stepford wives, they are not so much vacant as missing.

The paintings of Chris Ofili could be seen as gorgeous landscape fantasies, promises of a garden in the mind. Intricate webs of paint rise in the form of pearls and respirate back into reflective pools of lacquer. But, wait a minute, the body is here, too. The paintings are not hung; they rest on stubby little brown volumes—the same volumes that punctuate the paintings' surfaces, jutting out like sand-pail castings. These volumes are elephant dung and the dung comes from the balanced diet of zoo-maintained herbivores. Ofili's determination to undercut the exquisiteness of his surfaces with the basest record of life and loss throws the work into an insinuatingly confrontational position. There is something about it that understands how Charlie Chaplin could dance with the grace of Nijinsky while his pants were dragging around his ankles.

Slapstick and beastly longings also animate the recent work of Angus Fairhurst, whose drawings and animations of a gorilla with Left Bank anxieties simultaneously elicit a laugh and a sigh. Fairhurst's gorilla is game to try it all, but "all" is a limited prospect for a gorilla with his head in the clouds. In hundreds of simple ink drawings, the gorilla wanders through our world. Occasionally he sets out with a human companion but, like Don Quixote and Sancho Panza, their adventures are more a testament to indomitability than accomplishment. A videotaped auto-performance, *A Cheap and Ill-fitting Gorilla Suit* (1995) makes clear that gorilla and artist are one, that the aspiration to make art is as incomprehensible as that of a gorilla trying to melt into a cocktail party. Sure, he's a close relative, but he is disconcertingly not quite our class.

Fitting in is exactly what the collaborative work of Henry Bond and Liam Gillick is all about. Adopting the personae of newspaper reporters, they wander out into the madness of a world fueled by press releases and news conferences. They document and report on tag ends of events and their archive grows with a bland neutrality of tone that, in toto, becomes as nightmarish as any construct by Gilbert and George. Their bites from the Thatcher era and its aftermath make the period seem as levelingly miscalculated as the transformation of a crucifixion into a video game.

Steven Pippin also fits in. Looking like a curious combination of bank clerk and pallbearer, Pippin goes to outlandish ends to accomplish relatively simple things. In his primarily photo-based work, Pippin tinkers away at the low end of the technological ladder, creating cameras out of toilets and washing machines and bathtubs. Because he carries out his work in semipublic spaces, there is something of the flasher about his approach, but it's a flasher on fairly strong medication. The loony inventiveness of the process and the informed sophistication of the result constitute a curious marriage of performance and sculpture, with the photographs seeming to just happen as documentation. Naturally, the documentation is most frequently the artist in the landscape.

Tinkering could be seen as the province of Mat Collishaw as well, only his is a much darker game than Pippin's. If it weren't for the constant attempt to reach a moral center, Collishaw's aesthetic could be seen as unwholesomely morbid. Like Hirst, he returns continually to the fragility of life, but counter to Hirst, his productions are insistently modest, almost homey in their manufacture. Much of Collishaw's work deals with putrefaction, both literal and spiritual. Loss of breath and loss of ideals are simultaneously present in work that can be violently aggressive or tenderly abject. Whether he is engineering an unrelentingly visceral installation on our collective complicity in the psychology of rape or photographically hybridizing pelt-bearing flowers, Collishaw always assumes the posture of the questioner, not the provocateur.

Abigail Lane's work has often been referenced as Grand Guignol. Bodies and body parts recur relentlessly. Some are hers, some are those of fellow artists, and, recently, one is an anonymous Jack Russell terrier. The use of her own body is essentially a "take-back-the-night" strategy that neatly (very neatly, actually) recovers authorship for Yves Klein's anonymous, living paintbrushes. Using an ink pad, Lane has stamped out buttock-printed wallpaper rather like an antic deb during a wild party at the Omega Workshop. Other pieces, wax life casts such as *Misfit* (1994) and *The Incident Room* (1993), imply narratives keyed more to social workers and forensic technicians than to art familiars. *Misfit* depicts somebody's lovely boy fallen to the ground in full possession of everything but his pants. *The Incident Room* depicts someone's lovely girl run to ground in possession of everything but her life. They are troubling, morally uninflected reports from Tabloid Land. In the best of Lane's work, the horror of what she presents is not the victims but evidence of their victimization. Individuality, whether bloody handprints on wallpaper (taken from a New York crime-scene photograph) or the postautopsy cast of a house pet, is not the issue. The issue is what remains, and what remains is the observer and his or her relationship with the evidence.

Evidence is at the heart of Michael Landy's epic installations, which have included an abandoned garden market, a clearance sale on the scale of the Battle of Britain, and a demonic recycling service. Whatever the venue, Landy is charting nothing less than the fall of Western civilization. His installations alternate between spiffy finish and tawdry make-do, but the obsessiveness of the artist's need to create a social *Gesamtkunstwerk* remains unwavering. *Scrapheap Services* (1995) has, for example, been forming for years and references everything from the "disappeared" of Argentina's Dirty War to domestic kitchen recycling. It posits outrageous analogies and hints at deadly complicities. In his art, Landy is as daunting and enthralling as the Ancient Mariner, unable to disengage until his dreadful story has been told in its entirety.

Dinos and Jake Chapman are equally obsessed with the end, but it is the end of the Age of Reason. Their early work recast Goya's *Disasters of War* as hundreds of tiny scale models in which the most grotesque humiliations man could inflict on man were modeled to fit nicely into the palm of your hand on a little green bed of Astroturf. The culmination of the Chapmans' engagement with Goya was their scaling up to life and into three dimensions of *Great Deeds Against the Dead* (1994), an etching detailing dismemberment, castration, and the landscape of shame. The Chapman version uses display mannequins replete with noncompounded joints and bad hairpieces. The greatest attention is lavished on the wounds, but elsewhere all is intentionally artifice. In between the Goya caprices and afterwards are ludicrously, repellently mutated family members who sprout genitalia on the most unlikely anatomical grounds: Siamese twins with penile noses and vaginal mouths, mothers covered in penises and fathers pimpled in vulvae. It is genetic engineering that Mary Shelley never dreamed of and William Burroughs only hinted at. The sculptures are adolescent and anarchic and painfully human in their neediness to address the endless atrocities of the past, the realized horrors of the present, and the void around the corner. The true grisliness of the Chapman brothers' vision lies in its creepy acquaintance with the selfish expediencies of power and science.

Absolute facts are the subject matter of Anya Gallaccio, and her facts are digestible and arrangeable. Working with materials such as chocolate and flowers, Gallaccio creates installations that update the notion of memento mori. As in the Chapmans' universe, so too, Gallaccio's. Everything is mutating, moving inexorably toward decay.

Only, with Gallaccio, decay is regenerative. There is a curious optimism at the core of her work that implies that process is not futile, but rather essential to continuation. As Gallaccio uses flowers, Georgina Starr uses memories. She strings them together and lets them twist in the wind until they form something that has the weight of earned experience. Fictions are knit into realities and the weave of the whole becomes art. With her primary media being video and photography, Starr appears to be offering documentary evidence, unassailable facts. Nonetheless, her evidence is entirely controvertible and the self she documents so assiduously is often as much a fiction as the reverse. Starr's relatives are, in the end, entirely and wonderfully relative.

Tracey Emin is a biographical artist who never plays with fiction. Her compulsive interest in her own experience, unmediated and un-filtered, isn't just the basis of her work; it is her work. There is some-thing bullying about Emin's almost belligerent need to share her sexuality, her relationships, her memories with us. She molds her solip-sistic aesthetic into a kind of everywoman construct, but it is all Emin-world and, in truth, that is its sloppy appeal. It is as if someone glibly confided Joseph Beuys's philosophy that we are all artists to Emin over drinks and she went off to document her life in the style of a tabloid heroine, all screaming banner headlines and salacious sidebars and insinuating captions.

The signification of other people's communality is very much at the core of the programs of Gillian Wearing and Adam Chodzko. The big switch is that both artists understand that communality comes with a set of kinks that would give pause to the Marquis de Sade. Wearing is a somewhat aestheticized social worker who goes out into the world with a documentation kit and gets people to share. It's a daunting kind of egalitarianism whereby the person on the street is given permission to collaborate with the artist in the creation of a work of art. Without that other's input, there is no art. Fairly early on, Wearing also utilized newspaper advertisements to reel a portion

of her collaborators in for the video pieces, and the results are alternately charming and chilling. Chodzko came along a bit later and
also utilized newspapers. In them, he placed ads for everything from
people who thought they looked like God to people who were open to
fantasizing about a tryst in a sylvan glade (as illustrated by Chodzko).
Interestingly, Chodzko's other ongoing project, *Secretors* (1995), involves
the often surreptitious installation of blown-glass drips of "blood."
The drips, one of which was poised behind an unknowing politician
during a BBC broadcast, become peripherally sinister indicators that
we are all living in an updated House of Atreus. Chodzko engineers
games of chance that always have the possibility of hopeful resolution.
However, he is a good enough engineer to make sure that they don't.

Sam Taylor-Wood takes deadly serious issues and theatricalizes them
in ways that are alternately amusing and ominous. In all of her work,
there is a bit of Joe Orton's cuddly nastiness mixed in with Harold Pinter's menacing banality. Much of Taylor-Wood's subject matter deals
with turning male/female stereotyping on its knobby head. A series of
photographic self-portraits show a lovely British rose running randily,
unapologetically amok. Here is a good-time girl who is actually having
a good time. A pair of male video portraits are, initially, as wryly topsy-
turvy as the photos but the humor drains away as they gradually begin
to resemble case studies in self-induced hysteria and masturbatory
narcissism. Ultimately, they provoke a sordid, mutually isolate sense of
observing clinically representative patients from behind a one-way
mirror.

Isolation is also the theme of her installation *Killing Time* (1994),
in which four young Londoners sit in desultory solitude waiting to lip-
synch parts that Taylor-Wood has assigned them to a recording of
Richard Strauss's *Electra*. Trapped laconically in the camera's frame,
they might as well be waiting for a negative call-back to a job application or the foregone results of a lab test. Nothing is going on other
than a moment of exquisitely archaic passion that they can neither

identify with nor passively surrender to. Chillingly, this loss of emotional responsiveness—even mimetically—sets off little warning shudders in response to a generation whose members are immobilized like invertebrates trapped in jellied carapaces.

In the London of Sarah Lucas, all memory of Empire has been salted over and, with it, any grace note that might cushion the skeletal remains of a culture. The News of the Day is a mix of visceral jolts about suburban sex rings and hot flashes of surgically enhanced mammaries. Love is a cucumber reaming a slit in a soiled mattress. Hellos and good-byes are semaphored by the thrust of a right-angled forearm ending in a clenched fist. Concrete jackboots double as a proletarian monument. A cast of a bollard etched with the phrase "Fuck me while I'm sleeping" serves as a brutish tombstone.

The work looks rushed and careless and real. It could just as easily be traces of the soiled, improvisational decor in a vacated squat as art. It's not about despair—or hope—just debris to help shore up the abyss. Photographic self-portraits of the artist recur constantly and do nothing to help soften the blow. In each of them, Lucas smiles enigmatically, looking assertively comfortable in boy drag. From the smile and the pose, it's moot as to whether she is watching a man having his teeth kicked down his throat or waiting for an automatic timer to trigger the shutter release.

If there is a center to Lucas's work, it is amoral and impervious to editorial notions of right or wrong; things have gone too far for that. Like a battle-hardened correspondent, she simply records what she sees, and what she sees is a world as flattened and sordid as a domestic roadkill on an exhaust-clogged highway.

The annual meeting of the culture-keepers is in progress. It is being held on the HMS *Thatcher*, which is dry-docked in the Thames estuary. The keynote address, delivered by a senior keeper, is entitled "Whither Our Youth?" The address is supplemented with slides that are drawing nervous titters and irate asides. The visual aids click quickly forward: a young woman whose neck is scarred by love bites, an indigent holding a sign denouncing his exclusion from the dole, mutant flowers with fur-bearing petals, bloody handprints desperately pawing up a wall, a taxonomic display of stamped-out cigarette butts, globules of blood sweating from ceiling beams, a trash compactor disgorging an unwanted populace, a photo taken at a previous keepers' assembly. "When are you going to get to the art?" catcalls a bellicose junior. "That, you ninny," replies the senior keeper, "is exactly my point; sacred cultural boundaries have been breached while we were looking elsewhere." The audience petulantly stills and merges with the rhythm of the *Thatcher*, which bobs listlessly in the becalmed river.

Declaiming theatrically, the old man continues, "What we are witnessing are the seeds of anarchy. If you can't recognize the art, you can't monitor the activity. If you can't monitor the activity, you can't impose the criteria. If you dispense with criteria, you fan the winds of chaos." Crossing his white-flanneled legs, a moist-eyed young man plaintively asks, "Sir, what do you suggest we do?" "That, my son, is the dilemma we face," the senior responds. "Bollocks!" snorts a crusty veteran from the Dover watch. Rising and storming toward the nearest exit, he yells, "Go to the bridge and set a bloody course, that's what you bloody well do." The man's departure is followed by a funny little pop and a thump. The senior continues his address but the moist-eyed young man quietly slips out to the deck. There, he sees the Dover veteran sprawled in a pool of his own blood, an old dueling pistol clenched in his right hand. The young man kneels by the body.

The man is still breathing. The younger attempts to staunch the flow of blood. "No need," replies the dying keeper. "There's no help; it's finished." "What's finished, sir?" "The Levelers have won," gasps the suicide. "It's all one now that the children have crushed our ideals." "Oh," sighs the youth, "you never gave us any ideals." "Damn you to hell," hisses the veteran as he dies. "Oh, but sir, you already did," says the youth as he slowly rises and crosses the deck to look at the gray London sky.

On the shore stands a girl with a video camera; it is aimed at the young keeper in the bloody flannels standing on the deck of the listing HMS *Thatcher*. Silently she mouths the word "brother" and smiles.

Brilliant! New Art from London, ed. Richard Flood (Minneapolis: Walker Art Center, 1995), 48–55.

Slow. Fade.

I met Paul Thek in 1977 while he was installing *Processions* at the Institute of Contemporary Art in Philadelphia. Watching him madly attempting to create his kind of something out of a plenitude of other people's nothing was like stumbling on Hamlet directing the play within the play. Wrenching a cathartically redemptive environment out of the sterile, ungiving architecture of the ICA space perfectly suited Paul's psychodramatic persona. The first time I encountered him he was flailing around the gallery plaintively crying out for stuffed birds, which he wanted to hang from the ceiling. Components of the installation were pouring in all around him—bales of newspapers, oars, a bathtub, tons of sand, park benches—but he was missing birds and that was all he could think about. He was also working, essentially, alone. At the time, I didn't understand how different it was for him to be lacking the theater of collaboration. In Europe, he had put together a carnival of players whose contributions melded into his own and catalyzed the whole (rather like what Julian Beck and Judith Malina were doing with the Living Theater); in Philadelphia, there were certainly plenty of ICA-supplied assistants, but they were not collaborators and he knew it, and, by the time I arrived, they knew it.

I was naïvely enraptured by Paul's temperament and eagerly jumped at an invitation to have dinner with him and the director of the ICA, Suzanne Delehanty. Too quickly, it emerged that all three of us were raised as Roman Catholics, and I remember clinging to that odd unity of past history as an increasingly rocky evening progressed. Suzanne's religion was still in place; mine was long gone. Paul's religion, however, was a stigma that had never and would never heal. Something extremely scary emerged whenever Paul discussed his particular kind of Pentecostal Catholicism, and that night I remember being at once drawn in and repulsed. His messianic conviction could be extremely powerful and, although he was giving me the creeps, I was totally in the thrall of the emotive immediacy of his working process and the mercurial flow of his intellect. Paul's voice was his most seductive device. He would build his sentences with a kind of resonant, incantatory rhythm that suggested an intimate oratory. When he was going for sympathy, he'd slip into a singsongy, childish tenor. When he was angry, he would go Shakespearean behind clenched teeth. Nonetheless, it was a beautiful voice, particularly well suited for dramatically whispered asides. He was always theatrically drained or operatically energized. There was something of a specter about him as well; a faint rattling of chains echoed in his wake. I was hooked, but I honestly don't know if the art would have continued to mean as much if he hadn't been around to nourish it and poison it—if his persona wasn't pulling me through it. During that evening with Suzanne, I threw him Benedictine boarding-school anecdotes with increasingly baroque embroidery only to have him come back with a Grand Guignol crusher of his own. When we finally parted, I felt like an amateur apostate after a duel with Torquemada.

What Paul created at the ICA was, in the end, an extraordinarily moving conflation of his history and our history. There was at its center an overwhelming melancholy about the botch we'd all made of everything. Rising up from a bed of sand was a ramshackle tower sheltering a newspaper grotto with a bathtub that was alternately about escape and entrapment, shelter and exposure—a fitting sanctuary for Paul the Baptist. All around the tower were bits and pieces of past lives and past efforts. There was Thek's "Bandwagon," an environment celled off in chicken wire holding a shack of crating raised up on a trestle table containing, among other things, plaster casts of the artist's feet (waiting for the Magdalen who never came). While the piece was intended as a cautionary reminder of mutual interdependence, it had the feel of a juggernaut whose advance was stalled in the muck of its creator's psyche. Nearby there was an installation of Paul's newspaper paintings. Executed mainly in tempera on spreads of the *International Herald Tribune*, these pieces are, collectively, among the most exquisite meditations on self-imposed exile since Charles Maturin birthed his presciently existential anti-hero *Melmoth the Wanderer* in 1820. In another area were Paul's bronzes, *The Personal Effects of the Pied Piper*, which deal with the Outsider/Savior and serve as yet another fractured, self-heroizing, self-pitying auto-portrait. Finally, there were his notebook pages, which contained scripted reflections, study drawings, and doodles, both benign and deadly. Superficially, the exhibition was a retrospective hymn to mystical/mythical collectivism and intended to act as both a provocation for the America he had once fled and a consolation for the homeland he hoped to recover. Now, looking back, it was also a major piece of evidence to the awful psychic splintering that had begun to eat away at Paul's ability to create new work and control his demons. There was no whole, only a succession of parts—a sob, a torrent of tears, a giggle, a cynical *mot*. The totality of a *Gesamtkunstwerk* eluded him and would continue to do so during the long decline of his ultimate American experience.

In 1981 I did an extended interview with Paul for *Artforum*,[1] believing him to be the missing link between American and European art. There was an enormous amount of garbagy work and thought being promulgated at the time—wave after breaking wave of flatulent, instantly commodified painting washing up on the coast of Transavanguardia. Paul was still virtually unknown outside of a small band of loyalists, unknown primarily because his art left very few physical traces and that which survived the ephemera of the environments (or was created to the left and right of them) was not seductive enough for the market. Naïvely, I thought my interview might change that.

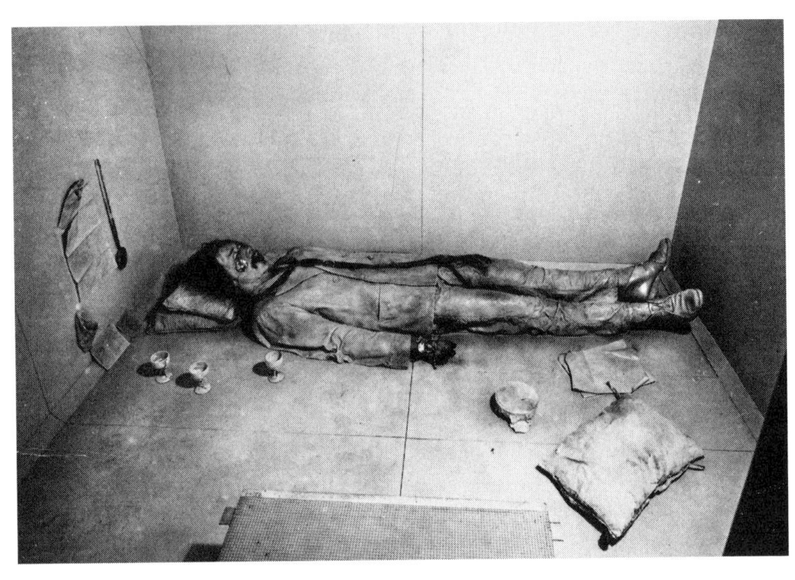

Paul Thek, *The Tomb* (interior view)
Stable Gallery, New York, 1967
Photograph by John D. Schiff

I would go and visit him and he would rummage round in the milk crates of memorabilia under his bed and fish something out and we would talk about it for a while. Sometimes, we would climb to the roof of his tenement where he had an ambitious potted garden under way. I was in no hurry to end the interview and taped far too much material. He would frequently digress and talk about joining a religious community, or about the girl who was waiting for him on the island of Ponza, or his makeshift home on Fire Island, or the succession of betrayals that defined the geography of his art world.

By the time I conducted the interview, the sexual repression of his queerness and the religious oppression forged in his upbringing had taken a terrible toll. Somewhere at the heart of his isolate anger was a psychotic misogyny capable of producing paranoid delusions. Regrettably, his ability to invent and live out corrosive fantasies had become a serious disability. Later on, during the controversy over Richard Serra's *Tilted Arc* (1984–88), he was able to turn some of his terrible, female-directed anger against a male power figure, and I tried to view his attacks on Serra as healthy rather than as a wrong-headed assault on another artist. The nuttiness of his proposed alteration of the *Tilted Arc* (cutting portholes occupied by silhouetted animals in Serra's Cor-Ten metal wall was one solution) seemed therapeutic. I never tried to analyze any of it, and I certainly never attempted to stay him from his course, which involved an editorial letter-writing campaign and proposals to New York City's Public Art Fund. There was a desperate inevitability about all of Paul's end-run decisions, which confounded any of the half-steps initiated by friends to introduce an iota of reality to his endeavors. In truth, Paul was seduced more by the determinism of his damnation than by any feeble tokens one might tender for redemption.

Doing the interview with Paul was a long, curious process. There was no clear demarcation between fact and fiction. I don't think it was intentional, but rather indicative of his aesthetic, whereby he assiduously avoided the straight line in favor of the meandering one, the pragmatic in favor of the emotive. What became increasingly clear was that Paul was seriously adrift, and unwilling or unable to stabilize. He wasn't working on anything at that time and inevitably, we went backward to when he was. The sixties were the defining decade for Paul, and his embrace of that period's social and political liberalism gave him a creative energy that resulted in his most important work. His deep mistrust of minimalism and Pop also galvanized his output and triggered the morbid poetry of his reliquaries. Being an American in Europe during much of the Vietnam nightmare further defined the installation work through the realization of meditative environments wrenched from the awfulness that was unfolding in Southeast Asia via structures of newspapers built on beds of sand. Mostly, Paul wanted to make art that was beautiful and healing, and many of our conversations were about that. When the interview was published, it changed nothing. Paul went on tending his garden and stuffing bits of his life in the milk crates. I continued to believe that no other artist quite captured the essence of a defining American decade as had Paul with his potlatch aesthetic.

In 1984 I was working with Barbara Gladstone and wanted to do a Paul Thek exhibition at the gallery. After negotiations, a date was set for a show, a studio was rented, and money was advanced for materials. As the months passed, Paul grew ever more elusive: studio visits were scheduled and abruptly canceled. It became increasingly clear that something was going very wrong. Eventually, Barbara and I were granted a visit. There were a handful of essentially unfinished paintings with one exception. It was the largest of the group and depicted an empty boat with a raised sail, bobbing in a desolate expanse of sea. It was a simple act of perfect poetry and, I am sure, the final self-portrait.

During this period, my relationship with Paul was limited primarily to late-night meals during which he poured out a stream of invective about the women in his life. He conjured up grotesquely vivid images of his dying mother wallowing in her own filth and misty images of the dark-haired girl in white waiting for him on Ponza. He launched into fantasy scenarios where female curators and dealers did every-thing short of castrating him in order to bend him to their rapacious goals. He recounted hearsay orgies where a European curator (male for a change) and his assistants poured wine onto the genitalia of the *Fishman* cast, lapped it up, turned the sculpture over and violated it.

At this stage I wanted out of the exhibition, but it was already too late. Then, less than a month before the show was scheduled open, Paul stopped talking to me. Three times a truck was dispatched to collect new work and three times it was sent away empty. When, fearing the worst, Barbara and I went to the studio, it was filled with primed blank canvases. Paul had disappeared. The show was installed without Paul's input and included what little new work existed in combination with what he had previously brought in. Several weeks after the open-ing, Paul called as if nothing had happened and said that he would be dropping by to go over prices and see the show. When he arrived, he looked around and said that he hated it. I agreed; he left. A bit more time passed and he called to say that he had decided to exhibit with another dealer. Occasionally, afterward, he would phone me at home and rant, or simply announce himself and lapse into silence until I hung up.

One night, late at night, in 1988, walking across Union Square I felt a hand on my shoulder and swung around. It was Paul. "Why is it that we never talk?" he asked. "Because we have nothing to say," I answered. It was a stupid, arrogant response, which I instantly regretted. I started to say something conciliatory, but Paul was already gone. Several months later, a friend called to say that Paul had died of AIDS (repor-ted in the *New York Times* as "complications resulting from hepatitis and gastrointestinal disease").

I've avoided thinking about Paul for years. I know there was nothing more that I could have done, but that's beside the point. The best of

Paul's contribution was the knowledge that you could wrest beauty out of absolutely anything—for a moment. His greatest work—the environments and paintings on newspaper—was doomed to literally illustrate that principle. He had the ability to redeem the unsuitably sentimental through the sublime simplicity with which he rag-picked his way through life and art. The most eloquent of his props were salvaged and reclaimed from the garbage pile to be given a dignity they never possessed in their original incarnation. Like the subject of Oscar Wilde's prose poem, *The Artist*, Paul "took the image he had fashioned, and set it in a great furnace, and gave it to the fire. And out ... of the image of *The Sorrow that endureth for Ever* he fashioned an image of *The Pleasure that abideth for a moment*."

Today, Paul's commingling of hope and despair feels emblematically correct for the 1960s. His nostalgia for a lost age of poetic heroes whose limbs he sheathed in carapaces of butterfly wings and his fear of living in an age of hemorrhaging humanism lend his art a schizophrenic appropriateness for the out-of-order 1990s. The *Technological Reliquaries* are terrifyingly accurate metaphors for a world beset by AIDS and directives for racial cleansing and class oppression in the guise of bureaucratic expedience. As the hysteria of jingoism spreads, Paul's self-sacrificing martyrs—the Pied Piper, Bo Jangles, Fishman, and the Hippie—are more necessary than ever to plow under the dragon's teeth sown by the Manchurian candidates who now rise to ever more precipitous heights. Paul's contribution was all about modesty and the power of one; it is important because it was responsive to the world and contra to the cynicism of the worldly.

Paul Thek: The Wonderful World That Almost Was (Rotterdam: Witte de With, 1995), 113–18.

Notes on Digestion and Film: Matthew Barney

Imperfect beings become agitated and couple in order to complete themselves, but purely beautiful things are as solitary as the grief of man.

MARGUERITE YOURCENAR, "SISTINE," IN *THAT MIGHTY SCULPTOR, TIME*, 1992

The final formation of the perfectly hermetic circle is when you are capable of sticking your head up your ass.

MATTHEW BARNEY, CONVERSATION WITH THE AUTHOR, SEPTEMBER 1995

Lacan focuses on the rimlike structure that is characteristic of all erogenous zones in the body (comprising both vagina and anus, as well as others). This formation is not casual (it is not simply that humans are biologically prone to be stimulated at the points where the body exhibits "openings"), but related to the intrinsic structure of the drive as it turns out from the body, circumvents some object, and then moves back on itself, receding once again in the body where it achieves "satisfaction."

KAREN PINKUS, *BODILY REGIMES: ITALIAN ADVERTISING UNDER FASCISM*, 1995

Twice, I've asked Matthew Barney to share lists of films that have influenced and informed him. The first time was for an article I did for the British magazine *Frieze* in 1993. At that time, his list was as follows: *Delicatessen* (Jean-Pierre Jeunet and Marc Caro, 1991), *Evil Dead II: Dead by Dawn* (Sam Raimi, 1987), *Female Trouble* (John Waters, 1974), *Hellbound: Hellraiser II* (Tony Randel, 1988), and *Tommy* (Ken Russell, 1975). The issue of *Frieze* also contained submissions by a variety of other artists and was occasioned by a series of attenuated screenings hosted by Richard Prince, who invited a semiregular cast of characters to drop by his studio with a pre-cued video sequence lasting no longer than five minutes. Over several months, a number of people tromped up the stairs to Prince's studio anxiously carrying their videos, ready to seduce the other guests through the power of their surrogate cinematic identity.

I particularly remember a night when Diego Cortez presented that exquisitely ridiculous argument between Brigitte Bardot and Michel Piccoli in Jean-Luc Godard's *Contempt* (1963), which ends with Bardot slamming out of their apartment with the line "I have contempt for you." Arto Lindsay popped in Glenn Gould playing a selection from the *Goldberg Variations*; Larry Clark ran a portion of an old kinescope where Patsy Cline sat reminiscing with members of her band; Meyer Vaisman featured the dance sequence between Michelle Pfeiffer and Al Pacino in Brian De Palma's *Scarface* (1983). I proffered a scene from Michael Curtiz's *The Egyptian* (1954) in which Bella Darvi teaches Edmund Purdom "the final perfection of love." Each of us piggishly exceeded our agreed-upon five minutes. Only Barney adhered to the contract with an amazing sequence from an otherwise forgettable movie called *Society* (Brian Yuzna, 1989) in which the protagonist shoves his fist up the antagonist's anus, grabs his head, pulls it into the body and out through his ass. Yikes! There really wasn't much to say when Barney killed the image. It wasn't a contest but clearly he'd won, as he had once before with a literally eye-popping sequence from *Evil Dead II*. At the time, I didn't give it much thought other than regretting that I had failed as miserably as had Daryl F. Zanuck in bringing his protégée Bella Darvi to a wider audience. Later, after seeing Barney's *Cremaster 4* (1994), I gave it more thought.

Like George Lucas and his *Star Wars* series, Barney tends to shoot his videos out of order. *Cremaster 1* went into production a year after *Cremaster 4* had been completed. It was while he was getting ready to shoot the latter in Boise, Idaho, that I asked for an updated list of influential films. The new roster included: *Dames* (Ray Enright, choreography by Busby Berkeley, 1934), *Flying Down to Rio* (Thornton Freeland, 1933), *Nekromantik 2* (Jörg Buttgereit, 1991), *Olympia Part 2 (The Festival of Beauty)* (Leni Riefenstahl, 1938), *The Shining* (Stanley Kubrick, 1980), and *Willy Wonka and the Chocolate Factory* (Mel Stuart, 1971). Since receiving the list, I've seen a rough edit of *Cremaster 1*, and the films offer an intriguing insight into Barney's preproduction thinking.

Before committing to the present, I should note that Barney's peculiar relationship with mainstream film has been in and out of my mind since he made *Delay of Game* and *Radial Drill* back in 1991. In both of these videos, his character briefly inhabited a female drag persona whom he characterized at the time as emblematically West and East Coast types. The West was attired in all white with a towel turban, one-piece bathing suit, terrycloth robe, mules, and enormous sunglasses. The East wore a long black sheath, opera gloves, stiletto sling-backs, drop earrings, and a stylized beehive hairdo. There was no doubt in my mind that the West was Lana Turner as the blanc-de-blanc femme fatale in *The Postman Always Rings Twice* (Tay Garnett, 1946), just as the East was Audrey Hepburn as the suicidally adorable Holly Golightly in *Breakfast at Tiffany's* (Blake Edwards, 1961). These drag personae were not really discussed in the initial critical responses to Barney's work other than as points of departure for reflections on the gender ambiguities suffusing the project. Yet, as precursors to the real woman who plays the protagonist in *Cremaster 1*, they now seem more human in their cosmetic limitations.

That they are simply bad drag queens whose disguises put them in additional societal jeopardy provides a kind of melancholic chord to the project. Barney has always been quite clear about the source of his masculine drag. Photographs of Harry Houdini and Jim Otto were included in his installations, and Otto's name was punningly woven through the titling of the videos. Critiques of the work compliantly targeted the literal and metaphoric alignment of Houdini and Otto with Barney's performative actions, but I think it would be a mistake to overlook the armada of fictive superheroes who populated comic books, movies, and television during Barney's formative years. The very tasks he set himself in his actions owe far more to Batman, Spiderman, Superman, and Tarzan than they do to those of Houdini or Otto. Unlike Houdini (whose life was made into a film staring Tony Curtis, directed by George Marshall in 1953) and Otto (a life as yet unfilmed although he was certainly a model for the Nick Nolte character in Ted Kotcheff's 1979 *North Dallas Forty*), superheroes inhabit a world of solipsistic inversion not dissimilar from Barney's performative persona whose need to accomplish an existential "personal best" supersedes all other goals.

Classic superheroes, cartoon-birthed or otherwise, all tend to adhere to a chivalric code that dispenses with pretty much everything other than essentially unattainable ends. They are the phallic warriors of futurism whose robotic perfection could be seen as key to Filippo Marinetti's dismissal of the settled volumes in the *Victory of Samothrace* in favor of a streamlined race car. The superhero, like Marinetti, dismisses the found-vessel-for-proffered-ideals in favor of the auto-erotics of the lubricated machine. Compliantly, the cult of the superhero as robotic gladiator moved from its futurist construct to a fascist epiphany in Leni Riefenstahl's numbingly rhapsodic documentation of the 1936 Olympics. Removed from any context other than pure competition, Riefenstahl's athletes are exemplary *uber*-autos, thinking machines mindless of everything except the end to which the purring motor is directed: their very own metabolic triumph of the will. It is interesting to note that the centerpiece of *Olympia Part 2* is devoted to the decathlon competition, which was won by the American Glenn Morris. For a moment, Riefenstahl took Morris as her lover but, ultimately, rejected him. The final irony was that, upon his return to America, Morris was a one-shot king of the apes in *Tarzan's Revenge* (D. Ross Lederman, 1938), after which he succumbed to alcohol and drugs and an early death. One wonders if by violating his auto-erotic mandate in Riefenstahl's arms, he had orgasmed himself back into mortality.

In 1993 Barney dropped the superhero persona of his own volition and entered an arcadian realm. In the video *Drawing Restraint 7*, Barney introduced an entirely new mythology to his work. The premise of the video is deceptively, albeit weirdly, simple. Two satyrs occupy the back of a limousine that enters Manhattan across every bridge and through every tunnel. As they are being driven, the satyrs engage in a wrestling competition that results in the loser having his Achilles tendon flayed by the winner. As the wrestling bout proceeds, the submissive satyr is forced to make a series of drawings with his horns on the transparent sunroof of the limousine. Meanwhile, the increasingly agitated chauffeur, played by Barney, tries to achieve the "final formation of the perfectly hermetic circle."

Barney's character is a sexually undifferentiated "kid" with cartilaginous buds instead of horns and a very long tail resembling a nasty permutation of intestinal tract and umbilical cord. As the wrestling satyrs escalate their struggle, the chauffeur coils repetitively under and around the driver's seat in pursuit of his tail. Because, according to Barney, the character is a "field of infinite possibilities," there is no resolution to the choreography. The activity is, however, a kind of hymn to guilt-free, anal narcissism particularly insofar as the ungendered satyr has no other option for truly getting to know himself, let alone anyone else. The video itself resembles a demented, suppressed sequence from Disney's *Fantasia* (1940). With its gorgeous Caribbean blues and cartoonish characters, its hybrid Greco-Roman sources, and its feeling of being totally, anomalously primal, it is reminiscent of Walter Pater's description of Leonardo de Vinci's painting of *Saint John the Baptist* in which he posits the "notion of decayed gods who, to maintain themselves, after the fall of paganism, took employment in the new religion."[1] In other words, Pan has donned Christian drag in order to assimilate himself into the present while Barney dons mythological drag to find continuity with the past. In the ambiguity of the painting, Pater continues, "we recognize one of those symbolical inventions in which the ostensible subject is used, not as matter for definite pictorial realization, but as the starting point of a train of sentiment, as subtle and vague as a piece of music."[2]

What Barney was composing turned out to be the *Cremaster* cycle. The cremaster, it should be added, is the "suspensory muscle of the testes" that contracts the male genitalia in response to a variety of stimuli, some as pragmatic as cold and others as subjective as fear. A leitmotif in the composition deals with a period in utero when the fetus is still sexually undifferentiated prior to descending into an ovarian or testicular determination.

Cremaster 4 is Barney's most ambitious video and most determinedly narrative. There is a definite beginning and an almost definite end. In between, there is a motorcycle race and a coming-of-age story dealing with Barney's most peculiar protagonist to date, the Loughton Candidate. Barney plays the Candidate as an anatomically rammy version of Laurence Olivier's pathetic vaudeville performer in *The Entertainer* (Tony Richardson, 1960). The similarity is primarily, but not simply, physical. Both performers wear Edwardian three-piece suits and spats. Both part their slicked-back hair in the middle. Both have a fatal need to play it out to the end. That Barney has extremely large, floppy ears is, over time, no more remarkable than the continental divide that Olivier has between his front teeth. These men are brothers in their difference. Whereas Olivier's character has to put out for bored provincial audiences, Barney must do the same for a trio of androgynous "faeries" who look like they've escaped from a hallucinatory Toulouse-Lautrec poster. Whereas Olivier had to find his way back through his vainglory into the carapace of a family, Barney has to find his way through something that looks frighteningly like a Brobdingnagian alimentary canal to his potential maturity. Whereas Olivier finds a sort of peace at the end of his ordeal, Barney is left in a state of suspended animation. *Cremaster 4* doesn't actually end so much as it exhales its way off the screen to the drone of a bagpipe.

Cremaster 1 is an entirely different story. The lead character is a woman (played by a performer called Marti Domination) and she is trying to remain sexually undifferentiated while hiding in a bifurcated persona split between two blimps. (I know this is confusing.) The blimps hover over a blue, Astroturfed football stadium filled with an army of chorus girls wearing two-tiered bell costumes of virginal white on the outside and vivid orange on the inside. The blimps are staffed by stewardesses in crisp, time-approximate uniforms and caps. The protagonist wears a white satin teddy and transparent plastic high heels. She is concealed under a white-clothed buffet that, on one blimp, is laden with white grapes and, on the other, with purple.

Each blimp has a quartet of exquisitely haughty stewardesses who primp and pose and pout. Far below, on a blue football field, the chorus girls move in and out of complicated dance formations. Above them, Marti Domination choreographs their movements by arranging grapes under the buffet. Suddenly, inexplicably, Marti is on the field with the chorines and becomes the centerpiece of a hallucinatory production number. And that is what I saw on the monitor in Barney's studio. What I heard from the artist was that the blimps are simply doing their jobs, trying to descend into ovarian or testicular differentiation and that Marti is trying to stave off that process in an effort to remain undifferentiated (although she looks quite differentiated to me). Lacking Barney's crucial final edit, I can't speculate as to how clearly any or all of this will play out in the finished product. What I do know is that his list of films provides a wonderful set of preproduction notes.

The clearest entries come from *Dames* and *Flying Down to Rio* in which the insanity of Hollywood choreography reaches new heights of kaleidoscopic madness. In these two films, one can see Barney adapting and shuffling bits and pieces of dance sequences to fit his football field. His mining of camera angles and kinetic routines is both a wonderful homage to the period and a fascinating perversion of the same.

What becomes gradually unnerving is the easy merger of the Hollywood musical with Riefenstahl's equally complicated editorial choreography in *Olympia*. The mesh between the madcap musicals (at the height of the American Depression) and the fascist follies (at the height of the German recession) is dauntingly seamless. Both Leni Riefenstahl and Busby Berkeley were animating enormous machines made up of flesh and blood: chorus girls and world-class athletes were all being deployed to create a syncopated engine moving to the will of their masters. In this context, Marti Domination's seemingly capricious movement of the grapes across the floor of the blimp grows ominous. Then, too, there is the football field and its cozy similarity to the Reich-constructed Olympic stadium in Berlin.

As to Marti herself, there is a kind of thirties-glamour in her champagne blonde, elegantly French-twisted hairdo. Unlike with Barney's own earlier drag personae, where the camera never encroached on the artifice of pancake makeup taming stubble, the camera is all over Marti and luxuriates in the flawlessness of her femininity. She is all peaches and cream and languorous moves. Like her false-sisters (in *Delay of Game* and *Radial Drill*), she is an iconic construct but, like the robotic Maria in Fritz Lang's *Metropolis* (1927), she can easily pass for real. She also drives the video forward; she is the reason for the action. Through her control of the "field," she becomes a superhero in satin, which is the most dangerous superhero of them all because you don't see her dangerous propulsion as she plows over you on the way to the finish line.

Kubrick's *The Shining* lends its pristinely chilly environment and crystalline colors to the project. It also contains some alienatingly illusive overhead shots of a garden maze in which the final nightmare of the film is played out. Much of *The Shining*'s power has to do with the disruption of order within an ordered environment, and the maze, in the purposefulness of its dysfunctional perfection, can be seen as another version of the football field as it is utilized in *Cremaster 1* and, in truth, of the Isle of Man in *Cremaster 4*. Both field and island function as organisms that have been infected with a virus that, in the convoluted elegance of its construct, threatens to dominate the host in which it has taken shelter.

Nekromantik 2 is one of the most operatic gross-outs in recent cinema. What plot it has is devoted to the insistent grafting on of fresher flesh to a corpse that hasn't got a lot left to give. *Nekromantik* is essentially about the refusal to accept the limits of mortality insofar as mortality equals change, and *Cremaster 1* is clearly devoted to a protagonist who will do anything to suspend the natural movement toward change.

Willy Wonka and the Chocolate Factory is a children's film for people who hate children. At least four prepubescents (there may, in fact, be a few more) meet horribly grotesque fates inside a Technicolored fantasy of a factory populated by a whimsically dictatorial industrialist and his staff of dancing/singing dwarfs. The factory becomes a kind of Baal ingesting and, none too obliquely, excreting the greedy children. Here the concept of the body as machine takes on a horrifying explicitness. As one child after another is metabolized to feed the carelessly voracious appetite of the factory, the idle play of *Cremaster 1*'s protagonist with the grapes is clear. Whether a grape is eaten or dropped into the chorus line is moot. Either way, the individual is only an integer in service to the sum. No wonder Barney's protagonists don't want to leave the in utero arena of undifferentiation. To leave is to be consumed and voided.

Matthew Barney: Pace Car for the Hubris Pill, ed. Matthew Barney and Gracia Lebbink (Rotterdam: Museum Boijmans Van Beuningen, 1996), 21–35.

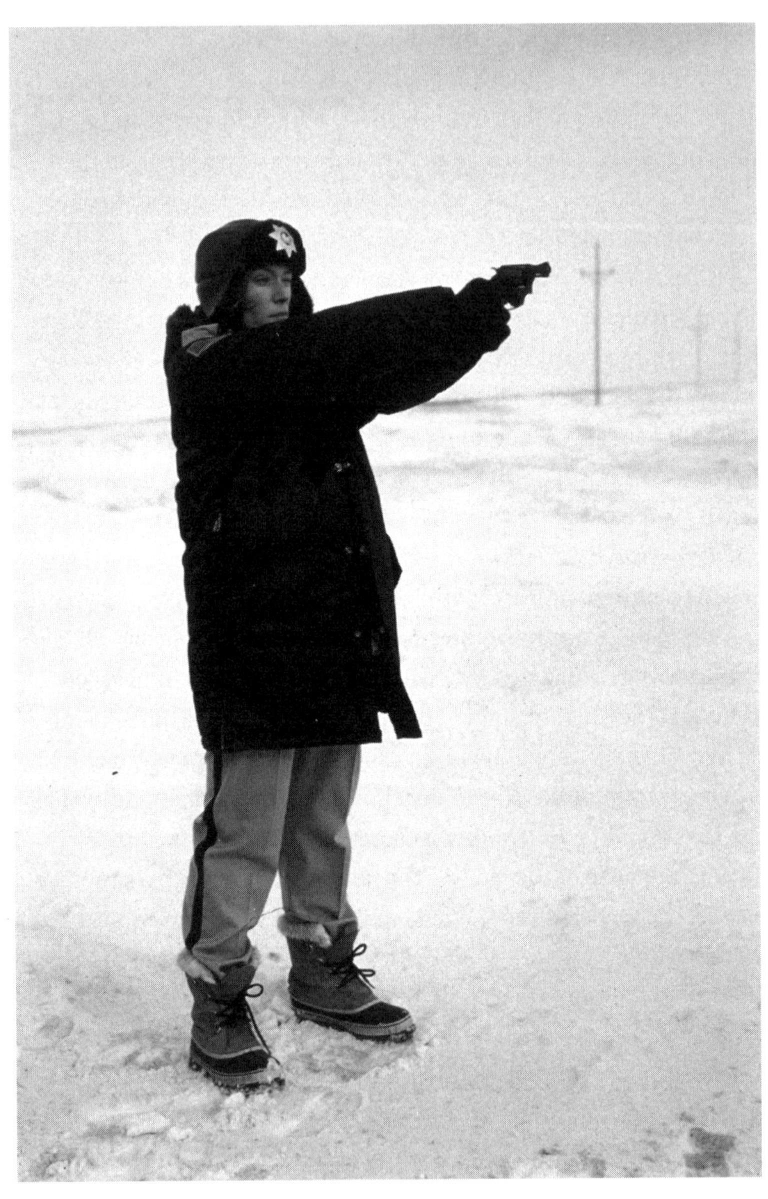

Frances McDormand as "Marge Gunderson" in *Fargo* (1996)

Minnesota Nice: *Fargo*

I've been thinking about the Joel and Ethan Coen movie *Fargo* (1996).
I've been trying to figure out why it left me elated and flattened all
at once. A big part of my mixed reaction is due, I'm convinced, to the
film's setting in the state of Minnesota (with a preface and afterword
in North Dakota). I happen to have recently moved to Minnesota [in
1994], and I went to see *Fargo* with all the anticipation of the newly
baptized to their first church meeting. Before Minnesota, I'd lived on
the East Coast, and trust me, nothing on the East Coast can in any
way prepare you for what is west of it. The Minnesota I'd been creating
for myself since my arrival was necessarily more exotic than prosaic.
I really wasn't interested in how it conformed to what I knew, only
how it differed.

The key to the difference was the Mississippi River, legendary
divider of America's East and West. The epic grain elevators that flank
its shoreline give the place a purpose that is mythic—feeding America.
Here was where the harvest of the Great Plains was distributed so that
a nation would never go hungry. A couple of car rides later, the grain
silos were joined by the ore docks, which spread up along the shore
of Lake Superior from Duluth. Unlike the wholesome volumetrics of
the concrete elevators, the ore docks are spidery and sinister. Railroad
tracks feed down to the lake from the Iron Range and disappear
behind chain-link fencing through jumbles of smoking outbuildings
and onto silhouetted trestles where the ore is loaded onto waiting
tankers. For me, ore is almost better than grain—more brutal, bigger
businesses and bigger bastards running them. Also the names of the

ranges—Cuyuna, Mesabi, Vermilion—have a great, moody poetic ring to them. The final component in my Minnesota is the lumber, the lost treasure of the state and its greatest shame. By the early part of this century, what had been one of America's biggest forests and Minnesota's greatest bounty was gone—cut, shipped, and banked. All that remains is a scattering of millwork and paper plants, the stench of which pulverizes the towns that depend on them.

However, Minnesota's vanished forests left another legacy, altogether weirder than the stomach-churning scent of paper pulp: Paul Bunyan, the satanic totem host of every tourist-driven village in the state. There are Paul Bunyan statues all over Minnesota, each one more grotesquely hearty than the next, each more gigantically and enigmatically welcoming than its predecessor down the road. Bunyan and his familiar, Babe the Blue Ox, first entered the ranks of American folk legends in 1910 thanks to the fanciful prose of a columnist for the *Detroit News-Tribune*. Nowadays, Bunyan's most unique contribution to mythology is that he was created as a hero for capitalism rather than evolving as a hero from necessity—a Frankenstein monster in the guise of a lumberjack, blithely deforesting the Midwest when not frolicking with his ox.

Paul Bunyan is the omnipotent, uncaring god who presides over the Coens' *Fargo*. He is present as an enormous, mute sculpture, a brother to the statue that arrives to take Don Giovanni plummeting into the bowels of hell. Bearded with a blood-red mouth, wearing a checkered lumberjack shirt and hefting an ax, the Coens' Bunyan is situated in the town of Brainerd, the film's moral epicenter. It is from here that *Fargo*'s undistractible and pregnant heroine sheriff, Marge Gunderson, sets forth on a journey to solve a grisly string of murders. Marge is set up as a bit of another regional cliché: she's "Minnesota nice." The modifier I've heard more than a few times from other East Coast transplants is "Minnesota nice, as cold as ice" and, indeed, it's true of Marge, who tracks her prey with the fuzzy, warm-blooded intensity of a starving wolf.

The corruption in *Fargo* starts in Minneapolis, Minnesota's mercantile capital where money is milled from grain, ore, and lumber. An everyman by name, Jerry Lundegaard has come up against a problem that only dollars can resolve. He constructs a kidnapping plot in which his wife will be harmlessly taken hostage by two goons-for-hire from Fargo. Her ransom will be paid by her affluent father and suburban life will prosaically continue. Of course, nothing goes right and a wrath as insatiable as that borne by Eumenides against the house of Atreus is unleashed in the wintery whiteout of a midwestern tract development.

Jerry's Minnesota is very different from my Minnesota. This is not to suggest the Coens' portrayal is inaccurate—they were, after all, brought up in suburban Minneapolis—only that I have so assiduously avoided the reality of the suburban islanding, driving by on my way to grain, ore, and lumber. Getting stuck in a split-level house of Atreus was not my idea of Minnesota and the awful, dysfunctional rhythm of Jerry's family could just have easily been enacted in New Jersey. This was part of what was so flattening about *Fargo*, the idea that all American suburbs are essentially the same. The suburbs have historically been the ruin of American cities: divide the behemoth up anyway you have to; just get Mister and Missus home to their glare of light on the horizon before the babysitter slips another dose of Ritalin to their heir who is gnawing on the shag carpet in the family room. *Fargo* gets the suburbs frighteningly right.

It is the arrival of the kidnappers from Fargo that throws the film back into an unmistakable Midwest as they drive into a Minneapolis that is cold and white and rich. Kidnappers and extortionist are suddenly, giddily let loose on a state filled with Scandinavian-accented, apple-cheeked victims and witnesses; everything that could go wrong does. The two parties are in tenuous communication through a paroled Native American, Shep, the only "other" in the film. It is Shep's existentially careless relationship with his "others" that sets the plot on its relentlessly fatal course. Once the exposition is out of the way, things just convulse and move on: flat accents lead into flatter landscapes as snow-bleached highway shoulders and lakeside cabins start sprouting bodies like the darling buds of May.

As in the best of the Coens' films (*Blood Simple*, 1984; *Raising Arizona*, 1987; *Miller's Crossing*, 1990; *Barton Fink*, 1991), the stakes in *Fargo* are remarkably low—chump change, really. All the escalating awfulness needn't ever have happened but, somehow, it's the pettiness of the prize that gives the film its curious moral gravity. At *Fargo*'s particularly American end, Jerry finds himself in a seedy motel and his response is equivalent to a child's tantrum over being sent to bed in the middle of a favorite cartoon. What he has wrought is nothing compared to what has been denied him. Jerry's tantrum holds within it the encapsulated, leveling power of *Fargo*. The film was never about the Midwest in general or Minnesota in particular. It was about America and the toll that the country's drift from entitlement has taken. Jerry Lundegaard is a spoiled everyman, one of an army of everymen brought up to believe there would always be a chicken in the pot. When there isn't, Fargo turns into Waco or Ruby Ridge or Oklahoma City. It's a national parable and the message is devastating.

Frieze, no. 29 (June–August 1996): 37–38.

Shadowland

Cut a chrysalis open, and you will find a rotting caterpillar. What you will never find is that mythical creature, half caterpillar, half butterfly, a fit emblem of the human soul, for those whose cast of mind leads them to seek such emblems. No, the process of transformation consists almost entirely of decay.

PAT BARKER, *REGENERATION*[1]

Art is not life, nor was it ever meant to be. Art is, at its most elevated, that triumph of the cognitive animal over banal necessity. History is not experience, nor a mirror of experience. History is, at its simplest, what has been remembered, or misremembered, for the record. Art and history are not congenial; they don't lie to each other, but they are incapable of telling the same truths. They can both approach the truth, caress it a bit, but truth is something other, something that is neither expressive nor linear. Art and truth are, however, sympathetically conjugal and dwell in the many-chambered cave of life and history. *no place (like home)* is an exploration of that cave and its inhabitants. What it reveals is a whispering darkness where an occasional pulse of flame illumines that which we fear the most and that to which we aspire most dearly. It is a darkness inhabited by ghosts and infants, those who have passed over and those who have yet to bear witness or wear the stain of complicity. What light exists is provided by artists who, from the beginning, have transformed caves into civilizations.

THE DUCHESS

I've done you so much harm in wishing to do you good.
    CLAIRE DE DURAS, *OURIKA*[2]

In 1823 a remarkable novel was published in France. Entitled *Ourika*,
it purported to be the autobiographical account of a young Senegalese
woman who, as a child, was rescued from slavery and subsequently
raised in the bosom of the French aristocracy. The book is brief; the
prose, eloquently spare. While the first of the San Domingo slave up-
risings in 1791 and the French Reign of Terror, which began in 1793,
play crucial roles in the narrative, history is not really the issue. Rather,
Ourika is concerned with a shadowland that eludes the map of history—
a place where souls are doomed to wander in search of the history that
has escaped them.

Ourika was the creation of Claire de Duras, an aristocrat and a survivor of the French Revolution. Her book, which introduced the first
Negro narrator in European literature, was an immediate best seller.
As slavery did not become illegal in the French colonies until 1848, it
was also a pioneering work of abolitionist literature—a moral fiction.
Duras's heroine was based on fact, but the sensitivity of the author's
characterization transcends the limitations of imaginative reportage.
Ourika is one of those extraordinary novas that illuminate the landscape over which they burn and presage that which is to come.

The tender eloquence with which Duras tells Ourika's story is more
than a graceful act of literary imposture; it is a transformative rite of
identification. While it is also tempting to view *Ourika*, by extension,
as a meditation on the status of women, that would be to miss the
greater achievement. Duras was a presiding member of the French
Enlightenment, authored novels, maintained a salon in the Tuileries
Palace, and served as an intellectual mentor to one of the era's greatest
diplomats, Vicomte Chateaubriand. With the exception of the novel's

narrator, the women in *Ourika* are liberated. The great achievement of the novel is that it gives voice to nothing less than utter loss. The hypnotic melancholy of Duras's heroine is more profound than self-pity; it is something vast and unchartable. *Ourika* crystallizes the unthinkable awfulness of those cast into the shadowland—of those forced to follow a road map that leads inexorably to no place.

What did it matter that I might now have been the black slave of some rich planter? Scorched by the sun, I should be laboring on someone else's land. But I would have a poor hut of my own to go to at day's end; a partner in my life, children of my own race who would call me their mother, who would kiss my face without disgust, who would rest their heads against my neck and sleep in my arms. I had done nothing—and yet here I was, condemned never to know the only feelings my heart was created for.[3]

THE GENERAL

I am sending to France with all his family this man who is such a danger to San Domingo. The Government, Citizen Minister, must have him put in a very strong place situated in the center of France, so that he may never have any means of escaping and returning to San Domingo, where he has all the influence of the leader of a sect. If in three years this man were to reappear in San Domingo, perhaps he would destroy all that France had done there.... I entreat you, send me some troops. Without them I cannot undertake the disarming of the population, and without the disarming I am not master of this colony.

GENERAL LECLERC, BROTHER-IN-LAW TO NAPOLEON BONAPARTE AND COMMANDER OF FRENCH FORCES IN SAN DOMINGO[4]

In 1803, a scant few years after Ourika's fictional death, a real exile died at Fort-de-Joux high in the Jura Mountains along the French-Swiss border. The exile was Toussaint L'Ouverture, the Creole son of an African-born slave and the leader of what would, after his death, become the first successful slave rebellion in the New World. He was fifty-seven years old and a loyal son of France. He died believing in the Rights of Man promulgated by the Revolution and in the man who murdered him through aggressive neglect—Napoleon Bonaparte. Fort-de-Joux was L'Ouverture's "no place." To the end, L'Ouverture believed that Bonaparte would negotiate in good faith, and as an equal, for the freedom of the slaves of San Domingo. Bonaparte, of course, had no intention of upsetting the machinery of slavery and simply sought to silence its most eloquent opponent. At Fort-de-Joux, shamed and separated from all he held dear, guilty of no crime that would warrant a trial, L'Ouverture wrote from his heart to Bonaparte asking for release from the historical cul-de-sac to which he had been condemned.

> *I have had the misfortune to incur your anger; but as to fidelity and probity, I am strong in my conscience, and I dare to say with truth that among all the servants of the State none is more honest than I. I was one of your soldiers and the first servant of the Republic in Santo Domingo. I am to-day wretched, ruined, dishonored, a victim of my own services. Let your sensibility be touched at my position, you are too great in feeling and too just not to pronounce on my destiny.*[5]

There was to be no justice for L'Ouverture in the shadowland. Perhaps, at the end, he took heart from the words he had pronounced to the captain of the boat sent to remove him from his Caribbean island to France: "In overthrowing me, you have cut down in San Domingo only the trunk of the tree of liberty. It will spring up again by the roots for they are numerous and deep."[6] The tragic irony of L'Ouverture's defeat was that the very citizens of France with whom he believed he shared a vision could not, by and large, accept the loss

that honoring the vision would entail. It was, after all, the growing
bourgeoisie who fostered and funded the French Revolution, and their
continued welfare was deeply and profoundly interwoven with the
slave trade. Even as the Revolution brewed in France, thirty to forty
thousand slaves a year were still being fed into San Domingo to reap
ever greater harvests in trade, harvests that spread the wealth not only
in France but throughout Europe.

Historical fact tells us that, in the twilight of the eighteenth
century, there were half a million slaves on the island of San Domingo,
the majority of whom were native Africans. The recent arrivals were
often at odds with their Creole predecessors and both were at odds
with the mulattos. Occupying neither world, the mulattos were
subjected to the caprices of eugenic classification (there were 128
shades of color culminating in the *sang-mêlé*, who was composed of 127
parts white, 1 part black, and classified as black) and the whimsy of
those who could offer or deny them freedom. It was a system that
promoted self-loathing and hubris in equal portion. To be robbed of
one's essential identity, and then blamed for the loss by the one who
has robbed you, was perhaps the cruelest practice in a litany of
atrocities enacted by the French overlords.

L'Ouverture sprang from the fatally abundant soil of San Domingo
and formed an army that would, in his wake, topple the French rule
and lead to the creation of Haiti, the first black state in the New World.
L'Ouverture was, however, much more than a brilliant insurgent; he
was a man of the Enlightenment and he believed that he was fighting
for the universal rights of man. Had he been less of a man, he might
well have survived to realize half of his dream. As it was, that which
made him great also destroyed him.

THE PRESIDENT

The whole commerce between master and slave is a perpetual exercise of the most boisterous passions, the most unremitting despotism on the one part, and degrading submissions on the other.

THOMAS JEFFERSON, *NOTES ON THE STATE OF VIRGINIA*[7]

One of the most chilling moments in *Ourika* comes when its narrator learns of the first massacre of the white planters by the San Domingo slaves and repudiates her own race, a race she knows nothing of. Later, at the height of the Terror, surrounded by her beleaguered white protectors, Ourika has a horrible epiphany that seals her fate as surely as L'Ouverture's idealism sealed his. "In any case," she reflects, "all the world was miserable, and I no longer felt alone. A view of life is like a motherland. It is a possession mutually shared. Those who uphold and defend it are like brothers. Sometimes I used to tell myself that, poor negress though I was, I still belonged with all the noblest of spirits, because of our shared longing for justice."[8] But, alas, Ourika had by then become a shadow and shadows cannot act; they are merely insubstantial echoes of that which they mimic.

Ourika, the metaphor, and L'Ouverture, the reality, are both seared by drawing too close to the tripart flame of *liberté, égalité, fraternité*. Shaped by the pen and scarred by the brand, neither ever had the possibility of escaping from the shadowland to see the fullness of themselves reflected in oneness with those whose reality they could only dream into being. The irony is that their dream had been constructed by others less generous than themselves—others whose moral order depended on the extension of the promise and whose economic order necessitated the denial of the promise. The contradiction in it all is bluntly caught in Dr. Samuel Johnson's questioning taunt: "How is it that we hear the loudest yelps of liberty from the drivers of Negroes?"[9] The tragedy in it all is made devastatingly clear in the words of

America's greatest advocate of the Enlightenment, Thomas Jefferson: "I tremble for my country when I reflect that God is just."[10] Jefferson (framer of the Declaration of Independence, American ambassador to the court of Louis XVI, and third president of the United States) was, at the time of his death in 1826, one of the largest slaveholders in the state of Virginia.

THE CURATE

The procession went on, amid that mixture of rites that characterizes idolatry in all countries—half resplendent, half horrible—appealing to nature while they rebel against her—mingling flowers with blood, and casting alternately a screaming infant, or a garland of roses, beneath the car of the idol.

CHARLES ROBERT MATURIN, *MELMOTH THE WANDERER*[11]

Two years before the death of Thomas Jefferson, Charles Robert Maturin, the Anglican curate of St. Peter's Church in Dublin, Ireland, died of an accidental dose of poison. He was forty-four years old and the author of the last, epic Gothic novel, *Melmoth the Wanderer*. Maturin was Irish (and a nationalist) but came from a Protestant family that had fled France after the Edict of Nantes was reversed and persecution of the Protestants began once more. His novel is a giddy orchestration of ever-mounting horrors within a rat's nest of related stories, all of which are driven by the dementia induced by otherness. Woven through the novel are narrative strands dealing with Thomas Cromwell's subjugation of Ireland and the Roundhead confiscation of Irish-Catholic properties, the nightmares of Bedlam at the height of the English Restoration, and the persecution of Jews and dissidents by the Spanish Inquisition. Everything is overheated and very little is without historical precedent. Maturin had, for example, seen in his own lifetime the long-dormant Spanish Inquisition brought back to papacy-sanctioned life in 1778, and felt the sympathetic, anti-British shock waves that respirated through Ireland during the heady first year of the French Revolution.

While *Melmoth* seethes with all the high discordancy of the Gothic form, it has a noble gravity missing in other examples of the genre. Its protagonist, the Wanderer, is doomed to be an exile from all that he knows, and it is his exile that Maturin designates as the novel's greatest horror. Maturin was a child of the Enlightenment and while Gothic (in its antirational hystericalization of all incident) would seem, on the surface, to be an absolute contradiction to the goals of Enlightenment, it served Maturin's humanist concerns quite nicely. The unspeakable despair of a man who belongs nowhere, whose life is an endless search for a resting place, further led Maturin to write one of the century's great soliloquies of the dispossessed: "The terror that I inspired I at last began to feel. I began to believe myself—I know not what, whatever they thought me. This is a dreadful state of mind, but one impossible to avoid. In some circumstances, where the whole world is against us, we begin to take its part against ourselves, to avoid the withering sensation of being alone on our own side."[12]

THE MARQUIS

In Marseilles, he had himself whipped, but every couple of minutes he would dash to the mantelpiece and, with a knife, would inscribe on the chimney flue the number of lashes he had just received.

SIMONE DE BEAUVOIR, *MARQUIS DE SADE*[13]

Not so curiously, one of Gothic fiction's most rational supporters was the Marquis de Sade (to admire him, wrote Georges Bataille, "is to diminish the force of his ideas").[14] For de Sade, who briefly profited from the Reign of Terror when he was freed by the mob from the Bastille, the Gothic novel evidences "the inevitable fruits of the revolutionary shocks felt by all of Europe.... For those who know all the miseries with which scoundrels can oppress men, the novel became as difficult to write as it was monotonous to read.... It was necessary to call hell to the rescue ... and to find in the world of nightmare the history of man in this Iron Age."[15] While it would be difficult to advance de Sade as a model representative of the Enlightenment, he was certainly a recipient of its "fruits" and a disenfranchised member of its aristocratic originators. Certainly, in his sense of victimization and authorial role of victimizer, he understood the consummate perversity of master/slave relationships better than his more idealistic peers. Georges Bataille, in his essay "De Sade's Sovereign Man," quotes Clairwill, one of de Sade's most ticklish fictional inventions: "I'd like to find a crime that should have never-ending repercussions even when I have ceased to act, so that there would not be a single instant of my life when even if I were asleep I was not the cause of some disorder or another, and this disorder I should like to expand until it brought general corruption in its train or such a categorical disturbance that even beyond my life the effects would continue."[16]

Here, truly, is the demonic understanding of how the well of reason is poisoned and of the monstrous implications when others, namely "we," drink its putrescence. In his summation of de Sade's frightening contribution to Western thought, Bataille states it all quite clearly: "And if today the average man has a profound insight into what transgression means for him, de Sade was the one who made ready the path. Now the average man knows that he must become aware of things which repel him most violently—those things which repel us most violently are part of our own nature."[17]

THE POET

Toussaint, the most unhappy man of men!
Whether the whistling Rustic tend his plough
Within thy hearing, or thy head be now
Pillowed in some deep dungeon's earless den;—
O miserable Chieftain! where and when
Wilt thou find patience! Yet die not; do thou
Wear rather in thy bonds a cheerful brow:
Though fallen thyself, never to rise again,
Live, and take comfort. Thou hast left behind
Powers that will work for thee; air, earth, and skies;
There's not a breathing of the common wind
That will forget thee; thou hast great allies;
Thy friends are exultations, agonies,
And love, and man's unconquerable mind.

WILLIAM WORDSWORTH, "TO TOUSSAINT L'OUVERTURE"[18]

William Wordsworth, the greatest of the English Romantic poets, died two years after the abolition of slavery in the French colonies and eleven years before the start of the American Civil War. By the time of his death, San Domingo had been the black republic of Haiti for forty-six years and Bonaparte had long been toppled and lay buried in his own island "no place," Elba. Wordsworth's tribute to L'Ouverture is filled with eloquent promise and the implicit acknowledgment that what L'Ouverture fought to attain is within reach. It was not, nor is it today.

What we are looking at in *no place (like home)* are artistic responses to legacies born centuries ago and oceans away to parents we never knew. The legacies—colonialism, slavery, cultural and physical displacement—received some of their worst interpretations and the proposal of some of their most eloquent solutions in what Charles Dickens called "the best of times and the worst of times," the eighteenth century. The most fluorescent heritage of the age of Enlightenment—the Rights of Man—was forged by the French Revolution and put to savage use during the Reign of Terror. But, once the guillotine was stilled, nothing much seemed really changed. Instead of a Bourbon king, France raised a Corsican emperor.

Now, in 1997, the progress toward a new age of *liberté, égalité, fraternité*—convulsive as it has been—still seems modest. L'Ouverture's tangled roots have put forth only the plainest of leaves, hardly the vibrant hybrid prophesied by the bloodied frenzy of cultivation. We have, as a civilization, washed up at no place in particular as the road to true Enlightenment has proved more treacherous than ever anticipated. And, while art is far too fragile a creation to significantly alter the course of history, it can allow us, if only for a moment, to draw perilously close to an understanding of what history and life have done to those fellow pilgrims we share it with.

Richard Flood, *no place (like home)* (Minneapolis: Walker Art Center, 1997), 8–15.

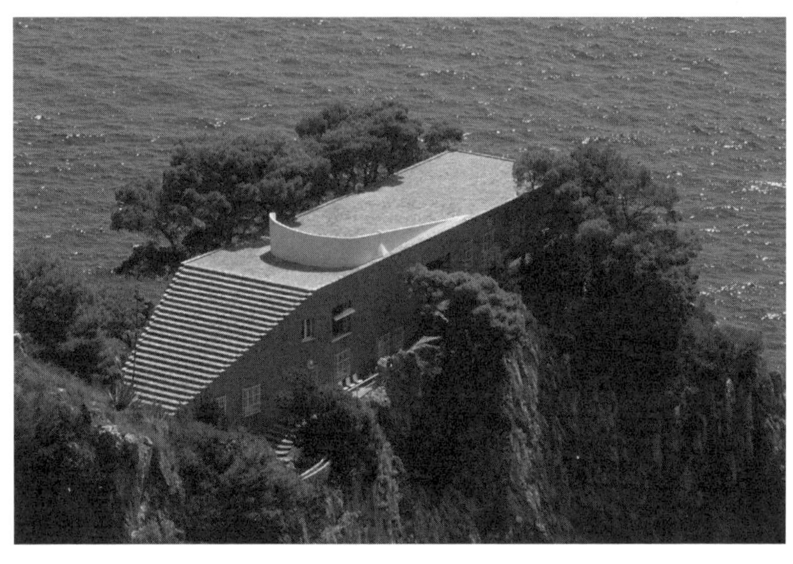

Casa Malaparte built by Curzio Malaparte, Capri, Italy, 1938–42

128

Curzio Malaparte: Casa Malaparte, 1938

When it came to writing, Curzio Malaparte was a man on fire. He was
a journalist and an essayist, a novelist and a playwright. When it came
to politics, Malaparte was a human weather vane. He was a republican,
a nationalist, a fascist, and a communist. While he was dying of cancer
in 1957, Malaparte turned the Roman clinic where he was undergoing
treatment into the set of a postwar opera buffa. Lying in state, he was
paid homage by the most notable of his countrymen, joined the Communist Party, converted to Catholicism, and then, totally synchronized
with the prevailing power structure, expired. The fifty-nine-year-old
writer left behind a literary legacy that, in its opportunistic relationship to historical "necessity," mirrored nothing less than the convulsive
contractions that led to the birth of modern Italy.

If there was one constant in the contradictory trajectory of Malaparte's life, it was his fidelity to a dream he embraced in 1938. The
topic of his fantasy was nothing remarkable—a retreat where he could
pursue his writing without distraction. The location was, however,
the stuff of legend. Malaparte fell in love with a rocky peninsula called
Capo Massullo on the coast of Capri. Barely 100 feet long by 30 feet
wide, bounded on three sides by cliffs plummeting 650 feet into the
Mediterranean Sea, Capo Massullo is a tapered finger sticking out into
an eternity of blue. In Curzio Malaparte, Capo Massullo found both a
lover and a colonizer.

The house Malaparte dreamed into being is arguably the century's
most eloquent marriage of landscape and architecture. Initially, Malaparte consulted with Roman architect Adalberto Libera, but the final

product is definitely more a concrete poem by Malaparte than a blue-print by Libera, who, in truth, never advanced his identification with the house's authorship. Lounging like a lizard in the sun, Casa Malaparte stretches the length of Capo Massullo. It is a simple rectangular structure made of native stone, sheathed in plaster, and painted a Pompeian red. The floor plan for the two and one-half levels is modest, austere really. If it weren't for two applied elements, Casa Malaparte would simply be a marvelously situated holiday villa. However, the two elements Malaparte chose to complete his house signify the difference between felicitous choice and ecstatic realization.

On the landward end of Casa Malaparte, a trapezoidal staircase ascends the exterior of the house, widening as it climbs toward the limitless sky. In profile, the shape cuts a sheer diagonal into the volcanic rock. Head on, the staircase is as ritually suggestive as a Mayan pyramid. Its purpose is rational—to provide access to the flat plane of roof terrace—but mounting the thirty-three steps to an altar of roof suggests an ancient, even sacred choreography. Once the roof has been reached, Malaparte's second element appears. An extended comma of white plaster, rising to around eight feet and creating a barrier wall at the summit of the steps, initially blocks the view toward the precipice. Move around it and the wall begins a gradual, insistent decline until it merges with the roof. The gesture is as insouciant as that of an aviator tossing a white silk scarf over his shoulder to catch the wind. Again, the purpose—privacy from prying eyes—is immediately perceivable. Yet architecturally, the effect is riveting. Crowning a house that is a hymn to the rational, Malaparte's comma is a diversionary and magical piece of lyricism. The writer referred to it as a "sail" and, indeed, it serenely guides the house into a celestially surrealist orbit that denies the right-angled mass of its core.

In 1943, one year after he was in residence, Malaparte wrote: "Today I live on an island, in a harsh, melancholy, and severe house which I have built alone, lonesome on a cliff hanging over the sea:

a house which is the ghost, the secret image of the jail. The image of my nostalgia."[1] The "jail" is Lipari, the island to which Mussolini exiled him in the 1930s. There he became obsessed with a staircase leading to the church of the Annunziata that would become his inspiration for Casa Malaparte. While the house may be the author's "image of the jail," he was truly a bird in a gilded cage—a cage that secured him a place in the twentieth century far more influential than did his writing. Casa Malaparte occupies that moment of rupture—of summation and advancement—that permits a culture to identify the best of what it has been and might be. At once, it provides closure and inspiration. It is a capriccio in which the classic and the modern are caught and held in an embrace by the same, never to be repeated melody.

When Malaparte died, he left his house to the People's Republic of China. As he had dubbed his legacy *casa come me* (house like me), his bequest was suitably perverse. Six years later, in 1963, Jean-Luc Godard (another occasional Maoist) assembled a house party at Casa Malaparte that would forever consign its then-moldering beauty to immortality. Godard's guests were Brigitte Bardot, Michel Piccoli, Jack Palance, and Fritz Lang. The occasion was the filming of *Contempt*, Godard's adaptation of Alberto Moravia's fashionably lassitudinous novel *Il Disprezzo*. Now, decades later, *Contempt* remains one of the most gorgeous, austerely giddy films ever made. It is also a love poem to the isolate splendor of Casa Malaparte and does what no documentary could, which is to show how the careless, solipsistic rhythms of the house's occupants are heightened simply by being framed within the house itself. Inside Casa Malaparte, surrounded by views of a beauty that would in earlier times have frozen the soul, the characters in *Contempt* indulge in idle flirtations, vainglorious pronouncements on the gravity of art, and games where power and its abuse are meaningless divertissements. Only the character of the director, played by Fritz Lang, functions with a goal as he shoots a very Godardian version of *Ulysses* on the roof, with only the sky as his limitless set. What Godard found on Capo

Massullo was curiously akin to what Malaparte found on Lipari: "Too much sea, too much sky, for such a small island, and such a restless soul." The ravishingly forlorn ending of *Contempt* is an astonishing cinematic equivalent to Malaparte's own epic despair: "The horizon is too broad, I drown in it."[2]

Artforum 35, no. 10 (Summer 1997): 122.

Douglas Gordon: *24 Hour Psycho*

Psycho was released in 1960 and provides perfect closure for the doomed, conformist utopia of America in the 1950s. Nothing awful would have happened to the movie's heroine if she hadn't accidentally been diverted from the freeway onto the highway it replaced—a highway turned into a back road to nowhere. In *Psycho*, once the freeway has been left behind, the nightmare begins and we are plunged into a parallel America where the darkest secrets lie perilously close to the surface, where truth and illusion are as one. The freeway may sweep past it but, off the fast road to the future, there exists a gridlock of blasted dreams—dreams that can kill.

Once seen, *Psycho* can never be forgotten. Neither can the experience of that first viewing ever be repeated. The insistent malady that hangs over an entertainment like *Psycho* is that its sting affects the nervous system only once and thereafter one grows increasingly immunized. Certainly a frisson lingers in subsequent viewings, but it tends to be analytic in nature and compromised by the coitus interruptus that is integral to the film's structure. Once the heroine (Janet Leigh) has been dispatched and her presence obliterated, the film has no goal other than a packaged resolution. All the film's propulsive, remorseless, essentially wordless energy sputters to a halt and another, infinitely more conventional film begins.

In his 1962 interview with François Truffaut, Alfred Hitchcock commented: "My main satisfaction is that the film had an effect on audiences.... I feel it's tremendously satisfying for us to be able to use cinematic art to achieve something of a mass emotion. And with

Psycho we most definitely achieved this. It wasn't a message that stirred the audiences, nor was it a great performance or their enjoyment of the novel. They were aroused by pure film."[1] Well, yes and no. When the "pure film" stops two-thirds of the way in, the rest of *Psycho* crawls on into a half-baked exercise in Freudian kitsch. The rather extraordinary performance of Anthony Perkins in the "pure" *Psycho*, for example, becomes a career-destroying cliché in the non-"pure" denouement. Janet Leigh, on the other hand, escapes the curse visited on Perkins by being terminated in the legend-making ether of the "pure" *Psycho*. Perkins, unfortunately, had to hang around for the Gong Show finale.

From its opening seconds, *Psycho* is undiluted, voyeuristic slime. No tracking shot in American film has ever quite so insinuated the phrase "invasion of privacy." The shot aerially traverses the city of Phoenix, Arizona, then slides up the brick wall of a hotel and slithers through a partially opened/closed window to reveal a postcoital couple at the end of a lunch-hour tryst. The audience is immediately complicit with the camera; that is *Psycho*'s dirty little secret. When Hitchcock referred to audience arousal, he was disingenuous in attributing the arousal to "pure film" as opposed to a much thornier goal: audience participation. Once you've partnered with Hitchcock's camera and gone along for the ride to the Bates Motel, your fingerprints are on the knife that violates Janet Leigh just as surely as those of her "pure film" murderer.

Douglas Gordon understands all of this, and his *24 Hour Psycho* (1993) is an inevitable corollary to the Hitchcock film. In the corpus of Hitchcock's work, *Psycho* is the one that adapts most readily to the kind of extended frame-by-frame autopsy to which Gordon subjects it. Discussing the genesis of his film in a 1993 interview in *Frieze*, Gordon commented: "I always wanted to make an epic for my first film—a real movie, not Super 8 or anything. I thought it might be interesting to take an existing film and re-make it. I wanted a picture with a story

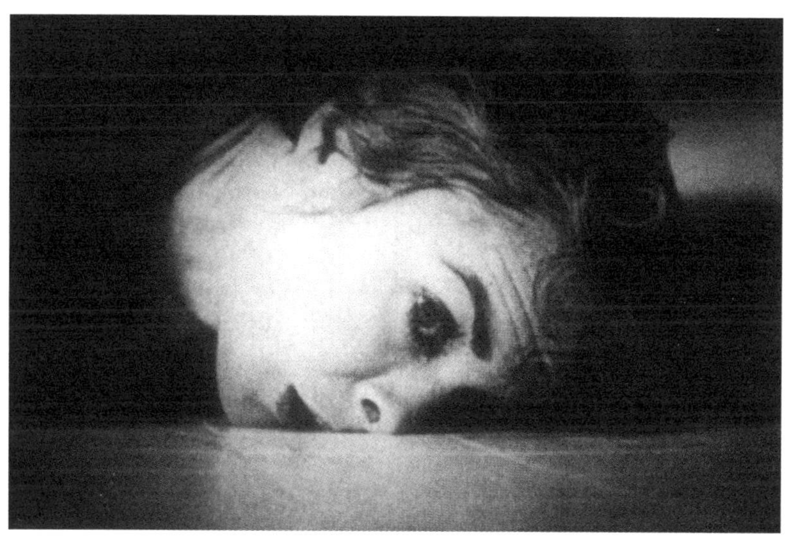

Janet Leigh as "Marion Crane" in *Psycho* (1960)

which was familiar to a broad audience; so I started to work with *Psycho*. What I decided to do was alter the narrative of the original by making it 24 hours long, and without sound."[2]

The absence of sound in Gordon's film turns out to be a major, formal asset. While Hitchcock's original had very little dialogue—two reels are virtually mute—it did have Bernard Herrmann's intense, anxiety-producing score. But take away the soundtrack and slow everything way, way down, and the film gets even creepier. With no audio cues to ground the scenes, the audience is rendered helpless, an impotent participant, caught in a prolonged, comatose awareness not dissimilar to being trapped in a car that is spinning out of control while seconds thud by like hours.

The opening pan into the hotel becomes, in Gordon's film, even more suggestive than in the original. Details that previously slipped by unnoticed suddenly loom large: an uneaten sandwich, neatly folded clothes; the excuse and the routine. Only when Janet Leigh's lover carelessly lifts a rumpled bed sheet to his nose does anything close to erotic spontaneity disrupt what otherwise looks like an affair that has gone on too long. Obviously, all of this information was available in the original, but there it was just a blip on the scanner, not a death knell. *24 Hour Psycho* is still Hitchcock's movie but, like a good therapist, Gordon is giving him the time to let it all out.

Psycho is crammed with great sequences—the hotel assignation, Janet Leigh's torturous drive out of Phoenix, her murder in the shower, Perkins's compulsive mopping up, the murder of the insurance investigator—and they lose none of their power in Gordon's version. If anything, they become more glacially mesmerizing as the drama peels off and the images take over. The shower sequence is arguably one of the most analyzed sequences in Hitchcock's career. Talking about it with Truffaut, he said: "It took us seven days to shoot that scene and there were seventy camera setups for forty-five seconds of footage."[3] In *24 Hour Psycho*, the scene goes on for almost half an hour and, without

136

Herrmann's screaming staccato strings and Hitchcock's blitzkrieg editing, the sequence plays like a muted, elegiac pavane. A hand endlessly clutches a shower curtain. Ever so slowly the curtain pulls away from the hooks that secure it. A field of white drifts down. Something darker than desire eddies around the drain. And so it goes on—inexorably. A death staged for audience arousal becomes an austere re-creation of a victim's will to survive. Gordon's appropriative strategy bestows a kind of dignity on the woman, which Hitchcock's desire to entertain denied her. In the end, *24 Hour Psycho*'s true virtue is that it removes the tawdry cynicism that informs Hitchcock's experiment in audience arousal and shifts the enterprise away from exploitation to something very much like tragedy.

Parkett, no. 49 (1997): 37–40.

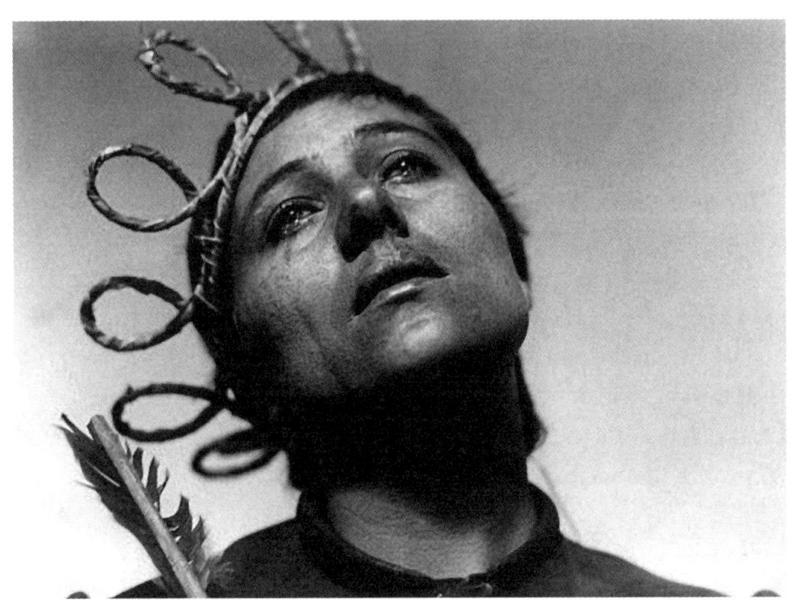

Renée Jeanne Falconetti as "Joan" in *The Passion of Joan of Arc* (1928)

138

Voodoo Auteurism:
Film Stills and Photography

Larry Johnson's suite of six photographs *Untitled (Movie Stars on Clouds)* (1983) imagines identical, sweetly elegiac credit sequences for two of Hollywood's most fatally iconic films, *Rebel Without a Cause* (1955) and *The Misfits* (1961). On fluffy white clouds adrift over Technicolor blue skies, Johnson simply imposes the names of the stars in each of the films: James Dean, Sal Mineo, and Natalie Wood signify *Rebel Without a Cause*, and Montgomery Clift, Clark Gable, and Marilyn Monroe signify *The Misfits*. The series is arguably the most effective double entendre about the promise and the lie of cinematic immortality in contemporary art. (Only Andy Warhol's faux-innocent silkscreens of movie stars occupy similar territory.) Dean died in a car crash, Mineo was stabbed to death, and Wood died by drowning—all violently fatal baptisms into legend. As for Gable and Monroe, *The Misfits* was their last film; Clift lingered on with increasingly apparent disabilities for three more.

While the cast of *Rebel* remains pretty much frozen in amber and emblematic of glittering youth, the stars of *The Misfits* are more like touchstones for the cruelty of illusion: all three had stayed much too long at the fair and the film shows each of them in an almost documentary state of naked disintegration. In Johnson's photographs, it is assumed that we know the names and, more important, can supply the faces as well as an emotional tenor to those names. He further assumes that we carry within us those signifying freeze-frames that confirm the emotional weight of who these people were, that we invest in the myth of artifice that is the cinema's greatest allure.

I don't remember exactly when I picked up Parker Tyler's book *Classics of the Foreign Film*. I do know that it was a used copy and that my purchase was well past the 1962 publication date. What I am certain of is that it was my first book of film stills and that afterward I never looked at a photograph in quite the same way. Prior to *Classics of the Foreign Film*, photographs were either things that were passed from hand to hand, eliciting cooing and clucking sounds in response to the frozen poses of family members and friends, or they were the most interesting parts of magazines. If the photograph was compelling, maybe the copy that it accompanied would be as well. Either way, photographs were essentially visual corollaries to facts and I tended to shuffle through them with less attention than I would pay to a spidery crack in the ceiling. Parker Tyler changed all that.

Classics of the Foreign Film was Tyler's attempt to widen the American public's nascent interest in, primarily, European film. The seventy-odd films to which the book is devoted are the selection of an aesthete rather than a critic, an enthusiast rather than a formalist. When I came into possession of it, I had seen none of the films under discussion and, even today, many continue to elude me. They range from the obvious, such as Robert Wiene's *The Cabinet of Dr. Caligari* (1920), to the obscure, like Curzio Malaparte's *Il Cristo proibito* (1951), to the debatable, as in Gustav Machatý's *Ecstasy* (1933), up to the sublime Satyajit Ray's *The Apu Trilogy* (*Pather Panchali* [1955], *Aparjito* [1956], and *Apur Sansar* [1959]). The text is wonderfully idiosyncratic but, for me at the time, more or less irrelevant. The stills were everything, and Tyler's copious captions seem to acknowledge and reinforce that hierarchy. That the stills happen to look exactly like photographs also occurs to Tyler who, in a number of the captions, goes out of his way to discourage such a misreading. For example, in referring to Alf Sjöberg's *Miss Julie* (1951) he writes, "Stills can be only modestly indicative of the superb flair for beautiful and picturesque action which carries along a hectic liaison." And, about a still of Michelangelo Antonioni's *La notte* (1961), he says,

"Reunion between novelist and wife (at dawn on the industrialist's estate) does not come as easily as the above glimpse of the final scene makes it appear." Say what the author will, the stills stand independently from their cinematic context and that is what makes them so incalculably seductive and instructive.

The stills reproduced in *Classics of the Foreign Film* offer an encyclopedia of photographic practice and, looking at the book again today, I am naïvely amazed at just how imitative cinematographers appear to be of that practice. It is unlikely that by now there isn't a single photograph of note that hasn't been edited into the ever unreeling history of cinema and, I might add, fed back into the galaxies of images that reside in the overpopulated minds of those travelers—us—through the twentieth century's fin de siècle. There is no shame in recycling per se; photography itself is a mechanistic parasite on the host of the real. Nonetheless, the film still is a glamorous fiction while the photographic setup is a constructed lie. The film still is an element of a completed act whereas the photograph brings with it no such assurance. With the film still, you are free to move the scenario forward with no onus of personal intent; you are simply massaging a fiction. The extension of a photograph's narrative is psychologically more politicized. One's involvement with the extended narrative of a photograph introduces the potential for a kind of voodoo auteurism. A movie is always in the can whereas life is endlessly mutable and idle intervention has been known to kill.

Looking again through Tyler's book, I started to imagine which director's stills would make the best two-dimensional exhibition. It was easy: Carl Dreyer (*The Passion of Joan of Arc*, *Day of Wrath*), Alexander Dovzhenko (*Earth*), Sergei Eisenstein (*Potemkin*, *Que Viva Mexico!*, *Alexander Nevsky*, *Ivan the Terrible*, parts I and II), Michelangelo Antonioni (*L'avventura*, *La notte*). Such an exercise is ridiculous, as these directors are represented by the best stills in a book that excludes any images from pre-1961 films by Jean-Luc Godard (*À bout de souffle*),

François Truffaut (*Les quatre cent coups, Tirez sur le pianiste, Jules et Jim*), Pier Paolo Pasolini (*Accatone*), Agnes Varda (*La pointe courte, Cléo de 5 à 7*), and Luchino Visconti (most notably *La terra trema, Senso, Rocco e i suoi fratelli*), among many others. Regardless of the omissions, my "classic" film stills in Tyler's book were, by 1961, the gateway to radically new ideas about the narrative potential of photography. The proliferation of books on film that emerged in the 1960s gave anyone who was interested the sense that he or she could diagram the emotive magic of film through a designer's layout of stills on the printed page. Ingmar Bergman, Marguerite Duras, John Ford, Alfred Hitchcock, Stanley Kubrick, Akira Kurosawa—all of them offered lessons in lighting, composition, and stylistic verisimilitude. In fact, all became accidental teachers of photography.

The influence of film on the visual arts has, in the last twenty-five years, been enormous. One need only think of a director like Hitchcock (represented in Tyler's book by *The 39 Steps*), who has provided content for such wildly diverse artists as Victor Burgin, Stan Douglas, and Douglas Gordon, to understand the thrust and parry between the relatively hermetic world of art and the box-office driven world of cinema. Obviously, movies rule, but postmodern art, with its incessant need to analyze and critique popular culture, is the ideal corollary to the movies and benefits enormously from its audience's pre-cued knowledge of the same. Artists like John Baldessari literally have constructed photographic collages from extant film stills. Others, like Burgin in his Hitchcock-inspired analyses of *Vertigo* and *Marnie*, shoot their own hybrid stills. The most obvious example of the film still to photograph and back again is in the work of Cindy Sherman, whose mining of B-movie clichés yielded an extraordinarily complex critique of genre films. In a more conceptual practice, Richard Prince rephotographed existing pictorial advertisements without their copy and enlarged the potential discussion as to film's influence on advertising images. Prince's series of men's hands with cigarettes look less like advertising vignettes than like stills from Godard's *À bout de souffle*, and his motorcycle girls illustrate the codependency of Roger Corman's biker movies and the motorcycle magazines that inspired him. Younger artists like Matthew Barney and Sam Taylor-Wood continue the relationship between film and photography. Barney has discussed the influence on his work of horror films and their directors, including David Cronenberg and Sam Raimi. The editions of "stills" that supplement Barney's films and videos are spectacular indications of how to semaphore "cult" iconography. Taylor-Wood's interests are more aligned with mainstream cinema, particularly the films of Martin Scorsese, but she brings to her photographs a kind of saturated mise-en-scène and narrative complexity that references in equal parts Visconti and Robert Altman.

To a certain degree, all of these artists can also be counted as the inheritors of Warhol, who was the self-identified love child of the coupling of art and cinema. His intuition about icons and the defining moment of iconicity was peerless, and his ability to generate (and market) his very own movie stills remains unmatched among visual artists attempting to make the crossover into film. Like Parker Tyler, Warhol was intuitive rather than analytic and, just as important (perhaps more so), he was a fan. He treasured the defining moments and, rather than wanting to debunk or analyze them, he elected to celebrate the established pantheon. When it came to film, Warhol's genius lay in his complicity and the sheer wonder at its ability to create indelible legends. Rather than complain or dissect, Warhol flat-footedly celebrated the marvelousness of it all.

Veronica's Revenge: Contemporary Perspectives on Photography, ed. Elizabeth Janus
with Marion Lambert (Zurich: Scalo, 1998), 203–9.

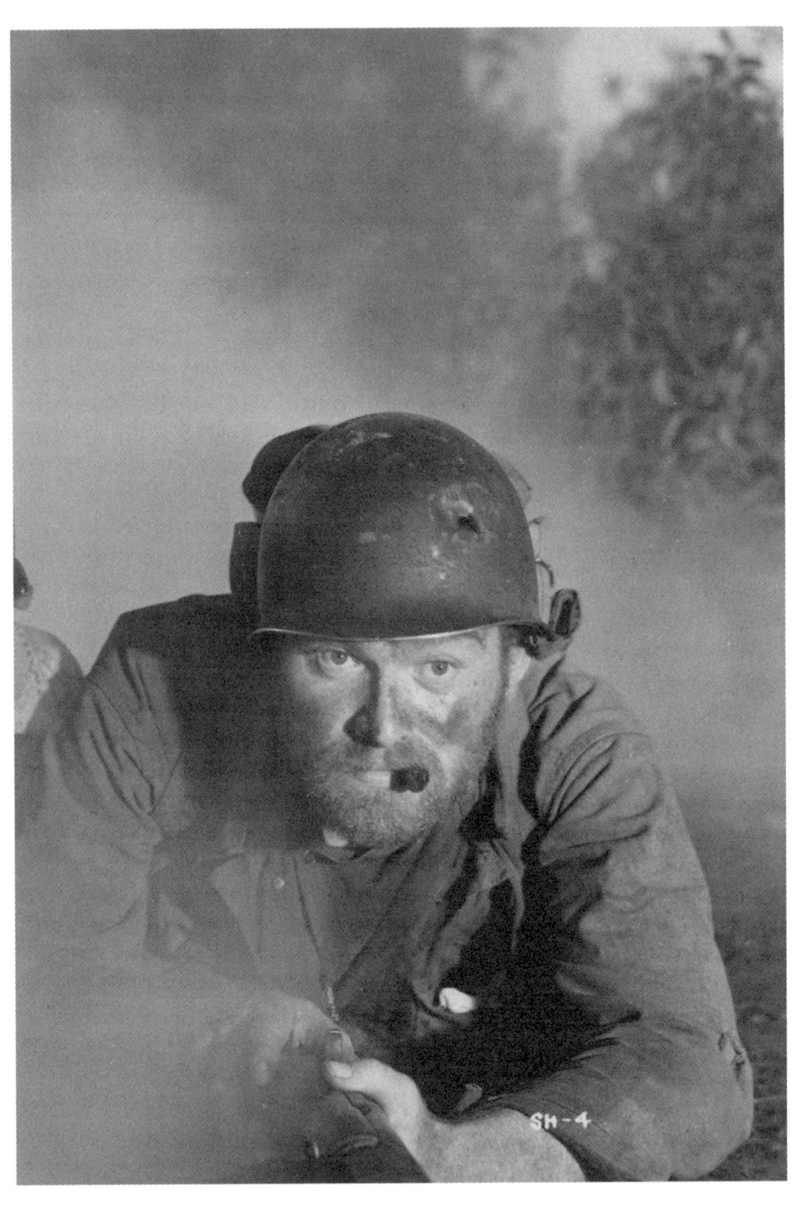

Gene Evans as "Sergeant Zack" in *The Steel Helmet* (1951)

144

Reel Crank:
On Manny Farber's *Negative Space*

Manny Farber is the Raymond Chandler of American film criticism. His adrenaline prose has been pumping since 1942, when he began reviewing for the *New Republic*. Over the succeeding four decades, he kept his writing lean and mean, florid and furious, absolutely unique. He reviewed for *Time*, the *Nation*, the *New Leader*, *Artforum*, and a parcel of other publications. In the late 1970s his successful career as a painter increasingly took center stage, and film gradually lost an important, always surprising apologist.

I first learned of Farber's criticism about twenty years ago, at the height of my enthusiasm for the films of the B-movie producer Val Lewton, who assembled a kind of atelier for writers, directors, cameramen, and actors to churn out low-budget horror movies of extraordinary beauty and, time permitting, intelligence (including *The Seventh Victim*, *I Walked with a Zombie*, and *The Curse of the Cat People*). A friend gave me a copy of the 1971 edition of Farber's *Negative Space*, a collection of his reviews that contains a brief obituary consideration of Lewton, written in 1951 for the *Nation*, and I became an instant convert, as much to the energy of the writing as to the writer's opinions, which were singularly cantankerous. At the time, I was so thrilled to have encountered someone else's thinking about Lewton that I didn't notice just how elegantly parsimonious Farber was in his postmortem critique, which, typically, leads with a vice to identify a virtue. He cut to the core of Lewton's methodology, observing that the producer "hid much more of his story than any other filmmaker, and forced his crew to create drama almost abstractly with symbolic sounds, textures, and the like, which made the audience hyperconscious of sensitive crafts-manship" and that "his lighter-than-air sense of pace created a terrif-ically plastic camera style." Obviously, "hiding the story" in "a lighter-than-air sense of pace" isn't really a great asset, but it is precisely what makes Lewton's films so stunningly different from any other contri-bution to the American horror genre.

The newly reissued edition of *Negative Space* (Da Capo) includes plenty of material that was not presented in the earlier edition of the anthology, notably Farber's collaborative reviews with his wife, Patricia Patterson (written in the 1960s for *Artforum*), which drag him kicking and, occasionally, screaming into the 1970s. While spousal collabora-tions can be among the most truly horrible pursuits a couple can in-dulge each other in, Farber and Patterson actually manage to pull off a not inelegant Pat and Mike impersonation à la George Cukor (not one of Farber's favorite directors). A major source of critical conflict between them is Marguerite Duras, whose *India Song* strikes a deep, vibrant gong for him and is a mosquito batting against a wind chime for his wife. What's lovely about the Farber/Patterson collaborations is their shared enthusiasm for certain directors, particularly Fassbinder (whose use of color and composition they liken to "Mondrian with a sly funk twist"). And it is Fassbinder who allows Farber to visit a European aesthetic on a guilt-free pass after a good twenty years of jingoistic Americanism. Let me give you a Whitmanesque example of the latter from Farber's 1957 essay "Underground Films": "The cream on the top of a *Framed* or *Appointment with Danger* ... is the eye-flicking action that shows the American body—arms, elbows, legs, mouths, the tension profile line—being used expediently, with grace and the suggestion of jolting hard-ness." Still, the real meat of the matter is Farber flying solo with his wild prejudices and enthusiasms boldly tattooed on the wing of his little single-prop plane of cinematic advocacy.

When the American Film Institute announced the winners of its troublesome contest to nominate the one hundred best American films last June, I thought of Manny Farber. I raced through the Institute's awardees and came up with one entry I thought he might approve of. At the very least, I assumed he had to like Charlie Chaplin, but when I consulted *Negative Space*'s index it led me to find Farber, in an interview with Richard Thompson, trying to ditch Chaplin in an attempt to champion Laurel and Hardy. I knew better than to check him on the Institute's numero uno film, *Citizen Kane*. Back in 1952, in an essay entitled "The Gimp," he tackled *A Place in the Sun* (no. 92 on the AFI list) and *A Streetcar Named Desire* (no. 45) and pummeled them until you could hear George Stevens and Elia Kazan screaming "Uncle" across the back lots of Hollywood. However, it was not really Stevens and Kazan that Farber was after. He was tracking much bigger game, the very agent of the chiaroscuro virus they were victims of: Orson Welles. At the core of Farber's critique was the notion that, although it was initially unsuccessful, "*Citizen Kane* seems to have festered in Hollywood's unconscious until after the Wylers and Hustons returned [after the war] from their government film chores; then it broke out in full force." His analysis (in "The Gimp") of Welles's first—and perhaps greatest—film is a wonderfully insightful reading of how Hollywood went about creating the postwar, A-film formula, exemplified by "a horse-drawn truckload of liberal schmaltz called *The Best Years of Our Lives*." Farber is relentless in his downsizing of what he calls "solemn goiters" bearing "the label of ART in every inch of their reelage." He is, at heart, a B-movie apologist. He's sensational on products like Sam Fuller's *Pickup on South Street* and Don Siegel's *Coogan's Bluff*, without ever implying that they are more than the brute propulsive unreelings that they appear to be: "a bit of John Foster Dulles, a good bit of Steve Canyon, sometimes so good as to be breathtaking." Farber also loves character actors, and much of his best writing is devoted to supporting cast members like Gene Evans in Fuller's *The Steel Helmet*, who "plays the hot-headed [*sic*] showing off, the endless chewing on a cigar stump with the blast effect of water issuing from a whale's spout, bestial and grotesque as a charm spot in a film dedicated to the U.S. Infantry." Or Elisha Cook in Howard Hawks's *The Big Sleep*, who as "a supporting player hit his peak and managed to dry out whatever juicy glamour and heroics were in the film so that it took on a slatelike hardness."

Farber is very much a sensitized kind of guy's guy. His writing peaks in the presence of idiosyncratic originals like Hawks and Preston Sturges, whom he assessed in a 1954 essay coauthored by W. S. Poster (entitled "Preston Sturges"), where he seems to be arguing for himself as a critic as much as for the director he is writing about. "The discrepancies in Sturges's films are due largely to the peculiar discontinuities that afflict his sensibility, although such affliction is also a general phenomenon in a country where whole eras and cultures in different stages of development exist side by side, where history along one route seems to skip over decades only to fly backward over another route and begin again in still a different period." In a rebuttal of Siegfried Kracauer's critique of Sturges's confusion of honesty and candor in *The Great McGinty*, Farber/Poster write: "Such criticism is about as relevant as it would be to say that Cubists were primarily interested in showing all sides of a bottle at once." The curiously parental-advisorial end of the Sturges essay can, in many ways, stand in for a self-defense tactic by Farber, for justifying his critical capriciousness. "Sturges may not be the greatest director of the last two decades; in fact, it can be argued that a certain thinness in his work—his lack of fully formed, solid, orthodox moviemaker's technique—prevents him from being included among the first few. He is, however, the most original movie talent produced in recent years: the most complex and puzzling."

It's hard to place Farber in any subdivided pantheon. He clearly adores the work of James Agee with, natch, serious reservations: "Agee was a brick wall against pretense in small movies, but, on Big Scale work, where the Boulevard is made of National Velvet and the Limelight's as stunning as the Sierra Madre, Agee's reviews suggested

148

a busy day at Muscle Beach: flexing words, bulging rumps of talent, pyramidal displays of filming cunning." I still love Pauline Kael, but not for a second would I put her in the ring with Farber; she simply doesn't have the chops for his kind of hamfisted finesse. The biggest problem with his criticism is the fact that he can't always slow down long enough to frame his passionate ardor for the art form he is alternately embracing and repelling. What is exhilarating about the best of his criticism is that it moves with the speed and linear clarity of the films he loves. It is unlikely that movies will ever again get the kind of tough love that Farber dispenses with such exuberant, bruising gusto.

Artforum 37, no. 1 (September 1998): 15–16.

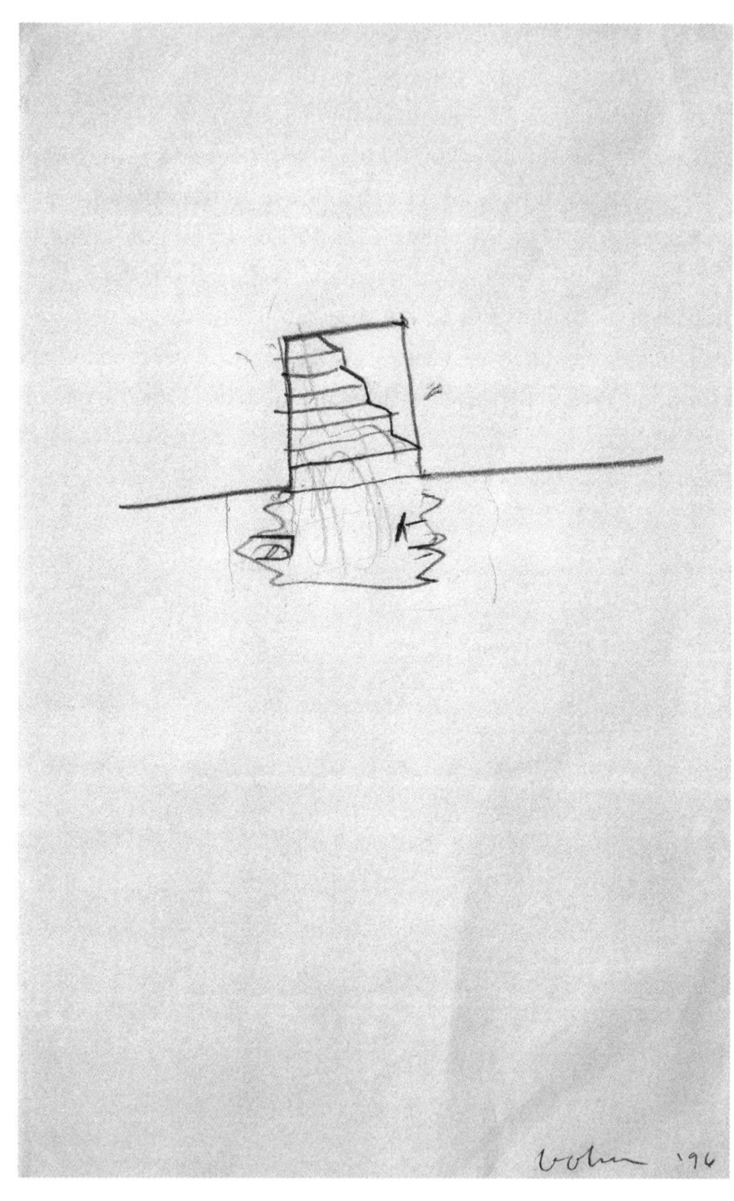

Robert Gober, *Untitled*, 1996
Graphite on paper, 20 × 13 cm (8 × 5 in.)

150

The Law of Indirections: Robert Gober

It is almost impossible to discuss Robert Gober's work without moving through it chronologically. It has been riveting to watch him assemble his cast of characters and deploy them, over time, in an ongoing drama that is at once autobiography and social history. Objects that initially appear opaque are gradually enlisted to serve in a larger drama that is revelatory in its psychological clarity. The topics he is drawn to—birth, infancy, adolescence, sex, death, loss, spirituality—are all scented with the smoke of Freud's cigar, and immersing oneself in a Gober installation can be as analytically trying as an hour on a therapist's couch. Gober is after much more, however, than therapeutic catharsis. Increasingly, he has involved himself in the creation of a mise-en-scène that invites viewers to become participants. It is as if it is no longer enough for him to have an audience see what he is presenting; they have to feel what he is feeling.

More than any other American artist, Gober reminds me of Walt Whitman. Like Whitman, he apprenticed in his field (Whitman began as a printer and editor; Gober was an assistant to the painter Elizabeth Murray). Like Whitman, he was devastated by the death toll of the young men around him (Whitman tended to the wounded during the Civil War; Gober was committed to AIDS activism). Like Whitman, he is enamored of the natural world and the careless, sensual grace of those who inhabit it. Like Whitman, he is a moral crusader with a very strong utopian bent and a definite point of view as to the nature of right and wrong. And, also like Whitman, he has a judgmental sternness and eroticized self-awareness that, in their coexistence, are

particularly American, male attributes. I also associate Gober with
Alfred Hitchcock and his uncanny ability to tap into a very American
kind of paranoia. They are both curiously outsiders, and their particular view of America is distinctively gothic. Like Hitchcock, Gober
understands the seductive morbidity of the commonplace and carries
into his work an awareness that innocence exists only to be tested.
Then too, in addition to a dyspeptic relationship with Catholicism,
Gober and Hitchcock share an understanding that, always and everywhere, there is a terrifying abyss lurking in what we perceive to be the
normal. They know that the land of the normal can be as dangerous
as it gets.

*All must have references to the ensemble of the world, and the compact truth
of the world,*
*There shall be no subject too pronounced—all works shall illustrate the
divine law of indirections.*
WALT WHITMAN, "LAWS FOR CREATIONS"[1]

There is a dogged tenacity in the development of Robert Gober's
sculptural practice. Once imagined, nothing ever completely departs.
Instead it is tweaked and nudged into a version of its original self,
which, while subliminally similar, is inevitably other. Observing its
permutations is almost like watching a child being persistently stalked
by the shadow of the adult he will become. Some things seemingly
consigned to the past—a tantrum, a bad dream, an injury—never really
go away; they lurk, awaiting artistic materialization.

The liquidity of Gober's visual vocabulary is paralleled by the per-
vasiveness of his references to water, both literal and implied. One of his
earliest realized pieces, *Prayers Are Answered* (1980–81), is a scale model
of a graffiti-covered Lower East Side church with a removable roof.
The interior of the church is engulfed by a plaster-modeled deluge

that swirls apocalyptically over the floor. The church was the last in
a series of meticulously detailed architectural models of houses that
Gober began in 1978 and completed in 1980. Today he refers to this
body of work as "oddly naïve,"[2] but in retrospect it establishes, formally
and thematically, a number of issues that he continues to explore.
The very process of moving from a domestic space to a religious space
was dramatically summarized in 1997 with the realization of his installation for the Museum of Contemporary Art in Los Angeles, in which
the two domains were conflated with a vengeance.

In a little house keep I pictures suspended, it is not a fix'd house,
It is round, it is only a few inches from one side to the other;
Yet behold, it has room for all the shows of the world, all memories!
Here the tableaus of life, and here the groupings of death.

The drowning pool of a church was followed by *Slides of a Changing
Painting* (1982–83), which documents the permutations of a single
painting that Gober endlessly added to and subtracted from, photo-
graphing each stage of its creation/destruction. When I first saw *Slides*
projected, I could barely take in the profligacy of images, let alone
what they depicted. Hyperbolically, I was reminded of the narrator in
Edgar Allan Poe's "The Fall of the House of Usher" and his description
of his host's art: "From the paintings over which his elaborate fancy
brooded, and which grew, touch by touch, into vagueness at which
I shuddered the more thrillingly, because I shuddered knowing not
why;—from these paintings (vivid as their images now are before me)
I would in vain endeavor to educe more than a small portion which
should lie within the compass of merely written words. By the utter
simplicity, by the nakedness of his designs, he arrested and overawed
attention."[4]

Seen today, *Slides* appears to be a Rosetta Stone for Gober's work, literally providing a key to the sculpture that would follow it. Image after transformative image predicts much of what would, over the succeeding years, become a substantial body of work. Of no small importance, the imagery in *Slides* is suffused with the relentless flow of water. It bursts from culverts, cascades down a mountain, eddies around a storm drain, cuts through a forest, comes to rest in a wading pond. The paths it describes are myriad, and nothing is safe in its course, least of all the human body, which it splits and swallows like a twig in a deluge. Although Gober would not use water itself as a sculptural medium until 1992 in his installation for the Dia Center for the Arts, the absence of water was a major theme in his work from 1983 onward. It was almost as if, after the cataclysm that overtook the church and threatened to inundate the world in *Slides*, the awesome promise of water had to be contained.

> *I do not doubt interiors have their interiors, and exteriors have their*
> *exteriors, and that the eyesight has another eyesight, and the hearing*
> *another hearing, and the voice another voice,*
> *I do not doubt that the passionately wept deaths of young men are*
> *provided for.*
> WALT WHITMAN, "ASSURANCES"[5]

In 1983 Gober began a serial body of work that would, intermittently, occupy more of his time than any other sculptural subject. The target of his investigation was a simple, old-fashioned domestic sink, and he kept exploring its possible permutations until 1992. Made of plaster over wire lath and finished with semigloss enamel paint, the sinks came with no faucets or drains; they are as mute and leeched of fluids as a body on a mortuary slab. Scores of preparatory drawings led to the production of some forty sinks. Many were simply untitled; others bore deadpan catalogue modifiers such as *Long*, *Double*, *Deep Basin*, and *Corner*. Still others came with anthropomorphic adjectives like *Sad*, *Silly*, and *Scary*, or psychological encumbrances such as *Subconscious*, *Split-Up Conflicted*, or just plain *Mixed-Up*. When the sinks were first shown in 1984, they were a startling revelation, reminiscent of minimalism in their insistent variation on a theme, but this was minimalism encoded with a haunting emotional resonance. While overtly mimetic of their source, they were also hieratic objects being offered up for contemplation—but contemplation of what? Drudgery, domestic order, women's work, purification, deification of the everyday? In the endlessness of possibilities lay the inherent strength of the object.

In 1984 Gober's first urinal appeared, and this motif would continue to put in an occasional appearance through 1988. In a way, the urinal was easier to assimilate, particularly in Gober's dysfunctional rendering, with its implicit reference to Duchamp's iconic readymade, *Fountain* of 1917. It was an ideal interpretive object for Gober insofar as it opened the sluice for a surrealist/dada critique while being crisply up-to-date in its strategy of appropriation, which mirrored that of immediate predecessors such as Louise Lawler, Sherrie Levine, and Richard Prince. Unlike the appropriationists, however, Gober was involved in a labor-intensive process that eschewed the cult of the readymade in favor of the adamantly handmade. So, while he was playing the prevailing intellectual game, he was also distancing himself from it and the criticism surrounding it. There was also the issue of content. Manhattan, in 1984, felt like the AIDS capital of the world, and an unplumbed urinal, often installed in groupings of two and three, conjured up much more than Duchamp. Not for the first time, the issue of surrogacy became manifest in Gober's objects. The politics of a sink are oblique; the politics of a urinal are not. Not for the last time in his sculpture, art history took a backseat to his story.

Gober's final evocation of the absence of water in the 1980s was an edition of pewter sink drains (an image that first appeared in *Slides of a*

Changing Painting), which he insinuated into an enormously ambitious and provocative 1989 installation at the Paula Cooper Gallery in New York. The drains (4½ in. diam., 3 in. deep) were installed in the gallery walls at the height of the artist's breastbone. Here, at last, were drains for the sinks and the urinals, but naturally they were useless. Again, the sculptural authority of the work was one with its denial of function. The drains, like the sinks and urinals, are evocations of the memory of water, and their strange, passive power is very much dependent on the viewer's instant comprehension of what they are and what they represent. They are not what they appear to be, but become part of the artist's dolorous game of bait and switch.

It is tempting to see the sinks, urinals, and drains cumulatively as surrogate portraits of gay men in the 1980s. Certainly they all looked exactly like what they were modeled after, but perversely they did not do what they were supposed to do. They were definitely *queer* in the most homespun sense of the word. When the sinks were begun in 1984, the gay community was already being sorely tested by the growing stigmatization of gay men as carriers of the AIDS virus, as pariahs being visited by a plague tailored to their heedless otherness. The Pentecostal fervor that sought to isolate the gay community, when combined with the community's own uncertainty as to how to cope with the politics of polarization, resulted in a schizophrenic program of psychological empowerment and physical denial. Across America, bathhouses and gay bars began to be closed by local governments, while organizations like ACT UP (AIDS Coalition to Unleash Power) and collectives like Gran Fury emerged to fight back against repression and federal indifference to medical initiatives. It was a time when the sweetly archaic, inherently passive term *gay* gave way to the more ambiguously differentiated term *queer*. The pink triangle of Nazi Germany was revived by activists and armored with the phrase "Silence = Death." In this context, Gober's inventory of muted, dysfunctional receptacles became an elegiac analogue to an era in which hope and anger were as one, and neither had an outlet. A sculpture from 1985, *The Sink Inside of Me*, with its bifurcated backsplash and basin, was designed to fail in its function; it simply could not of its nature contain what utility would demand of it. In a universally expanded catalogue of sinks, it is "queer." Nonetheless, it is what it is: complex, unique, one of many, and beautiful in its otherness.

> *And I say that clean-shaped children can be jetted and conceived only where natural forms prevail in public, and the human face and form are never caricatured.*
>
> WALT WHITMAN, "SAYS"[6]

In 1986 the absence of the body began to be apparent in Gober's sculpture. Playpens, cribs, beds (three for dogs, three for their masters), and a chair came into being. The playpens and cribs were singularly ominous in their evocation of the isolated child trapped in a cage imbued with its own Skinnerian agenda. These pieces mark the first appearance of what would become an ongoing theme in Gober's chilling evocation of childhood; they are also particularly naked in their equation of infancy with imprisonment. The compound word *playpen* is itself rife with contradiction; each half of the word seems hell-bent on nullifying the other. Each of these little cages—whether it is *Pitched*, *Slanted*, *Distorted*, *Tilted*, or contorted into an *X*—is an indictment in three dimensions. Here, that which was intended to protect the child is retrofitted into an arena for penitential modification. Nurturing and punishment coalesce into a regimen of denial. Even the potentially hopeful *Open Playpen* (with one quadrant of bars missing) became, at best, possible evidence of parental carelessness rather than liberation. As emblems of the realm of infancy, the crib and the playpen are absolute, and the normalcy of their function is unquestioned. Yet, in Gober's analytic lexicon, they are as bent on redemptive brutalization as the hellish arsenal of Victorian child-taming inventions meant to cure everything from bed-wetting to bad posture. Clearly, to be young is to be a victim.

Whereas the cribs are as loaded as land mines, the three beds that Gober made between 1986 and 1988 are insistently lacking in overt emotional inflection. Each is a basic, generic design, and each is made for a single occupant. All three have undersheets and blankets. The first has one pillow, the second has two, and the third has none. They have the simplicity of storybook illustrations, perfect for each of the three little pigs (or Mama, Papa, and Baby Bear). Yet their chronological proximity to the cribs and playpens chafes. One begins to inspect their orderly rightness for a psychic wrongness. Are these beds intended for the adolescents who were once confined to the cribs? Do the vertical rungs that make up the backboard and footrest of the third allude to a hospital bed? Does its whiteness? Is that an indentation of a body on the blanket? Was the pillow removed after the body? Is this what the beds looked like in the Darling family nursery after the children had fled with Peter Pan to join the Lost Boys?[7] A sobering melancholy suffuses the empty beds, which remind us of all those things that were never truly ours to possess: our youth, our innocence, our lovers, the dependency of our children, the mortal continuum of our friends. (In 1991 Felix Gonzalez-Torres generated a billboard project that occupied a number of sites in and around Manhattan. The image was a black-and-white photograph of a rumpled, white-sheeted double bed bearing the imprint of two now-absent bodies. Seeing it, one could not help remembering Gober's more sober single beds and realizing that an empty bed had, through the 1980s, become much more than an empty bed, that the continuing toll of the AIDS virus was changing the way we in the queer community front-loaded our collective image bank.)

The dog beds, of which there are also three, are probably best known for the fact that Gober taught himself basketry to construct them. They are also fascinating for the hand-painted pillows they contain. Two have the kind of repeat patterns (painted on flannel) that one associates with the lining of sleeping bags. One shows vignettes of geese; the other, stags. In the American wilderness both arc most often seen at the other end of a gun barrel, and their relationship to a dog is that of prey to predator. Yet here the predator is invited to curl into a blameless doggy sleep while perhaps subliminally absorbing the images of that which it has been taught to stalk and retrieve. The dog beds are oddly disquieting in their bland recognition of our domestic accommodation of the feral and our complicity in channeling that which is most base into that which we invest with so much surrogate affection. It is the last dog bed, however, dated 1988, which stands as one of Gober's most troubling works and which would, in 1990, occasion a contained, yet serious, controversy.[8] In this dog bed the repeat pattern alternates between two images: one of a sleeping white man and one of a lynched black man. Both were appropriated, the former from a Bloomingdale's print advertisement, the latter from a 1920s cartoon found in the New York Public Library. The combination of the dead and the dreaming appears to be a horrific three-dimensional paraphrase of the old adage "Lie down with dogs and wake up with fleas." The resultant sculpture is not a dog bed; it is an incident. This is Goya territory, where the sleep of reason begets monsters. The allocation of guilt is not the point. The fact that the dreamer possesses the image of the dead is enough; the guilt is implicit.

Contemporaneous with the children's furniture was the first of Gober's chair sculptures, *Slip Covered Armchair* (1986–87). The painted linen slipcover is cloying in its dense patterning of pastel pansies and daffodils, lilac sprigs and robins, dragonflies and redbirds, water lilies and ferns. The pastoral riot is almost too abundant, particularly juxtaposed with the spartan meanness of the beds. One looks in vain for the rot in this domestic arcadia, but none is there. That it is mother's chair is unquestioned. Only a wild child fresh from the forest would not be alert to the aggressive female encoding of the slipcover's pattern and trim of schoolgirl pleats. The chair is a child's safe harbor for a lullaby or a fairy tale—except for the fact that it is as hard as a rock and as abrasive as sandpaper. Its niceness is all feint and parry. Its nurturing promise is denied both parent and child. Yet, in the "please do not touch" environment of an art gallery, it is an unambiguously tender object.

Gober returned to *Slides of a Changing Painting* for inspiration in 1988. Invited to participate in a show with Christopher Wool at 303 Gallery in New York, he attempted to realize a sculpture from the painted image of a woman's sleeveless dress hanging from the limbs of a tree. When he found it impossible to resolve the sculpture, he decided to make a photograph. Wool applied one of his stencils of intertwining tendrils to the dress, which was then hung from a tree in the woods and photographed. Other photographs (not exhibited at the time) show three similarly installed dresses receding into the depth of the forest. Either singly or in triplicate, the dress is an extremely unsettling image. The tree is almost identical to that in the hanged-man cartoon portrayed in the dog bed, but there is no overt evidence of violence, only the suggestion. The creepy, fetishized display of the dress or dresses suggests an intent to either warn or document. Either way, the image is unsavory in its evocation of an unseen perpetrator and an undiscovered act. Of all Gober's body stand-ins, the dress on the bleakly naked tree is the most overtly Grand Guignol but, naturally, in the most understated possible way.

Around this time Gober began another serial body of work that was
in many ways another demonstration of his expertise in the kinds of
radical permutation that informed the sinks. This time his subject was
a door. It wasn't just any door, but an elegant, somewhat antiquated
formal door defined by a central grid that articulated three pairs of
inset panels (two square over four vertical). That the center of the organizing grid resembled a stacked cross was most congenially obvious in
the artist's least-manipulated door, part of an untitled installation for
the 1988 exhibition *Utopia Post Utopia* at the Institute of Contemporary
Art in Boston. There he built a room, leaving the studs exposed on
its exterior. One entered through a refined, fully painted door frame,
across from which, propped against the facing wall, was its missing
door. The room was painted a misty blue and held three works of art
selected by Gober. In the center of the floor, between the door frame
and the door, lay Meg Webster's *Moss Bed*, a mattress-sized berm of
earth covered in velvety moss. On one of the opposing walls was a
small gilt-framed landscape by Albert Bierstadt; on the other was an
aluminum-framed handwritten joke about a fireman and a drunk by
Richard Prince.

Wryly, elegantly, simply, Gober summed up the exhibition's title
while letting his own divided sculpture act as its hyphen. He also captured something more delicate: a sense of impalpable, late twentieth-
century loss. When Bierstadt raced west in the 1860s to capture a
utopian American landscape, the East was already industrialized, and
the trains he took across the Great Plains passed through a landscape
that was home to a growing number of hardscrabble farmers who were

unknowingly on their way to the Dust Bowl, thanks to the government's fiction of dry-land cultivation. Bierstadt's *Lake Tahoe, California* (1867) wasn't an idyllic destination; it was a target waiting to be absorbed into the nation's metropolitan expansion. Webster's dreamy *Moss Bed* (1986–88) was a further reminder of the promise of something perfect far beyond the gallery walls, but it was nature on a respirator and had the strange effect of turning the installation into an oddly serene trauma unit. Prince's *Untitled (Joke)* (1985–87) was the sobering foil to Bierstadt and Webster. Distinctly unfunny, it read: "*Fireman pulling drunk out of a burning bed*: You darned fool, that'll teach you to smoke in bed. *Drunk*: I wasn't smoking in bed, it was on fire when I laid down." It isn't too difficult a stretch to see Prince's "bed" as Gober's earlier hanging man/sleeping man dog bed or Webster's endangered *Moss Bed* and to understand what has always been America's dilemma: when the first immigrant lay down to take a nap, the bed was already smoldering, and by the time the first slave ship docked, it was aflame. In the *Utopia Post Utopia* installation Gober doesn't merely open the door to all of this, he literally removes it.

As fascinating as the *Utopia Post Utopia* installation proved to be, it did nothing to prepare anyone for the installation Gober would execute at the Paula Cooper Gallery in 1989, which was as tightly constructed and nakedly efficient as a noose. While he had been involved in curatorial-collaborative installations earlier in his career,[10] none of them was as rife with complexity as the one at Paula Cooper's, which felt like a perfectly, horribly apt end to the leveraged mess that was the 1980s. There were only six elements in the exhibition: two differently patterned wallpapers, a series of identical pewter drains, several cat-litter bags, a wedding dress, and a bag of donuts. In combination, they were as psychologically orchestrated as the dream casino Salvador Dalí whipped up for Hitchcock's Freudian-driven *Spellbound* (1945).

The installation space was basically carved into two interconnecting areas, both defined by unfinished, framed walls. The first space was wallpapered with the hanging man/sleeping man motif, and in its center stood a wedding dress whose materials (silk, satin, muslin, linen, tulle, welded steel) are ominously descriptive. Leaning against the three walls were hand-painted bags of "Fine Fare Cat Litter." The second space was wallpapered with "graffitied" male and female genitalia printed in white on black.[11] In its center, on a pedestal, stood a bag of donuts. Pewter drains were embedded chest-high in the wall, spaced equidistantly around the room. For all the unoccupied space, a horrible claustrophobia hung in the air. No single object dominated this unwholesome ensemble. The wedding dress was a vacuum—either an iron maiden in waiting or a muted destroyer that had already consumed the absent bride. It was as much a failed container as the sinks and urinals. (Gober would later have himself photographed in a facsimile of the dress in a conflation of Saks Fifth Avenue merchandising and Duchampian genderbending, but for the time being, the dress was simply another kind of drain.)

In conversation, Gober has speculated about the relationship between the bride and the sleeping man in the wallpaper, suggesting that they could be viewed as husband and wife.[12] It is a provocative arena for interpretation, and I can't help but think back to Kate Chopin's much-anthologized short story "Désirée's Baby" (1893) or Jean Rhys's last novel, *Wide Sargasso Sea* (1966), two works in which the ambiguity of Creole bloodlines leads to death and degradation for the heroines. In both fictions the women are presumed by their husbands to carry the blood of slaves, and as a result, one is driven to suicide and the other is virtually buried alive. In "Désirée's Baby," the heroine, shunned by her husband, takes their mulatto baby and wanders away from his plantation, where "she disappeared among the reeds and willows that grew thick along the banks of the deep, sluggish bayou; and she did not come back again."[13]

While this overlay of fiction is surely to the left of Gober's intent, it is accurate insofar as it indicates the loaded relationship between

Wedding Gown and the surrounding wallpaper. It also alludes to that which has been drained from the conduit of the wedding dress and the judgmental predetermination of blood in our culture. As for the cat litter, Gober has called it "a metaphor for a couple's intimacy—that when you make a commitment to an intimate relationship, that involves taking care of that other person's body in sickness and in health."[14] Cat litter also absorbs and camouflages waste; it is the perfect medium for those who want to avoid confronting their own mess. It's no wonder that the dress is empty because, in Gober's configuration, it has a weight that cannot be borne; it is the "sluggish bayou" that drags down Chopin's Désirée.

The second room—with its black wallpaper covered in crude, chalk-white renderings of penises and vaginas—offered no antidote to what preceded it. If anything, the air grew more miasmic. It was like being trapped and stalked in the awful suite of rooms described by Poe in "The Masque of the Red Death," where "there were much of the beautiful, much of the wanton, much of the *bizarre*, something of the terrible, and not a little of that which might have excited disgust."[15] Sunk into the wallpaper, the drains looked horribly at the ready to evacuate the myriad fluids that churn through our bodies. Punctuated by the drains, the wallpaper filled the room with the absence of sperm and blood and urine and tears and feces and sweat. It was like an abattoir for the yearning of the flesh.

Located at the center of it all was the insidious bag of donuts, which felt not at all nourishing, a sort of "let them eat cake" aside. The fact that it was simply a bag of donuts (deep-fried by the artist)—or, as Gober has referred to it, "a sculpture of a bag of donuts"[16]—didn't alter the feeling it brought to the room. The white paper bag began to morph into the wedding dress, and the donuts began to resemble the drains. This totally innocuous object (a snack for the coffee break) felt tainted. Where had the donuts been? What had been done to them? I remember somebody at the exhibition's opening grabbing one out of the bag and, in the ensuing scramble to get it out of his hand, wondered if they were trying to protect the art or him. The bag of donuts was an essentially humorous object, an odd salute to American pop consumables. Still, spotlit on its pedestal, it was unlikable and as benignly menacing as the glass of milk that Cary Grant offers to Joan Fontaine in Hitchcock's *Suspicion* (1941).

The totality of the installation was emotionally numbing. You could almost hear a subliminal soundtrack monotonously intoning, "You're born, you do some shit, and you die." Prior to this installation Gober had certainly been a provocative artist with an often disturbing vision, but never had his anger and social intent been manifested so clearly. This was a portrait of an America that was wandering down the same lost highway taken by Janet Leigh in Hitchcock's *Psycho* (1960), a road trip that ended with her blood pouring down a bathtub drain. These rooms were Gober's very own Bates Motel, and that bag of donuts was all of us waiting to be consumed. The American Gothic undertow that had been in Gober's work since the early architectural models now surged to the surface. Serialist and surrealist sources were still there (and would remain), but the artist's kinship with American film images and literary themes was now also clearly apparent.

Ribs, belly, backbone, joints of the backbone,
Hips, hip-sockets, hip-strength, inward and outward round, man-balls, man-root,
Strong set of thighs, well carrying the trunk above,
Leg-fibres, knee, knee-pan, upper-leg, under-leg,
Ankles, instep, foot-ball, toes, toe-joints, the heel;
All attitudes, all the shapeliness, all the belongings of my or your body.
WALT WHITMAN, "I SING THE BODY ELECTRIC"[17]

The first legs appeared in Gober's work in 1990. They protruded horizontally from walls, visible from the foot to the knee or mid-thigh.

They were clothed in a cuffed pant leg, a sock, a shoe. A small expanse of hairy flesh showed between the sock and the cuff. In *The Body in Pieces: The Fragment as a Metaphor of Modernity*, Linda Nochlin takes a look at some late nineteenth-century legs. Her legs are specifically French, female, and male imaged. Nochlin posits that her cut-off legs have three possible readings: fetish, metonym, and "signboards advertising commodities." While she takes pains to point out that "the male fragmented leg obviously signifies very differently from the female one,"[18] my guess is that it is the nature of the artist that determines the meaning, and as Gober has stated, he saw the expanse of flesh between the sock and the cuff as an erogenous zone.[19]

It is important to note here that, in the mid-1960s, another American artist (one with whom Gober shares some biographical similarities) also explored the fragmented male body in a series of reliquaries containing wax legs and forearms. Unlike Gober, Paul Thek overtly and poetically heroized the limbs, often girding them in archaic or talismanic sheaths of leather and butterfly wings. Thek's reliquaries are widely acknowledged to be meditations on the sacrifice of America's young in Vietnam, but they also handily fulfill Nochlin's reading of the "cut-off." The fetishistic component is instantly apparent in the romantic costuming, which conjures up an eroticized gladiatorial arena where Spartans stand shoulder to shoulder with archangels. Metonymically, the limbs are not simply male indicators; they are male warriors who are poetically doomed to fulfill one's fantasy, be it Roland or Kilroy. As "signboards," they offer a commodity that is complicated. They indicate legions of valorous warriors and the solitary unknown; they also summon up a kind of erotic morbidity that reached its apogee early in this century through the poetry of British writers such as Rupert Brooke, A. E. Housman, and Wilfred Owen, which eulogized the casualties of World War I (i.e., "Dead and divine and brother of all, and here again he lies").[20]

Whitman, no stranger to the erotics of the fragmented body, wrote:

Gober's legs do not occupy the high dramatic ground claimed by Thek. They are commonplace, not heroic. Their very lack of glamorous costuming gives them an indeterminate status, which actually makes them scarier than Thek's blighted Olympians. The heroic is not really Gober's metier, but the nuance of the everyday is, and the everyday, as Whitman preached, is charged with the erotic. The vignetted body has powerful erotic connotations that are often greater than the sum of its various parts. Gober's nondescript limbs could belong to anyone, and in that fact, fantasy is nurtured. The vulnerability of the leg protruding from the wall lends it a sexual charge similar to that of the anonymous penis poking through a glory hole in a bathroom stall.

The leg could just as easily semaphore victim, however, or mark the scene of a crime. Hitchcock memorably fetishized disembodied male legs in four very different ways. In *Spellbound* (1945), the viewer follows a pair as they speed down a balustrade and into the back of a child, who is summarily pitched to his death on a spiked rail. In *Strangers on a Train* (1951), two cabs pull up to a train station, and two pairs of legs get out. One is shod in decorative, two-tone oxfords; the other, in plain, sensible shoes. The camera moves with the shoes as they become temporarily aligned inside the station. Minutes later, it is established that the oxfords belong to the effete villain and the sensible shoes to the tennis-playing hero; masculinity and motive are handily signaled by footwear. In *Rear Window* (1954), Jimmy Stewart's plaster-cast leg precedes him everywhere, alternately an emblem of impotence and arousal. In *The Trouble with Harry* (1956), the title character starts dead and stays dead, but his body's presence is inevitably indicated by its legs protruding from a place where it has been temporarily stashed. For Hitchcock, as for Gober, the leg acts as a stand-in for the corpus and allows a certain willed distancing from psychological intent and viewer identification. It helps in telling the story, but you create the fiction.

In a 1991 exhibition at the Galerie nationale du Jeu de Paume in Paris, Gober installed three new works that were surprisingly lyrical and unexpectedly emotive. Two consisted of trunkless bodies sprouting from the wall. Each body faced the floor and extended from the small of the back to the feet. One wore shoes, socks, and long black pants that had been cut away to reveal three candles growing up from the skin. One wore tennis shoes, white socks, and cotton briefs; it was perforated by five flesh-colored drains. The third was naked, legless, and mounted facing the wall; a musical score was transcribed across its buttocks and thighs (evolved from a vignette of a musically tattooed body in Hieronymus Bosch's *The Garden of Earthly Delights*, 1500).[22]

Gober has commented that the three works "seemed to present a trinity of possibilities—from pleasure to disaster to resuscitation."[23] Obviously, "pleasure" is the property of the musical score, which can't help but be seen as the homoerotic counterpart of Man Ray's *Le Violon d'Ingres* (1924), which turns the naked back of Kiki of Montparnasse into the swelling volumes of a violin. Gober has never played the musical fragment inscribed on the body, but that is irrelevant; whatever the tune, it is clearly the music of desire. Even the decision to mount the piece on a bucolic forested wallpaper lends it a kind of Attic sweetness, as if Ganymede had extracted himself from a frieze in an antiquities museum and was heading back into the pansexual grove. The body with the drains, by contrast, is soberingly headed nowhere. It represents the epidemically informed end to the carnal. Even the clothing that covers the body—white socks, sneakers, and underpants—is a shortlist of fetishized locker-room souvenirs. This is everybody's son/lover/fantasy reduced to a humiliatingly vulnerable icon of submission and loss. The final body, with its sprouting candles, is as much an altar as a sculpture. In its merger of flesh and symbolized spirit, it suggests the kind of passive hope one expresses in lighting a votive candle. Mediating, as it does, between the joys and the sorrows of the flesh, the sculpture affords a measure of solemn promise. If it were to bear an inscription, these lines from Whitman might serve it well:

And if the body does not do fully as much as the soul?
And if the body were not the soul, what is the soul?[24]

A fourth sculpture, also premiered at the Jeu de Paume, provides one of the few belly laughs in the artist's career. Simply and accurately titled *Cigar* (1991), it occupied the center of the gallery's floor like an enormous turd. The image was taken from René Magritte's 1959 painting *The State of Grace*, in which a bicycle sits atop a smoking, floating cigar. Gober's *Cigar* clocks in at a whopping, Brobdingnagian six feet and is composed of tobacco leaves rolled over a wooden armature with a hand-painted cigar band circling its center. Much has been written about the work, alluding to its various connotations (masculinity, practical jokes, Groucho Marx, Sigmund Freud, celebratory token for the arrival of a baby, oral prosthetic for fat-cat artists and entrepreneurs),[25] but it also seems to have an inevitable relationship to *Wedding Gown*. Both are made essentially to the measure of the artist (six feet), and while the *Gown* is a vacuum, the *Cigar* is the properly engorged stopper to plug it. The likelihood of ever seeing the two works in a shared space is extremely remote, but, for a curatorial moment, imagine the possibility; it's a surrealistically brutish image equivalent to a satyr raping a dryad (or Popeye going at Temple Drake with a corncob in Faulkner's *Sanctuary*). The pieces exist on the same creative arc and within the same archetypal construct, and they are very gothic.

A 1991 edition of *Parkett* was devoted in part to a series of essays on Gober's work.[26] It is the magazine's custom to ask featured artists to do a limited edition to benefit the publication. For his contribution, Gober created a facsimile of a page from the "Metropolitan" section of the *New York Times*. It was dated October 4, 1960, and, in the midst of wedding announcements and lottery results, carried a one-paragraph story with the headline "Boy Drowns in Pool." The article reports the death of a six-year-old boy named Robert Gober in Wallingford, Connecticut, going on to note that the boy's mother has been detained for questioning. Gober was indeed six in 1960 and lived in Wallingford with his mother. Obviously he was not the child in the pool, but what are we to make of this fabricated report? Certainly there is something of every lonely child's "you'll be sorry when I'm dead" lament contained within its starkly terse narrative. But does it go back to the water-engulfed church of *Prayers Are Answered* or the empty beds for those who have been disappeared? Was it a pre-AIDS Robert Gober, released from the specter of death?

The obituary was, and remains, one of Gober's most curious self-references. At the time, he was getting ready for the exhibition that essentially cemented his place among a handful of living American artists (along with Mike Kelley, Bruce Nauman, and Charles Ray) who were continuing a narrative sculptural tradition in ways that both advanced and consolidated the genre. The occasion of the exhibition was an invitation to do an installation at the Dia Center for the Arts in New York. The installation had been postponed once (to make time for the Jeu de Paume), and by the time it occurred, in mid-September 1992, Gober was ready to literally pull out the stops. He has stated: "I wanted the feeling of the show to be positive and mature. And I think I felt that making the sink functional wasn't only an internal imperative of expressing who I am, but maybe it was also a response to so much of the interpretation that had to do with the nonfunctioning sink and the epidemic and myself as a gay man. I think I felt a need to turn that around and to not have a gay artist represented as a nonfunctioning utilitarian object, but one functioning beautifully, almost in excess."[27]

What resulted at Dia was an exhibition by an artist working at the peak of his form. The merger of forest mural, plumbed and running sinks, stacks of bound newspapers, prison windows, fire exit, and boxes of rat bait all melded into an installation that was as emotionally liberating as it was dense. As he had done in previous projects, Gober left the exterior walls unfinished so that the forested interior space was like exiting a cave and emerging into a sylvan glade. The light felt dappled, and the sound of rushing water permeated the room. Only secondarily did one notice the gushing sinks and see the progression of prison windows high on the forest walls. The windows were barred, and beyond them were radiant, cloudless blue skies. On the floor, under the sinks, were boxes of "Enforcer Rat Bait" and, stacked throughout, orderly bales of New York's daily newspapers, their cover pages subversively collaged by Gober to reflect the interstices of art, gender, and politics. The conflation of interior and exterior was perfect in its resolute fatalism, as were the reminders of yesterday's news and today's predators. Soon the lavish artifice of the forest became more insistent and began to merge with the brilliantly maudlin, illusory cinematic ambience of the prison windows. It was like being trapped on the set of an existential remake of Sam Fuller's *Shock Corridor* (1963), in which the psychotic episodes of asylum inmates turn their very prosaic institution into a fragmented environment where the real and the hallucinated are constantly in uneasy flux.

The chilliest element in the installation was a cul-de-sac that left you facing a locked metal door over which a red lightbulb was mounted; a band of incandescent white light, coming from behind, defined the lower margin of the door. Stacked around it were more newspaper bales. The door was, of course, locked, and if there was a way out, this certainly wasn't it. This exit was not an exit, but an emblem of the escape from which there is no escape. We've left the cinema of Sam Fuller and entered the theater of Jean-Paul Sartre.

GARCIN: *Open the door! Open, blast you! I'll endure anything, your red-hot tongs and molten lead, your racks and prongs and garrotes—all your fiendish gadgets, everything that burns and flays and tears—I'll put up with any torture you impose. Anything, anything would be better than this agony of mind, this creeping pain that gnaws and fumbles and caresses one and never hurts quite enough.* [He grips the doorknob and rattles it.] *Now will you open?* [The door flies open with a jerk, and he just avoids falling.] *Ah!* [A long silence.]

INEZ: *Well, Garcin? You're free to go.*

GARCIN: [meditatively] *Now I wonder why that door opened.*

INEZ: *What are you waiting for? Hurry up and go.*

GARCIN: *I shall not go.*

INEZ: *And you, Estelle?* [ESTELLE does not move. INEZ bursts out laughing.] *So what? Which shall it be? Which of the three of us will leave? The barrier's down, why are we waiting?... But what a situation! It's a scream! We're—inseparables!*[28]

No Exit was first staged in 1944, and it caused a sensation in the nascent new theater of postwar Europe. It was the perfect, icily chic vehicle to popularize haute existential angst. Coming almost half a century later, Gober's manifestation of anxiety is far more complicated than Sartre's. If anything, the surrealist impulse in Gober's work aligns it more closely with the work of the last great surrealist, Luis Buñuel, whose film *The Exterminating Angel* (1961) both politicized and problematized Sartre's closed, existential formula. The guests whom Buñuel assembles for his cinematic house party simply won't leave, which is a subtly different dilemma than that of the characters in Sartre's play, who cannot leave.

The passivity of the former remains more stunningly modern than the entrapment of the latter. I think Buñuel's Catholicism creates another essential difference, which Sartre's rigorous atheism wouldn't permit, and that is the tantalizing possibility of redemption (or condemnation). Buñuel's houseguests do eventually leave but, following a Mass celebrating their liberation, find themselves unable to exit the church.

Gober's mise-en-scène certainly genuflects, through the presence of its closed door, to Sartre's existential determinism, but the main room is invigorated by Buñuel's more complicated misanthropic humanism. In addition to those twentieth-century currents of existentialism and surrealism, Gober's room also evokes the kind of sobering lyricism associated with Britain's nineteenth-century Romantic poets. I remember going home, after seeing the Dia installation, and sitting down to read William Wordsworth's "Ode: Intimations of Immortality from Recollections of Early Childhood." Indeed, Gober had created a visual analogue for the ode's fifth stanza:

> *Heaven lies about us in our infancy!*
> *Shades of the prison house begin to close*
> *Upon the growing Boy,*
> *But he beholds the light, and whence it flows,*
> *He sees it in his joy;*
> *The youth, who daily farther from the east*
> *Must travel, still is Nature's Priest,*
> *And by the vision splendid*
> *Is on his way attended;*
> *At length the Man perceives it die away,*
> *And fade into the light of common day.*[29]

The notion of the pastoral that Gober created was clearly no more modeled on a nineteenth-century ideal than was the environment he created for *Utopia Post Utopia*. It was a Warholian paint-by-numbers mural that repeats itself endlessly and whose paths lead nowhere other than back to the foreground. Its illusionary status was reinforced by the prison windows, which were instantly familiar from dozens of Hollywood movies in which the hero gazes through the bars at a too-blue Technicolor sky waiting for release. Only, in Gober's universe, as in Wordsworth's, the prisoner is already on the other side; he's simply forgotten what it looks like. Even the sinks confounded expectations. Their collective gush was more primal than domestic, and then, too, they wouldn't stop. There was a belligerence to their functioning that was almost nightmarish. Positioned below them, the containers of rat bait were clearly a warning that there was something feral in this anti-natural idyll. In the latent dampness of the plumbed forest, things were gathering underfoot, and those things were foul and pestilential. The piled newspapers, with their Gober-collaged contents mixing art news and obituaries and transgendered bridal advertisements, looked an awful lot like potential nests for whatever the rat poison was attempting to hold at bay. Curiously, it was as if there were two rooms hovering in parallel universes. One room, while cautionary, was essentially imbued with promise. The other, while engineered with alternatives, was filled with dire portents. Both held their truths.

I am a man who, sauntering along, without fully stopping, turns a casual look upon you, and then averts his face,
Leaving it to you to prove and define it,
Expecting the main things from you.
WALT WHITMAN, "POETS TO COME"[30]

After Dia, Gober was the subject of a survey co-organized by the Serpentine Gallery, London, and the Tate Gallery, Liverpool, in 1993. No new work appeared until a show in 1994 at Paula Cooper Gallery. It wasn't exactly an installation, more a tersely edited selection of recent sculpture and one strange drawing. There were six pieces, and with one exception, each pointed the way to installations the artist would undertake in 1995 and 1997. Wedged in a corner, a truncated torso of a woman gave birth to a male leg accessorized with a shoe and sock. It was titled *Man Coming Out of the Woman* (1993–94), so one knew that it wasn't "Man Going into the Woman," which was the horrible other possibility. (A later piece would depict a similar birth, only confined within a fireplace: a child's leg emerging from a man's anus.) The piece's direct, almost sophomoric rudeness begged a quick, tactical response. In the simplest of interpretive scenarios it would appear that a certain amount of predetermination takes place in the womb or that the process of gendering a child begins literally at birth. But there are two bodies involved, and the brutal violation of the female by that which she is delivering shouldn't be overlooked, because Gober would stage another, more ceremonial violation only three years later in Los Angeles.

Also on the floor of the gallery were two enormous sticks of butter lying naked on their open wrappers. Like the artist's earlier cigar, they were mostly strange because of their physical inflation. And, like the enormous helmet that crashes murderously out of the sky onto a young nobleman in the first chapter of Hugh Walpole's eighteenth-century howler *The Castle of Otranto* (1764), they are also gothic in their illogical scale. Walpole's clarification of his fictional impulses might well serve to contextualize Gober's butter sticks in that they released "the great resources of fancy dammed-up by common life."[31] The same explanation might be further voiced by the character played by Marlon Brando when he introduces the century's most notorious stick of butter to Maria Schneider in Bernardo Bertolucci's *Last Tango in Paris* (1972). Appropriately, what Brando's character was looking for was less about sex than it was about the liberty achieved through anonymity. As a functional depressive, Brando's character, like Walpole's Prince of Otranto, "could know no happiness, but in the society of one with whom he could forever indulge the melancholy that had taken possession of his soul."[32] In *Last Tango* the melancholy was lubricated by the butter.

Another overscaled object included in the show—an enormous box of Farina (*Untitled*, 1993–94, 80 × 52½ × 24 in.) with a deadpan re-creation of a smiling, spoon-fed moppet—offered a somewhat sunnier presence, with its benign promise of nurture. Given the right parental presentation, a box of Farina might well assume such formidable proportions to the obediently receptive child. With its Norman Rockwellesque little boy and comfortably recognizable logo, the Farina box was like a homely, antidotal beacon for those who had previously been exposed to the artist's bags of kitty litter or containers of rat poison.

Perhaps the oddest entity in the show was an enormous work on paper. The fact that there was much more paper than drawing was somewhat perplexing. The overall dimensions of the work, 80 by 138¾ inches, belie the tiny drawing of a cellar door contained on the vast whiteness of its field. As a subject in Gober's work, the cellar door had appeared in an early painting and in one of his architectural models. In and of itself, a cellar door is a thoroughly prosaic thing, a little functional wedge stuck onto millions of houses, great and small. But a cellar door is also mysterious, offering a descent into the submerged. It is the threshold to that unassigned area beneath the domestic. It is where things are not so easily fixed and more easily hidden. In popular entertainments, a descent into the cellar is rarely the equivalent of a walk in the park unless the park borders a cemetery and there is a full moon and something is howling in the darkness. Gober's tiny, somewhat tentative drawing sitting on all that unclaimed ground conjures up the enormity of what lies in wait once the cellar door has been opened; beneath all that white whispers an ocean of dark.

The most surprising piece in the exhibition was a storm drain installed flush with the floor. Peering down into the murk of the drain, one could just make out the naked torso of a man with a sink drain embedded in his chest. A steady stream of water washed over the blanched whiteness of the body. It was an incredibly sobering vision, particularly because it was so abjectly unobtrusive, with only a distant sound of water directing one to it.

The pierced chest and storm drain had both been previsioned in *Slides of a Changing Painting*, but not in this set of codependencies. (The sequence in *Slides* from which the chest was excerpted had previously resulted in an untitled sculpture from 1991 that depicted a hermaphroditic chest that had been cast from the volume used to create the cat-litter sacks from 1989.) The water that had nuanced the Dia installation never, for an instant, implied this kind of potential obliteration. Its properties in the forest were essentially those of cleansing and purification. Now the water turned ominous, and it was chafing against the illusion of flesh, not porcelain.

Caught in the drain, the body became another sluice as well as a kind of sacrificial offering. The storm drain itself is associated with loss; one thinks of the countless movies in which someone drops something essential into a drain (most viscerally imagined in Hitchcock's *Strangers on a Train*). The tension in the situation arises from our shared awareness that, once the object disappears, it's way beyond recovery. The pathos in Gober's sculpture is that the lost object is not only unrecoverable but is also lodged in plain view; it refuses to be swept away.

Gober's fresh mining of *Slides of a Changing Painting* continued into his installation for the Museum für Gegenwartskunst, Basel, in 1995. The centerpiece of this installation was *Split Wall with Drains* (1994–95), a kind of Apollonian alternative to the man in the drain. Additionally, *Split Wall* drew on two other previous works: *Slides of a Changing Painting* and the door frame and exterior walls from the *Utopia Post Utopia* installation. It was a paean to harmonious recycling and one of the artist's most eloquently understated works. Standing slightly higher than 10 feet with a width of almost 18 feet, *Split Wall* was evenly pierced by two identical doorways, each with an elegantly modeled door frame. Between the doors, on either side of the wall, were two storm drains mounted in the floor; a violent current of water tore through the drains over a congestion of autumnal leaves and crumpled beer cans. In the drain from which the water initiates, an envelope is lodged and resists the current. Passing through the doorway, one notices that the wall has been cleft lengthwise so that the illusion of one gives way to the reality of two. The doubling of doors, walls, and drains turns what initially appears to be an elegantly simple structure into what is literally a house divided. That the multiple fractures are so surgically clean only adds to the disquieting psychology of the work's inherent bipolarity. The only element that is not mirrored on either side is the envelope, which functions somewhat like a failed neurological impulse that, once sent, is incapable of locating its receiver. The tension imparted by the envelope, in its prosaic recognizability, makes this installation more lambently melancholy than the more feverish man in the drain. The envelope also provides an implied narrative for the doubling and splitting that belie the piece's initial formal coherence.

The other three sculptures in the exhibition were variously penetrated by a culvert pipe, a motif that dominated *Slides of a Changing Painting* but had never previously assumed three-dimensional form. Unlike drains, which are fixed in place to deal with an existing system, culverts are more improvisational and tend to be utilized to accommodate seasonal spillways or to divert the kind of occasional flooding caused by beaver dams and wandering streams. Gober's use of the culvert takes into account its inherent interventionist properties. In an untitled work (1994–95), a very large, flower-patterned tissue box is longitudinally speared by a bronze culvert. An oval aperture on the top of the box frames the pristine tissues inside. In *Lard Box* (1994–95), a gargantuan replica of a box of "Armour Lard" is penetrated lengthwise and crosswise. The third work, *Chair with Pipe* (1994–95), is a conventionally scaled, upholstered easy chair whose back has been pierced by a culvert, which is uneasily supported by its cushioned seat.

Each of the pieces is singularly strange, and the culvert's relationship with each is strangely singular. The box of tissues disassembles with the least interrogation, insofar as it is utilized for the shedding of tears or, tissues untouched, the repression of the same. In Gober's version the culvert gives permission for the manly sublimation of emotion (and, of course, the resultant psychological constipation). *Lard Box*, penetrated by its cruciform culvert, is less forthcoming. The odd marriage of Jewish taboo (rendered pig fat) and Christian icon (cross) provides a decidedly weird confrontation between Old and New Testament scriptural hierarchies. It is just as likely, however, that the Pop pull that Gober had previously experienced (from, for example, Farina) had resurfaced in the colorful (red, green, white) "Armour" box, with its promise of a "hydrogenated" product. It is worth noting that hydrogen, when oxidized, forms water, which implicitly turns the lard box into a suspension chamber for liquidity.

Chair with Pipe is at once the simplest and most resonant of the three sculptures. It is very pure Gober in that the original model for the chair was salvaged from the streets of New York and the collision between the chair and the culvert has a narrative possibility that is denied by the enlargement of the tissue and lard boxes. The narrative is grotesquely available in the media at least once a week (i.e., "Load from tractor trailer narrowly avoids gutting toddler in Connecticut suburb"). Then, too, the upholstery for the chair was inspired by an apocalyptic sequence in *Slides of a Changing Painting*. The fabric's digitized pattern is a basket weave of waterfalls and human limbs, based on a collaged combination of blue ribbon and photographs of Gober's legs. There is also a kind of deus ex machina finality to the work, as evidenced by the lugubrious ease with which the culvert occupies the overfreighted easy chair. In Basel, Gober's variations on a theme were fast-forwarded and freeze-framed with singular clarity. One of the particular pleasures dominating the exhibition was the permission it gave to see Gober working out so many long-dormant issues in his never-latent image bank.

The female contains all qualities and tempers them,
She is in her place and moves with perfect balance,
She is all things duly veile'd, she is both passive and active,
She is to conceive daughters as well as sons, and sons as well as daughters.

As I see my soul reflected in Nature,
As I see through a mist, One with inexpressible completeness, sanity, beauty,
See the bent head and arms folded over the breast, the Female I see.
WALT WHITMAN, "I SING THE BODY ELECTRIC"[33]

After Basel, Gober began to work intensively to fulfill an invitation that he had received in 1993 from the Museum of Contemporary Art in Los Angeles to create an installation for its warehouse space, the Geffen Contemporary. The resultant work was an epic environment in which the devotional and the psychological achieved a ratio of harmony that was both anxiety-inducing and unaccountably serene. Echoing Buñuel's career-long attempts to reconcile who he was with what had formed him, Catholicism, Gober engaged in a psychic battle to reclaim that which he had been denied by virtue of his sexuality.[34] Buñuel began his filmic assault in 1928 with the image of two priests tethered to a grand piano in *Un chien andalou*, made in collaboration with Dalí, and achieved his masterpiece of pictorial reinterpretation in 1961 with *Viridiana*, a film whose depiction of the Last Supper as a beggar's banquet brought down the wrath of both the government of Spain and the Church of Rome.

What Gober created was essentially less pugnacious than Buñuel's work; he simply constructed a chapel in a secular environment. It wasn't architecture, but it was architectural in scale, at 56 by 56 by 23 feet. It wasn't designed for nondenominational meditation, like Houston's Rothko Chapel, but it was an inescapably meditative environment. Dominating the installation was a six-foot-high concrete Madonna standing on the grate of a storm drain. Driven through her midsection was a six-foot-long bronze culvert. Beneath the drain was a tide pool teeming with life and littered with oversized American coins, all inscribed with the year of Gober's birth. Behind the Madonna was a doorway framing a flight of wooden stairs, down which poured a torrent of water (180 gallons a minute) that emptied into another storm drain at its base. This drain was, with the exception of the frothing water, dark as a tomb. To the right and left of the Madonna were two open, silk-lined suitcases whose bottoms were, again, storm drains over identical tide pools of crystalline intensity. Wading in the tide pools were mimetic vignettes of a man holding a baby over the shimmering water. Only the legs of the man and the infant were visible, but the pose suggested nothing other than stability.

The figure of the Madonna was pitted and eroded like a weathered lawn ornament. Her pose, arms extended with palms up, is the most generic of all populist depictions of Mary, the one most often seen sheltered under upended bathtubs in the front yards of the defiantly pious. In that pose she is most often referred to as Our Lady of Peace, and her closest rival is Our Lady of the Rosary (painted yellow and turned into an unlimited edition by Katharina Fritsch). Made out of plaster (for the home) or plastic (for the dashboard), these images are ubiquitous totems for the disciples of Mariology. They exist to advertise one of the intrinsic articles of faith in Catholic dogma, the virgin birth of Jesus.

Gober's decision to core the Madonna with a culvert was, to say the least, confrontational. For a Catholic-schooled boy, however, it was also understandable, because to be raised a Catholic is to be raised with a heightened awareness of and carelessness toward wounds. Classrooms are presided over by crucifixes, and one gets used to greeting the school day with an image of an almost-naked man frozen in aestheticized agony on a cross; blood streaks his face below a crown of thorns, and an open wound punctuates his side. One gets to know him well because the parish church holds the Stations of the Cross, a devotional aid depicting Jesus's progress from the court of Herod Antipas to Golgotha, ending with Mary holding the body of her executed son. Jesus and Mary are always the central players, but around them are a galaxy of secondary and tertiary characters, all of whom bear instructional wounds and often warrant side chapels of their own. They are missing breasts and eyes; they are crucified upside down and roasted on gridirons. Just when you think there are no more indignities left to be suffered, a new twist on martyrdom is introduced, and you're left slack-jawed at the infinite variety of it all.

In this context, two other standard classroom accessories are worth a mention: the framed depictions of the Sacred Heart of Jesus and the Immaculate Heart of Mary. Often hung side by side, they depict Jesus and his mother with their chests decorously opened to reveal their hearts, which are frequently surrounded by flames and topped by a cross. Gober's decision to turn Mary herself into a cross through the intervention of the culvert is no stranger than any of this. The oneness of the mother with the suffering of the son is brutally cohesive, and the analogy of the womb to a spillway for that which can no longer be contained or borne is dramatically encapsulated. Mary's positioning atop the sewer grate is itself a kind of poetic abbreviation insofar as gift-shop versions of Our Lady of Peace and Our Lady of the Rosary often portray Mary balanced atop a globe, one foot crushing the head of a serpent. In Gober's version, the serpent has been replaced by the sewer, and beneath the grate, in place of the globe, lies a glistening pool, strewn with the coins of those who wish for something more, something other. Framed by the conduit, the torrent of water descending the stairway becomes an analogous stand-in for her Immaculate Heart. It is as if all the domestic disorder semaphored by the water on the staircase were being contained by the culvert and redirected into the regenerative tide pool. Of course, it isn't, but such are the mysteries of faith in the modern age.

Because the installation is so adamantly biblical in the fulcrum of its imagery, it would be neglectful to overlook the religious symbolism of the abundant liquidity in Gober's environment. Water is, first and foremost, a baptismal fluid. It is also the prime element of Jesus's first public miracle, the Marriage at Cana, when he turned water into wine, and that which he walked upon when he chose to convince those he wished to follow him of his divinity. In the Old Testament it is the agent of the ultimate apocalyptic chastening of the earth and what buoyed Moses into the bosom of Pharaoh's family and later turned to blood as Pharaoh's warning.

Water had, from *Slides of a Changing Painting* forward, played a major role (absent and present) in Gober's work, and at the Geffen its potential to destroy and renew was finally brought into a balanced equation. The water that had originally wreaked havoc on the church in *Prayers Are Answered* in 1980 was, by 1997, contained and functioned as the focus of a series of liturgical markers in the installation. Behind the high altar designated by the Madonna, the stairway occupied that space often given over to a representation of the Last Judgment, and the torrential force of its disposition proved fully equivalent in impact to some very good frescoed versions of the same. The paired suitcases functioned as baptismal fonts. What, after all, is a suitcase other than the baggage you carry? In this case, Gober's baggage was Catholicism. Glimpsed through the grating, the infant's sponsoring elder was about to administer the sacrament of baptism, which is generally symbolic of regeneration and, specifically, in Catholic ritual, the cleansing of original sin. The tide pool did not contain simply water but, rather, baptismal water. The roiling maelstrom caught in the drain at the foot of the stairway had, in its passage under the Madonna, undergone a rite of purification as well. Its violence had been stilled and transformed into a dream of serene placidity. Here was where life began; here was where life was affirmed. In Los Angeles, Gober was the architect of a chapel that could accommodate him and the author of a religion that could sustain him.

I need no assurances, I am a man who is pre-occupied of his own soul.
WALT WHITMAN, "ASSURANCES"[35]

The most recent piece of sculpture I've seen by Gober is a generic child's chair positioned over a slop drain. A brightly colored, floral-patterned box of tissues occupies the seat. It is a portrait of the American child as an absent analysand, circa the millennium, and it is an indictment of a culture that has stopped listening to its children. Not present in the chair are the latest statistics for national analysis: Barry Loukaitis, aged fourteen when he killed three classmates in Moses Lake, Washington; Evan Ramsey, aged sixteen when he killed two in Bethel, Alaska; Luke Woodham, aged sixteen when he killed three in Pearl, Mississippi; Michael Carneal, aged fourteen when he killed three in West Paducah, Kentucky; Andrew Golden and Mitchell Johnson, aged eleven and thirteen, respectively, when they killed five in Jonesboro, Arkansas; and Kipland Kinkel, aged fifteen when he killed four in Springfield, Oregon. Lost boys all; all lost in America.

Gober's sculpture accompanies me throughout my America. It is the sink left behind in an abandoned Vermont homestead by the family living in a trailer down by the highway, or the urinal vacated by a biker in the fluorescence of a Wyoming roadhouse. It is the playpen in a day-care center in California, or the khaki-clad legs in the next stall at a prep school in Pennsylvania. It is the bed in a VA hospital in Minnesota, or the culvert diverting a clear stream of water before it reaches the cattle-fouled trough in Texas. It is a forest-glade mural in a taco joint in the Nevada desert, or the salvaged mansion door in a county museum in Georgia. It is the breakfast cereal we eat, the products we use to sanitize the pets we keep, and the domestic poisons we employ to kill the predators we fear in the dark. It is the religion we practice and the primitive magic we use to guarantee that religion's efficacy. It is a paragraph buried deep in newspapers across the country until one day it erupts onto the front page. And then Barry or Evan or Luke or Michael or Andrew or Mitchell or Kipland tells us how much it hurts to grow up in America. Gober is listening to their voices and telling their stories—our stories. That, after all, is what his art is about: America and its law of indirections.

Robert Gober: Sculpture + Drawing, ed. Richard Flood (Minneapolis: Walker Art Center, 1999), 9–31.

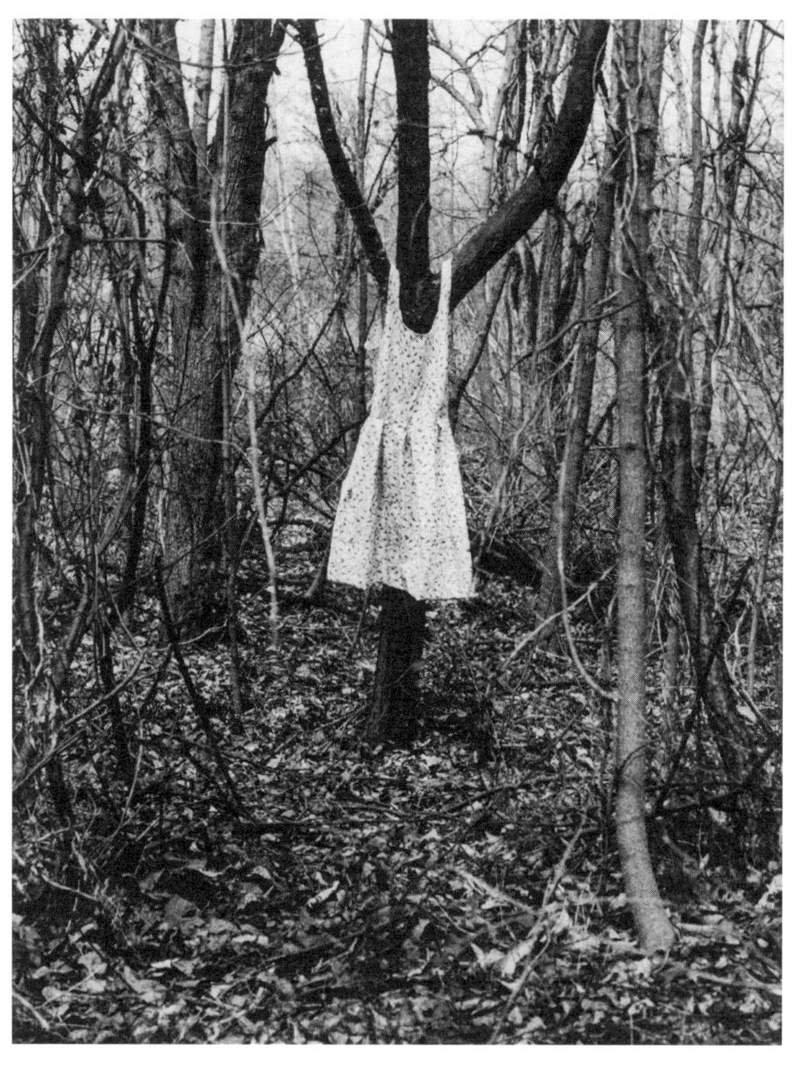

Christopher Wool and Robert Gober, *Untitled*, 1988
Black-and-white photograph (edition of 10), 35.2 × 27.6 cm (13⅞ × 10⅞ in.)

186

Interview: Richard Flood and Robert Gober

In 1990 Jacqueline Brody, then publisher of *Print Collectors Newsletter*, asked me if I would interview Bob Gober for an edition of that publication. I said "yes" and Bob said "yes." For me, it was a wonderful, illuminating conversation. Later, in 1993, Judith Nesbitt, then of the Tate Gallery, Liverpool, invited us to have another conversation to be published in a catalogue commemorating an exhibition of Bob's work that she co-organized with the Serpentine Gallery, London. Again, Bob was extremely generous in sharing information about his creative process and patient with my tangents. When Bob agreed to participate in the exhibition that this catalogue honors, we decided to keep talking. What follows are edited versions of our original exchanges with two new interviews conducted at the dawn and dusk of 1997.

INTERVIEW 1 (January 21, 1990)

RICHARD FLOOD: *I remember your first exhibition of sculpture at the Paula Cooper Gallery, in 1985, very distinctly. The works were all creamy, slightly surrealistic, quite recognizable variations on domestic sinks. I walked in, and I thought, "This is a beautiful show." The work was very restrained, but it was also brand new at that moment. With the next show, in 1987, the psychology of the artist seemed more visible somehow. You left the sinks for cribs and urinals and dog beds, and suddenly the implication was that you were dealing with something more personal. By the time one gets to the third show, this past October, you have a wedding dress, wallpaper, drains, kitty litter sacks, and a bag of*

187

donuts. I began to feel that this wasn't just formal sculpture making a simple, formal sculptural statement; there was something else going on. I reacted very strongly to them; they were very upsetting to me. When you go into creating a piece of sculpture, is it about exploring a formal sculptural concept, and then it becomes something else?

ROBERT GOBER: It's more a nursing of an image that haunts me, letting it sit and breed in my mind, and then, if it's resonant, I'll try to figure out how, formally, this could be an interesting sculpture to look at.

If the first show was very much a formal exhibition of sculptural objects, and the second show moves more toward a feeling of installation, the third exhibition seems to me to be completely loaded in the sense that it is *installation—that each piece becomes quite aggressively dependent on the context it's viewed in.*

Definitely. And now I'm interested in going a step further in that I want to create dioramas about human beings seen from one perspective.[1]

Hmm. So then, in the last show, when you introduced the wallpaper, was it important for you to find out that you could control the wall through the wallpaper?

I think so, in a number of ways. One thing no one ever addressed about the wallpaper was that wallpaper itself was a medium. They would talk about the images I used, but not the nature of the medium— wallpaper. It was useful because of how it allowed me to envelop the room and how that reverberated. It made more of an enclosure, don't you think?

It also did a domestic thing that really skewed the focus. Correct me if I'm wrong, but the Wedding Gown *was central in one room, and the* Bag of Donuts *was central in the other room.*

The structures mimicked each other from room to room, the wall-paper, the multiples around the wall, and one central object.

People who follow your work were familiar with the hanged-man image, as you'd used it several times in other contexts. How did the genitalia graffiti come about?

It was inspired by a Joyce Carol Oates story that I was working on for the Whitney Museum's artist/writer publishing program.[2] But I had so much trouble getting the Whitney to print the images of the genitals that I think that was part of my impetus to blow it up and use it as wallpaper.

Were those drawings originally the endpapers for the book?

Yes, but much reduced in size.

So you were able to work out some of the frustration of the endpaper controversy through the wallpaper?

Yes.

When I first saw your image of the hanged man and the sleeping man, it was as upholstery in your dog bed sculpture. I thought, "My heavens, this is really interesting," because it wasn't what you were supposed to see there, but at the same time it didn't look that wrong there. No warning buzzer was being pushed that said, "Whoops, this is really the wrong image to upholster a dog bed in," because it looked like the inside lining of a sleeping bag or something. It was just drawn in such a generic way that it could have been somebody shooting a duck.

Yes, very much so. That was the formal inspiration.

I don't know why the image seems as inevitable as it does—

I know, I don't understand that either. I've worked with it for years, and it's still mysterious, even though it seems, as you say, inevitable—partly, I think, because the man is sleeping, so there's the possibility that he might be dreaming. I think that lends an unreality to the logic of it; you can't quite pin it down, but that's why it's such a good image, I think, because it yields so many different responses about what's happening. And then something's literally missing in the story—if you look at it as a story—and you kind of have to. You have to supply that: what was the crime, what really happened, what's the relationship between these two men.[3]

Let's talk for a minute about the objects embedded in the wallpaper of the last show. They seemed to be a conscious attempt to reference the earlier sink sculpture. How did they come about?

I took a rubber mold of the drain in my kitchen sink, and then I cast that in plaster, and then I wanted the foundry to cast that, but we got very confused in our communication because the fabricator didn't speak English very well. He wanted me to take the drain out of my kitchen sink so that he could cast from that, and I said I would not take the drain out of my kitchen sink, so I went looking for a comparable drain, but of course they don't make them anymore. So I brought three drains, and we cut them up and soldered them together to make what I found was a quintessential type of drain, and then we cast from that.

I was obsessed by the cross in the bottom of the drain. That was what I went to immediately. I thought, "My God, I never realized a drain was Pentecostal."

Actually, the cross was not cast from an existing drain, now that you bring that up. I couldn't find one with a cross. Old ones have them, like the one in my bathroom, but I couldn't find one now, so actually that was constructed before the casting.

That's funny, because that was what I kept going willfully back to, how absolutely strange that in the end, as everything is sluicing down the drain, it's also sluicing over this major, major symbol.

Yeah, exactly.

I thought the drains were so provocative, and in the critiques about the show, there was really wonderful writing about the drains. It seemed to me that every time I picked up a review, they got out of the show through the drain, and I thought it was very appropriate.

That is true; you're right. I thought of the drains as metaphors functioning in the same way as traditional paintings, as a window into another world. However, the world that you enter into through the metaphor of the drain would be something darker and unknown, like an ecological unconscious.

Can we talk for a moment about the wedding dress, which, to most people, was the landmark sculpture in the last show? Initially it appeared to be little other than a conventional white gown. But, looking closer, it got weird very fast.

That was a very tough piece to make, not just technically—with all the welding, draping, cutting, and sewing—but emotionally. For days I would wear a bra around my studio when I was alone to help me begin identifying with the form.

Did you go through any particular selection process to arrive at what size wedding dress?

Oh, sure. I looked at wedding dresses; I looked at a lot of brides' magazines—I probably still have pictures around. I looked at patterns, and then I looked at mannequins, and it was, I guess, looking at the mannequins that helped me start to get a handle on it, because I needed to work off a feminine form. The old mannequins were so much more aesthetic to work off of than the new adjustable ones. You buy them used; they're made for specific sizes. So we shopped around for a few days for a mannequin that just felt like the right size. Her shoulders were like 45 inches, and her bust was, I think, 39 inches, and her waist was 30 inches. If she were to become flesh, she would have been a bit Amazonian and out of shape, but it was perfect.

Oh, it's so funny. I thought it looked like Suzy Petite.

She did look petite, but if you took her measurements, she was actually quite a big girl. But a lot of that had to do with the armature being completely concealed within the outer and inner lining. That was a lot thicker than it appeared, not right at the ridge at the top, but as it progressed downward. When you looked inside, it was a much smaller waist than the outside dimension.

See, I had this theory that it was an idealized body.

It was, in a sense.

But I guess to me it was more like: this is what happens to the cheerleader who goes to the right sorority, who marries the right fraternity brother—it was something so about order. It was all about order on the outside, and the maintenance of order, but that the thing itself was a void. You know, it was a very long story; it wasn't a one-take about a wedding dress. But to me, also, there was a very interesting choice—it would have been so easy to put the wedding dress in the room that was wallpapered with the genitalia.

It wanted to be in that room, but it wouldn't have been as interesting in that room.

Did you ever indulge yourself in its proximity to that?

I never actually put it in there, but I thought about it a lot. But ultimately it was more provocative against the background of the hanging man/sleeping man wallpaper, because in a sense she becomes the sleeping man's bride. It takes on deeper overtones, or undertones, of complicity. I thought it was so fascinating—the wedding dress in general, what it symbolizes in terms of that moment in your life. There's no comparable costume for a man that symbolizes this moment; we've only created this outfit for women. A man's tux could be interchangeable for a funeral or a wedding; it's really only with women that we insist on this image of purity. But what was so fascinating to me about this outfit is that the thing that makes it a wedding dress, as opposed to a prom dress or a princess costume, is the train, which literally drags in the dirt. It's a fascinating symbol; it was so loaded, so simple and so loaded.

And the kitty litter bags resting against the walls ended up there because...?

The kitty litter I never saw as being that far a step from the wedding dress. I think people had a lot of problems making the connection between the kitty litter and the dress, whereas for me the kitty litter was to a large degree a metaphor for a couple's intimacy—that when you make a commitment to an intimate relationship, that involves taking care of that other person's body in sickness and in health. If I had chosen to do a box of diapers, which is an equivalent of a bag of cat litter, it would have been obvious. But because I was juxtaposing a low symbol with a high symbol and a deflated symbol with an inflated one, people had a very hard time reconciling the two, and they had a hard time, I think, seeing that I could be connecting the two with some respect.

Do you ever find yourself going back over the objects you've made—

Yes.

—and—I'm trying to think of a literary equivalent—you are writing this narrative about daily life and the ritual practice of daily life that is quite eloquent and quite strange. Is that something that ever occurs to you, that you are in some way documenting your culture?

I would object to the word *documenting*. I wouldn't say documenting—*reflecting*, maybe. But I think you're right. I think your idea of a literary equivalency of what I'm doing is accurate.

It's just that there is this narrative pull to so much of the work. I keep going back to the muteness of the sinks, which now, retrospectively, seem much more psychologically loaded. I'm remembering the particular configurations and what frustrations they offered. When I first saw them, I was not viewing them as things that would frustrate human activity. I was misreading them then, I would say, in light of what future work has shown me.

Yeah, I could see that.

I do also think that the work could never be mistaken as work coming out of another culture.

Or country. No, I don't think so. Without being self-conscious about it, I think I feel a responsibility toward that.

So much of what you do is so labor-intensive...

It actually isn't though; it just looks like it is. I always read that about my work—"painstakingly, laboriously handmade"—which I think is really interesting because I wonder, first of all, how do people know? I think I have a knack for making things that look like they take a long time to make, but it's a trick. It doesn't actually take me that long. I'm not interested in being bored; that's why I don't want to work for someone else or have a job. My dad worked in a factory; I want to entertain myself. I also think there's something peculiarly American in the degradation of manual labor. If I make it myself, it has to be "laborious"; it has to be this painful, boring process that I go through, and it really isn't. That's something I've actually wanted to clear up for a long time.

Don't you think part of it is that a lot of the work ends up looking ideally like it is a hairbreadth away from the real thing? Maybe this compromises people's own sense of creativity; the work comes too close to what is already available, so they have to heighten the theater of what is being done to achieve this. I think it's somewhat of an attempt to heroize the activity.

Oh, really? See, for years I thought it was used to diminish me, because I was not doing the respected masculine act, which was hiring other people to do your labor for you. There's something inherently suspect in the American imagination if you're not hiring other people to do labor for you and if you're not acting in an entrepreneurial sense about your work. That, at least when my work was becoming known, was the avant-garde critical discourse mode of being a sculptor. I heard a lot of words like "quaint, homey, homespun"—I think, basically derogatory words, slightly feminized words.

Women's work.

Yeah, and that's interesting because the generation of women that I've followed—with Cindy Sherman's show up now, Jenny Holzer's[4]— it's amazing. They can be so meaty, yet so popular, so enjoyable, yet so erudite.

What artists do you enjoy looking at, or anticipate work by?

Well, as I said, I followed the most amazing generation of women. Cindy and Jenny have to be two great American artists, and then there's Barbara Kruger, Sherrie Levine, Louise Lawler. It's the women who affected me. The men were all like bad examples, and then the women were almost all good examples.

INTERVIEW 2 (January 15, 1993)

RICHARD FLOOD: *When we left off in January 1990, you had just been asked to do an installation at the Dia Center for the Arts. But that only came to pass in the autumn of 1992. What happened in between?*

ROBERT GOBER: The Jeu de Paume [Paris] exhibition came in the middle. It was supposed to be a three-person show and wasn't going to be that big a deal. But it evolved into a one-person show, and Dia got postponed. I had an image of woods for Dia very early on, so I started researching the image for Paris, thinking I'd make wallpaper. As the Jeu de Paume show grew, I wanted to do a new installation for it, so I began with that forest idea.

What was the source of the Jeu de Paume wallpaper?

It came from the picture library at the New York Public Library. I sent my assistant, Daniel Oates, to look for a New England forest with a horizon line and depth, and he came back with a whole variety of choices. I eventually chose a small portion of a watercolor, then flipped it kaleidoscopically four different ways so that it could repeat vertically and horizontally.

The Jeu de Paume was the first time you showed the butts. I remember a leg in the studio when we did the interview in 1990. You were just starting to tweeze hairs into the calf. One of the leg pieces has enormous importance for me.

Which one?

The one with the drains, because somehow when I saw that piece, it was everything I was feeling. It hit a chord. In a way it was one of those pieces that managed to sum up a moment in a city that's feeling the same thing. I suppose the legs with the candles allowed me to go away from the drains and feel more hopeful, but it was the one with the drains that I believed.

The three for the Jeu de Paume formed a kind of trio of emotions for me. There was the butt with music, the butt with drains, and the butt with the candles, and they seemed to present a trinity of possibilities from pleasure to disaster to resuscitation.

Do you have a hierarchy among them for yourself?

I loved the butt with the music when I made it, and I still really do.

Have you ever played the score from the butt?

No, never. That never had any interest for me. I still have the original score, which I found on the street.[5]

Do you recall the source of the legs in general?

Kind of. I hate to travel, but whenever I do, I usually get images. I'd gone to Bern and to the Natural History Museum there and was surprised that there were no humans depicted in the dioramas, and suddenly this seemed a wide-open area to me—to do natural history dioramas about contemporary human beings. Then I was in this tiny little plane sitting next to this handsome businessman, and his trousers were pulled above his socks, and I was transfixed in this moment by his leg. I came home knowing that I wanted to make a sculpture of that part of the leg. I didn't know how far up I'd go on the leg or ... what it would be made out of when I started.

And then you got up to the butt...

And then I got up to the butt, finally, and I thought the whole body would follow, and it still might.

The oddest object at the Jeu de Paume was the enormous cigar lying on the floor.

Well, for years I had wanted to make a sculpture of a corrugated rain culvert.[6] I could never understand why it would be interesting as a symbol, but I knew that I was fascinated with it as a formal object. You know what it looks like? It's a cylinder that's wrapped on a diagonal, and that's kind of what the cigar ended up being. That happens a lot when I have an object in mind, that it's really only some quality of that object that gets brought forward.

But why a cigar? I associate cigars in our particular community with a certain group of artists.

Definitely, and Freud's cigar and a turd and all those symbols.

It's a cut cigar.

196

Yes. It has an internal wood structure. The ends are faked with four inches of rolled tobacco. The band is paper, gold and red paper with maybe a little painting on it. It was an amalgam of cigars that we bought and used as models.

Your first big show was at the Boijmans Van Beuningen [Rotterdam] in 1990. I remember you came back saying how wonderful it was not to have put a lot of things in a space.

Yes, it was. I forget the size of it, but the one gallery was around 100 by 100 unpillared feet. It made me not very scared of big spaces. Dia was very manageable to me space-wise.

Certainly the Jeu de Paume was very sparsely installed. Didn't the half-man, half-woman torso also somehow come from the Boijmans show?

The Boijmans catalogue published images from *Slides of a Changing Painting* (1982–83). One image was the chest of a half-man, half-woman, and I'd forgotten all about it. I hadn't looked carefully at these slides in a really long time. I decided I really wanted to make that image into a sculpture. Again, like the legs, you have the image, but then where does it start or end and how do you make a sculpture out of an image?

That piece is such a curious bag of groceries.

It developed from the cat litter bag. It was cast from a 100-pound bag of plaster. Then I didn't know what to do with it once I'd cast it, until I saw the original image again and thought about putting the two together.

Let's talk about Slides of a Changing Painting. *What was the process?*

Technically? I had this little board on a table, about 11 by 14 inches, on which I painted on and off for a year. I had my camera and lights mounted over it. I would paint, take a slide, add more paint, take a slide, scrape the paint off, take a slide. I took thousands of slides over the course of a year and then edited them down and showed them with a dissolve—basically a memoir of a painting.

Was the end result always intended to be a kind of documentation?

Yes. I knew in the beginning what the end form would be, that they'd be slides. I always thought of myself as a painter, but I could never make paintings. I was never interested in the physical abjectness of a painting, but the process and imagery really interested me, and it was the heyday of neo-expressionism, and I had a kind of allergic reaction to it. So, in a way, my intuitive response to that gluttonous situation was to make a surfeit of paintings that didn't really exist.

How did the newspaper stacks come about for the Dia installation?

There was a benefit for Printed Matter[7] where I was asked to read, something, anything, and I read newspaper clippings that I had collected over the years. I had a big file with no particular agenda, and I began to organize them to create a flow from the serious to the mundane to the stupid to the galling and to make a sort of entertaining and meaningful flow of stories. That reading might have actually been the synthesizing moment. It's funny the things we never expect and maybe don't even want to do that make something happen. And then I don't think I did anything again with them until Dia. I knew the form early on, but it was a real struggle to understand the content. I had the image of this room with piles of bound newspapers, but I didn't know what the content should be, and I worked on that right until the opening of the show.

In the end how many stacks were there?

There were 320 stacks with sixty unique cover pages.

What was the genesis of the forest mural on the walls behind the sinks?

I knew that I wanted a 360-degree forest. I went looking for existing photographs, couldn't find what I wanted. Spring was coming up, and I knew a forest in Long Island where I could shoot, so we hired two different landscape photographers, who took a number of 360-degree shots in four-by-five format with panoramic cameras. I spliced those together in a scale model of the space and made a collage. We[8] then interviewed and hired a group of scenic painters, and they spent two months in the space painting, transferring the photographs from my model to a scale painting on the wall. It was a very tricky thing to paint something as romantic as a forest. I wanted a very flat-footed approach. As the process we chose was essentially paint-by-numbers, it immediately limited the colors to a range of maybe seven or eight, which was very useful in its deadpan quality. Anytime it started to get impressionistic, it was horrible. When it was impressionistic or layered paint, it also brought up the whole history of painting, which I wasn't so keen to engage.

Did the prison windows come later in the conception?

I knew right at the beginning that I wanted to do a forest with prison windows, with sinks with running water. Then it was a matter of accepting that idea and finding the confidence to do it.

The windows were the one completely unexpected element for me. In a funny sort of way, they were the element that pushed the installation most toward theater. Were they intended to do that?

Not so specifically like that, Richard, because that is more your history of my work and your take on it. I don't think that was really my intention with the prison windows. It was to create the double bind of the prison cell and uninterrupted nature, to wrap those two together.

In people's response to the installation, there was a lot of emphasis on the nature of the running water, that the sinks had finally been plumbed. People were talking about liberation and pure water and the ecological implications.

When I first made sculptures based on sinks, it never occurred to me to plumb them. I don't know how to describe the change, why I did it. It was a visual correlation to what I was feeling. It was about possibilities. I don't quite know how to talk about the water running without it seeming really simplistic. I knew I wanted to turn the image around and make the functionless functional and to turn around what had been a symbol of the inability to cleanse yourself. I was interested in the beauty of the multiple sounds of the water running, hoping that it would be transporting. I wanted the feeling of the show to be positive and mature. And I think I felt that making the sink functional wasn't only an internal imperative of expressing who I am, but maybe it was also a response to so much of the interpretation that had to do with the nonfunctioning sink and the epidemic and myself as a gay man. I think I felt a need to turn that around and not to have a gay artist represented as a nonfunctioning utilitarian object, but one functioning beautifully, almost in excess.

When we talked in 1990, you were what might be termed "an artist of promise." Now you are internationally known. Has that caused any conflict?

I don't feel conflicted, at least about that. I feel like I've been very lucky, because things change fast, people go in and out of fashion, careers have ups and downs, people have fallow periods, bad things happen to good people. Now I feel extremely lucky to have maintained my health and to have had the luck of finding someone I care about.

People are always categorizing your work. For a while you were seen as the inheritor of surrealism, then dada. Do you feel that you have to address that kind of critical gamesmanship?

Maybe without thinking about it. I do have a big, stubborn streak of perversity, and perhaps without analyzing it, I do go in the opposite direction. But it was always my artistic nature and talent to work with diverse images whose meanings interweave, and that's what I keep doing. It just took a while for me to understand what the images were that interested me and how I could use them.

RICHARD FLOOD: *One of the things that I really want to talk about is Basel because it knocked me out when I saw it.[9] Somehow I got a really strong feeling about narrative lines in the work. Each piece told a very discrete, impacted story. The conduit puncturing the chair was somehow about the random photographs you see in a newspaper where a car runs off the street and slams into the baby's room and stops inches from the baby's head. It wasn't a moment of total obliteration, but it made me nervous, and it was a domestic kind of anxiety. It was also in the* Split Wall with Drains *installation with the letter trapped in the drain. There was something so poignant about it, like, "Oh God, that could have been me. It's that one letter I didn't get that could have changed everything." Could you talk a little bit about your relationship with narrative in the work in that show? I could be throwing out a red herring.*

ROBERT GOBER: I don't think it's a red herring. I think it's too broad. Can we narrow it down to a piece?

Let's start with the Split Wall. *Looking at it formally, I found the way it related to early work really wonderful because there was just the nuance of things that had happened before. And there was this solid move forward formally. Yet when I got to the other side and I was looking down in the drain and I saw the letter, everything changed. It was unlike the earlier storm drain piece where the impact was, "Ouch, there's a torso down there." This one was much more wistful, much more poignant. Tell me how the letter got there because, when we originally talked about it, there was no letter. You were talking about the leaves, you were casting the leaves.*

The leaves and the beer can I knew from the beginning. The letter was the last addition. It was clipped out of tin and painted, which means that I didn't plan it far enough ahead to go to the foundry, where you need six months. That was the last addition. I think about that piece much more formally: the water passing under and you passing above. What isn't symmetrical are the items within the drain; they're varied from side to side. I don't know how to take the narrative issue any further.

Am I alone in commenting on this?

Yeah, so far. But most of the reviews were in German.

And with the beer can, did you at all think of Jasper Johns?[10]

I cast the beer can in plastic here in the studio, and I think it probably had a lot to do with wanting to not make an homage to Johns. In its very nature it was different. It was not a bronze beer can; it was a plastic beer can. And I'm pretty sure I did that to avoid the easiness of that reference, because beer has to do with a lot more than Jasper Johns.

And what would some of the other things beer has to do with be?

Drinking and marketing and the beauty of refuse.

What kind of beer can was it?

It was Budweiser, I guess a 12-ounce. I never drank Budweiser beer, but it's such a classic American thing. Whether you drink it or you see the can discarded, the logo classically says "beer in America."

And was it important that the piece have that moment of reading "made in America"? Because the show really was conceived for Basel from the get-go.

I guess that it was because when I used to drink beer I would drink Heineken, but I wouldn't put a European beer into the drain. It wouldn't make sense to me. Whereas an American beer can makes sense.

The volume of the water running through the drain also seemed really intense compared with any of the previous drains. Was it mimetic of the Rhine? That museum is so specific.[11]

Yeah, I wanted a nice rushing stream.

At the time of our last interview you were still working with the drawings of the conduit but had not found any way to apply it. Which of those pieces in which it is used came first, the lard or the chair or the tissue box?

I don't remember.

Again, I may be in red herring land, but the tissue box seemed to be about therapy on some level. If you're in an impacted therapy, they don't let you lie down; you sit, and you've got the box of tissues next to you.

Did I tell you this?

No, but when I was in intervention therapy, the shrink wouldn't let me lie down; I had to sit in the wing chair with the tissues at the ready. So I thought it was like the whole idea of the spillway, the box of tissues...

Absolutely. When I conceived it, it seemed meretriciously absurd to me—a pipe going through a Kleenex box—but there was something gripping enough that I went ahead and made it. It wasn't until later that I was sitting in therapy and I realized that I sit in a chair, the therapist sits in a chair, and this kind of silly third companion is also sitting on a chair, the Kleenex box. It began to make me realize that what the pipe was about was an underground conduit of things that flow—maybe sorrowful things, but not necessarily. Things that flow beneath the everyday.

When I saw the chair and the lard, the chair somehow became an emblem of domestic violence, which is something I have never experienced. And then the presence of the lard really seemed to me to be very sexual.

Yeah. The chair ... I think I maintain a kind of willful naïveté around some of the images, like the pipe going through the chair. What I want to say is that it's not actually violent. I didn't take a chair and thrust a pipe through it or "violate" a chair. The pipe is built to organically be a part of the chair; the two things are built together.

They accommodate each other.

Yes, but then I know that there is this other side, that it is penetrated. It looks a bit like a cannon. The pipe is a stand-in for myself in a broad sense. It's tubular and six feet long like a body and is a twisted vessel that things pass through—similar to your body, and even to the sink sculptures in a sense that water comes in and water goes out.

And the upholstery, how did that come about? The latticework with the ribbon and the legs.

It was an image from *Slides of a Changing Painting*. But I don't remember the moment when I said I should turn it into a fabric. I do remember, though, the physical re-creation of it. It seemed important to me that it be my arms and legs. So Daphne Fitzpatrick photographed me, then we made color prints in the scale that I wanted, which was life-size, and then we set up a three-dimensional maquette in the studio with the flat photographs and three-dimensional blue ribbon curling through it on a black background. We took an overhead four-by-five transparency of that and scanned it into a computer. Then I worked with a photo shop on that image to make the shadows. The photographs of the arms and legs were flat, so we worked to make them volumetric. It's an Iris print, jet-spray computer-generated printing on cotton fabric.

With the box of lard, where you actually have this cruciform going through the box, I couldn't help but think it was like a marriage of the sacred and the profane.

Yeah, I think, to a degree.

I have never in my entire life used lard. But in a funny sort of way, I felt like I was entering Richard Prince territory.[12] I did have this feeling that it was definitely this Christian sexual thing, but I may be overloading it.

Lard is one of the grossest things—boiling down the by-products of butchered animals. It's a gross product in and of itself. I think that you're right, although to me it's not the sexual reference, but a broader material reference to human grossness.

And then the cruciform, the marriage of the pipes. Is that something you were curious about formally?

Yeah. I tried to take it further, to go upward and downward with it from the center, but that didn't really work out. Then I tried putting it into other objects, and that didn't work out.

And then the large drawing of the cellar door. The cellar and the woodshed seem to me to be the classical areas where punishment is meted out, so I found that tiny rendering of the cellar door in the middle of that vast expanse of paper really scary. I think formally it's a really beautiful thing, and it's so big that it takes on a sculptural presence as much as a linear one. I'm also thinking back to your early painting with a cellar door,[13] and it's a really similar cellar door. I'm trying to remember if the early burned-house sculpture has cellar doors ...[14]

Yeah, they both have the same type of cellar door.

Did you include that drawing in the Basel show because that was a missing element? Was it something you had been thinking about as a sculpture and the drawing became a prelude or—

Twofold. It wasn't completely pure. The institution owned the drawing, so they wanted to include it. But it wasn't inappropriate, and it's one of those images like the pipe that I'd been trying for many years to build a sculpture of but could never do. It was never interesting enough. I wouldn't say that the basement is just about badness. It's also the unconscious, the unknown within you. I think that drawing to me was like a warning or a reminder. If it existed in words, it would say "Don't forget this."

The scale of the cellar door itself becomes very important in terms of the huge volume of white around it. So it's a bit of a Pandora's box.

Yes, it is. But the way it works is by isolating it on white because then you have a contradictory knowledge of it visually. It's not the vast, expansive darkness, but it's the cellar door on the vast expanse of whiteness.

I don't know if this is true or not, but when we were at the dinner with your mom, she said that the first sink that you cast was based on the sink in the basement of your house in Connecticut.

Yeah, it was.

So the basement is also a source of creative material.

The basement is basically where my father lived, and I think, in a non-dark way, you learn as a young boy unconsciously about being a person and a man from your father. The sink was in my parents' basement, but it was also in both of my grandparents' kitchens when I was a kid. I was struck by its form and its beauty as much upstairs as I was downstairs. Also, in the basement we had windows, and I remember washing peaches in the sink and sunlight coming in through the cellar windows, hitting the water and the peaches in the sink. And, even as a young boy, being struck by the magical beauty of water and sunlight

in these beautiful white structures of porcelain sinks. So, yeah, it was
in the basement, but …

Okay, back to Basel for a moment and the Split Wall with Drains
*installation. Why was it important for you to pull the walls apart? What was
that non-crawl space in there about?*

That's a good question. What I had wanted was a wall that looked
like it had been sawed in half lengthwise. I didn't exactly achieve it,
although I think if you look closely, you would get it. I suppose in part,
on a superficial level, it's a thwarting of expectations because you can
cut a hole through a wall, which is what a doorway or a window is, but
I'd never thought about a wall split down its length in that way.

*Formally, the one thing that occurred to me was this odd pairing, with all
that water coursing under the wall and this silent passage of air through the
wall. It's a very calming piece, whereas the previous drain[15] left nothing but
anxiety. It was so resolved that you really could respire quite evenly with it. There
was a balance between what you couldn't see, the air, and what you could see
and hear, which was the water. Now let me go for a minute to the prison window.
The window is beginning to potentially be a character in the work in a way that
I find really interesting.*

When we go to the other studio,[16] you'll see that I'm trying to work
out another window there, but I'm very conflicted about what it should
be and what it means. But the split of the wall, I'm having a hard time
listening because I'm thinking back to that. It's very important that
you walk through the doorway, both of those doorways. I think when
you really notice the split is when you're walking through the doorway
and it's very close to your body and face and intimate to you, the split.
I think part of what I'm saying is don't take for granted the thing you
pass through.

*We didn't get very far with the cruciform thing. I just want to push it a little
bit. Was it a conscious decision at some point that you were indeed making a
cross?*

I wish. It's become more conscious. I have a tendency to work toward symmetry. It has its own value and meaning to me. The revisiting of the symbols that I studied or worshiped as a boy is becoming more self-conscious now. But, if you make a cross and each piece is equal in length, it is cruciform, but it's not necessarily about the crucifix. It's when you alter the lengths and three are short and one is long that you have the story of Jesus.

What hangs on a parochial classroom wall really is a distinctly other thing.

Yeah, and the cruciform is also an *X* tipped on its side, which is also a plus sign. It can be a larger symbol unrelated to a crucifix. The form of the drain is the same, which to me is a classic urban sewer drain cover. It's used to penetrate the floor again, but its use is different. It's set into the bottom of an open suitcase.

Was the more naturalistic drain in Basel an attempt to get away from the heavy emotional load in the earlier work?

People expect there to be a body in the drain. It's a quick cliché, instant gothic. So you want to thwart that as the only understanding of what flows beneath the surface, because it's often ... it was about a kinder memory or reverie, the beautifully colored autumn leaves.

Had the torso in the previous drain originally come to you as an image with the drain embedded in the chest cavity, or had it for a moment been just a torso?

I don't remember, but I do know that I wanted the water to drop to a lower level, and I do know that when I installed the pewter drains in the wall, the height I would use was 53 inches, right at my sternum. I wanted the drain in the wall to have that relationship to your body, so there was also that setup prior to it. I just took the two and put it together.

Was the torso a body cast?

It was sculpted out of clay from a model and then cast in wax. It had to be distorted to fit the scenario.

And the distortion was elongation?

The torso had to extend beyond your available view, so I had to elongate it, I think, widthwise and lengthwise, although it appeared normal from above.

A lot of people actually didn't see the torso the first time out. That was very interesting to me in that it was easier not to see it. But then the fireplace pieces came along, and you had no choice but to see them.[17] They were in a way the most confrontational. And the nature of the permutation of the body parts in there was also the most violent in your whole body of work, and the most shocking. Whether it was the children's legs or the child's foot coming out of the—

Out of the man's rectum.

Was there a combative stance in those sculptures?

Combative toward?

Toward the viewer.

Well, I am saying, "Stare into this firebox."

And?

And this is what you see when you do.

But, no, more than that. The child's leg coming out of the anus is such an odd image.

It is. I wish I could remember better. I do remember that it was one of those ideas that I didn't belabor. I had the idea. I ran to the studio. I said, "Stop what you're doing, grab the clay, and try to make this." It was a continuation of *Man Coming Out of the Woman*, if you squinted. It was a sculpture about being a boy and a man and a son and a father. It was a sculpture of a man giving birth, which is protean, kind of a myth.

And the children's legs in the fire, which I found absolutely terrifying.

It has a kind of storybook horror to it, a Hansel and Gretelish kind of horror. But at the front of it were the three prison bars. Four, actually, with two of them bent into the classic symbol of escape. Fireplaces are not exactly decorative. I think they're a deep ... not really a symbol, but a deep thing to have in your home. And I can understand from having one where, aside from warmth, the need originated from, because fire is so powerful and its ability to destroy you so swift that I could understand why you would want to have a contained fire in your home.

To sit and contemplate the beauty in something that has the ability to destroy you. So the legs enter into the story around that, and then there are other stories of a kind of abuse. I don't mean abuse in the literal sense of you saw someone's legs off and you make a fire and burn them, because that's not doable physically, but of children being used for other people's fuel. Yet you can escape from that.

The cycle of abuse in American culture around the child has become so strong of late. I couldn't help but think about that. Every time I see another headline, I keep thinking, how could you take a child and do anything other than nurture it. It just seems so grotesque.

But so human. I would doubt that it's anything new.

Oh, I agree.

But there is a particular fascination at the moment. The Metro section is the most harrowingly entertaining, but disturbing, section of the *New York Times* because of the stories of what people do to other people, to their families. You know how on the front of the *Times* it says "All the news that's fit to print"? Don[18] always says that the epigraph on the front of the Metro section should be "What's wrong with people?"

Okay, so you have the fireplaces and the drain and this idea in some way of containers that we're totally familiar with, that we're comfortable with. I'm just thinking now that there is a desire that draws you to things that are very, very prosaic within the culture. Things that are utilitarian, things that we're totally, totally familiar with. And then somehow skewing them so that the difference is less jarring because the context is so familiar. The crib then becomes probably the scariest piece because, if you go back, you can't help but think about the crib without knowing that after the crib came the prison windows and the fireplace with the bars. From the beginning was the crib a formal element that was also about being imprisoned and the psyche being imprisoned and one's ability to get to the next step and one's own freedom into the world? I don't want to overdo it, but was the crib in some way a metaphor for an arena? Was it like a gladiatorial ring, in a way?

Yeah, but if it is, then one contestant's outside and one's inside.

Well, that's the way it is, I do believe.

Not exactly a fair fight. Yeah, it was always a cage, but it wasn't a cage I invented. I think it was a cage I saw or felt. It was an interpretation of an object, but it wasn't an object that I invented. People say to me that they think I'm cruel for depicting it, but I'm not sure that's true.

I think everybody's got a memory of having their hands wrapped around those bars and being mad as hell and not able to articulate it while somebody makes faces or holds back or leaves the room or moves an object of affection very slowly to you or away from you. There were always these children in your work. There's a whole family of children who have come through. I mean the little girl's red shoe is one of the most poignant pieces you've done. What's the origin of the piece?

I think I found it right here on Tenth Street, and I've had it hanging around for years.

Like the music for the butt.

Yeah, there are a lot of things that hang around for a long time that I don't quite know what to do with.

A lot of people bring a lot of things back in off the street. And there's something instantly appealing about the activity. But they don't take it to the next step and cast it so that it becomes this incredibly fragile thing. Did the shoe ever have a story for you?

Just that it was lost. Somewhere there's a little girl without a shoe. Well, it probably came out of the garbage. Somebody had probably thrown two away, and they got scattered—rather than some little girl being swept off her feet so that the shoe was left behind. It was a symbol of loss to me and a symbol again of ... I seem to be interested in things that connote a type of transition.

What was the candle about?

I think it was a very neat, wrapped-up symbol of mortality and sexuality. Because you've got a candle that is basically the size of a man's erection, kind of the same color. It's clearly a candle, but around its base is hair, which gives you the erection pretty clearly. Yet the tip of it is still unburned, which gives you the possibility of igniting. You have the clichéd metaphor of life as a candle, etc.

And the wick is…

The wick is actually my venetian blind cord; it was the right scale, so I cut it off and used it.

The other container that got me really interested recently was the bag of donuts. Again, you had this other totally known container, which, unlike the wedding dress (which more and more begins to remind me of the conduit), was full.

That's true.

The bag of donuts got people really annoyed.

It still does. If I go and talk about my work, I almost always get angry questions about *why* is this a sculpture? Which is interesting because to me the reason why it's a sculpture is so familiar and old-fashioned; it's a portrait of something. It's like a bust. It's a sculpture of a bag of donuts.

Or a still life.

Yeah. A sculpture of a bowl of fruit. It's the naturalism, I think, that gets people confused and maybe gets them a little angry. If I'd carved the donuts out of marble, no problem whatsoever. But the fact that I deep-fried the donuts and then went to some scientific length to preserve them so that what you have was made of real materials, I think that continues to be very perplexing to people.

And the bag itself, was that treated?

No, the bag was just archival white paper with a pencil-drawn logo on it.

What compelled you to do the bag of donuts? I really liked the relationship between it and the wedding dress.

Yes, the high and low symbol.

I can see it happening in the studio where you have this one gorgeous voided thing that is hopes, aspirations, dreams—everything flies through at the speed of light. And then you have this other thing that is just about an instant, the lowest form of quick gratification imaginable.

It's true. It's a joke—a bag of donuts.

The donuts ended up in a Cyclatron or something, didn't they?

Oh, gee, I always get this wrong. I sent them to Christian Scheidemann,[19] who degreased and preserved them. I don't think it was a Cyclatron, but I do think that it was a type of vacuum pump. He went to great lengths to get the grease out and then inject them with a preservative.

I want to ask again about superficial affiliations in terms of the way people try to accommodate your work within the standard canons of "the known." There are always references to surrealism. There are occasionally references to dada. Much less in terms of Pop. Certainly with things like the kitty litter bag or the cereal box,[20] it does seem like there's a Pop discourse going on. I really do think a lot of Warhol, that early moment when he was interested in the hand-drawn image and the commercial logoing and stuff like that. Does it drive you crazy?

You've left out minimalism and folk art. No, as long as it's so broad, I find it very flattering actually.

Is there any one area where you think the work could be really interestingly enlarged upon in terms of an existing history?

What would you call religious art or art that's made with God in mind?

Probably ecclesiastical.

I would say that is maybe an area to be poked around in.

In terms of being made for a higher purpose?

More like an attempt to understand the mysteries of faith.

What brought you back to that?

It's too early to say, but I think that it is a meditation on faith, and these were the symbols I've studied. As a very young kid, I was forced to sit down or kneel down and stare at them. It's a rich repository.

Why have these visual symbols been so enduring for so long to so many people?

Do you have a conscious recollection of when you lost the faith, so to speak, or stopped practicing Catholicism?

Yes. It was the battle within myself of understanding what my nature was as a gay man and the conflict of that in the system that doomed me. Because of my God-given nature, that conflict was undoable, and I had to flee.

Around what age was it that you let it go?

Well, I would say probably through puberty and early teen years. It was a very deep battle within myself.

And at this stage in time are you finding yourself okay about the imposition of all that material on you? I mean all of that early childhood propaganda.

I wish that other people could see how damaging it is to children to be raised with that image of themselves as doomed, when we are in essence all God's children.

Again we could go back to the whole notion of sin and redemption and to the fireplaces.

And also the transubstantiation from three-dimensional and touchable to smoke.

When you were growing up, were there things that you were looking at with greater interest than other things? As a kid in suburban America, the way information reaches you is very ad hoc. You don't have a lot of control over what images are available to you. I can remember at some point I'd stumbled on a book of reproductions of Francis Bacon paintings and thought, "Whoa!"

How old were you?

I was about fourteen or so.

I didn't see them until I was a freshman in college. Actually I didn't know much about art, and I went to see *Last Tango in Paris* by myself at the local cinema, and I went back the next three nights. I didn't know what I was seeing, but I knew I had to see it.[21]

It's funny; you bring up Last Tango, *and then the stick of butter comes back to play such an important role in your own work.*

Well, the other thing that had actually almost equal, well maybe not equal, but … in the house next to us lived a priest. A Catholic church was built on the vacant land across the street from us, and until they built the rectory, the priest rented the house next door. I remember seeing his underwear on the clothesline. And the fact that a priest wore underwear, washed it, and you could see it was very interesting to me. But when the priest moved out and into the rectory, in moved a circus family. The mother had grown up in the circus and was now retired. Did I ever tell you about this? The Flying Zacchinis?

Never.

Her father originated the human cannonball, and she grew up to be a human cannonball, her profession in life, until she broke her arm three times in the same place and had to retire. They rented the house next door. That was an amazing influence on me as a kid. We would go to visit the circus, and their relatives—who were still performing and were part of, I would imagine, a kind of circus aristocracy—would oftentimes come to visit her.[22]

And were you on casual terms with them?

Oh yeah, I was in their house all the time. And they just led such a different kind of a life. I had not come from a family that traveled. So they brought other cultures to us. The boys were raised in circus tradition. Their hair was not cut until they were two years old. They were given Christian names, but then they were called by their circus names. One was named Boo-ba, and one was named Zee-zee. The cannons were mounted on trucks, and they were painted to resemble an object, like one was the X-15 missile. But this was also their family car as they traveled around the country with the circus. So when they took a detour to visit family, they would park the X-15 missile in front of the house. It was incredibly exciting and exotic and about visual symbols and performance as a thing to do with your life. To be shot out of a cannon is a pretty remarkable thing.

214

And were the children around your age?

They were a little younger than me. I think her sister was a trapeze artist, and I believe her uncle took out a lawsuit that went to the Supreme Court. A local news station filmed the person being shot out of the cannon and played it on the news. The Zacchinis sued. The issue was how much can you excerpt from a work of art. Even though the clip was three seconds, it was the entirety of their act, which was the entirety of their livelihood. And they won the case, and it now defines how you can excerpt something.

That's amazing! When did this take place?

I was an adult, and I was in New York and remember watching it at a great distance. Daphne's going to look it up. But that's my memory of it.[23]

The interview continues on West Twenty-First Street, where Gober temporarily rented a studio that could accommodate the large-scale pieces for the MOCA installation.

A lot of elements have changed. The water flooding down the stairs remains pretty much as originally envisioned, but the walls went away. Below the surface, where originally you were thinking the water would be turbulent, has turned into this bucolic serenity. I know a little bit about the transition, but if you could just talk about that process, because it changes the piece a lot.

Well, it was going to be set in a house, and I had a lot of problems with the house, metaphorically and then technically. Metaphorically going down into the basement was almost too heavy a burden in terms of what the meanings were and what I could do with them. And then technically it was very difficult because the house was going to be 30 by 30 feet, so you had a 30-by-30 expanse of water within the space. So in terms of evaporation and moisture within the room, it was very difficult because of the denseness of the humidity. Then, if I wanted to make a real foundation and a real footing and build the house realistically above that, you had technical problems with wheelchair access and safety within a structure within a museum. I wasn't really freed up until I jettisoned the idea of the house. Even though, when I took it out, I missed it. Even last night, where was I? Oh, I was at a concert, and I was daydreaming about how I could bring it back.

How did the turbulence of the water underneath get resolved into—

Well, I had a kind of natural ... I guess from making the man in the drain, and the idea of a drain and what's below, that I just always thought about it as darkness. But something wasn't feeling right to me about darkness as being the underneath part there. It just didn't fit with what I was feeling and with what I wanted to communicate to people and tell people to look at. And then Don and I were on vacation in Maine, and it was from being out in this pristine water landscape that I had the kind of simple idea of just flipping the project completely and making the underground something natural and something brightly lit by daylight. It's actually an idea that I've had for a really long time but had forgotten.

Was there any pleasure in determining these as tide pools just in terms of tide pools being where life is, the point of origin ...

Oh, yeah, definitely.

So the pools themselves are very optimistic given the nature of what lies above. And the legs were ... that was always an idea in there either way, right?

The legs were sort of the originating idea and came from a slide in *Slides of a Changing Painting*, which was always reproduced upside down, so nobody knew what it was. There were two legs in dark water, two male legs. I started with that image for the man in the drain actually. We tried to make two legs down in the drain, and it didn't work out, and little by little that turned into the man's chest down there. So I thought that it would be through the suitcase that you would see the man's legs. I don't remember where the baby came from, to have the baby's legs coming down between the man's legs, but I think it happened after I already had the reversal to the optimism of the tide pool.

And the suitcase came about how?

That was early. I think I had the suitcase before I had the drain. I remember I had a suitcase here with a child's leg in it. But it was too easy and so bourgeois-ish in its use of metaphors. It was just too easy—black suitcase with a kid's leg.

And the addition of the Madonna with the conduit came about…

Well, I'd sent Renny[24] out to find images of cannons. I'm thinking about the Flying Zacchinis, you know, and about what that would mean, what it's about. Then we made some clay cannons, but they weren't really all that interesting. And then I can't remember the moment of joining the conduit through the Virgin. But it's not that big a leap if I've been doing it with the chair, with the tissue box, with the lard box. So I do it with the Virgin. And so the conduit is, in a sense, like the cannon visually. It's a tube, it's an iron tube, but it's also … the cannon is kind of like a birthing image in a far-fetched way. A tube that something comes out of.

Well, especially if it's a member of the Zacchini family. It gets pretty literal there.

Exactly. So all that stuff kind of hazily comes together into an image. And I think standing her on the sewer drain is to me still problematic. I can justify the pipe through the Virgin, even though it's a penetration and I know that's not supposed to happen with a virgin. My associations with the pipe, it being a natural water runoff, make perfect sense in a way through the Virgin: water running through her, tears running through her, like the stream of life goes through the Virgin. But then putting her on this sewer drain gets me a little anxious. Partly about how it will be received, because I know that it's such a sacred symbol, yet … I think that goes back to what you were talking about, the sacred and the profane. And in a way how I do like to try to reconcile opposites in the objects. That tension to me is fruitful and an interesting one to pursue. It's important that her drapery mold around the sewer drain, that there's a relationship, an organic relationship. But then the view through the sewer drain, if you look through, is one of earth's beauty and life's fortune by the placement of the pennies in it. I mean fortune in the sense of luck. It's a glimpse of optimism within the tide pool. So it's a mixture of images that keep layering up in a totem pole kind of a way.[25]

It was hard to figure out what she was actually going to be made of because I really wanted to sculpt her out of clay. This I knew. I wanted this big physical thing in front of me, and I wanted to get my hands dirty. And I wanted to carve drapery. But I didn't want to reproduce a kitsch figurine, and I had a lot of problems around the face because I'd never made a face and I don't want to make a face. Faces are what you really focus on, but with the Virgin her face really isn't important. It's what she stands for and her posture. The open-palmed, arms-out approach felt right to me. A lot of times you look around for one thing, and you end up finding something else. I'd been looking around for a cement deer for my yard on Long Island. But I couldn't find one any-where. You find them in fiberglass now. And I kept thinking maybe I'd find an old one, but I never found one, new or old. But I knew there was something about old cement work that I wanted to possess, and then I was walking between here and home, down Tenth Street past those fancy antique stores, and somebody had a beautiful stone naked woman, life size. But very crude. And she's holding an apple in her hand, so maybe she's Eve. And I began to think, "Oh, she'd be so beautiful standing in the woods." But I didn't want to even go in and ask how much, because God knows what this would cost even for a third-rate stone sculpture on Tenth Street, you know. So then I think that I began to put those things together. The desire for concrete sculpture com-bined with seeing this full-size sculpture of a woman. She was in stone, but concrete seemed right because then I could control the detail on the face through sandblasting. So you're getting the gestalt of the Virgin without the detail of it. And, if anything, it's rooted in worn-out garden statuary, which I hope should give it a kind of a dignity. And I think it should be beautiful with the pipe, the old concrete with the bronze of the pipe.

So you really wanted a quality of erosion for the statue?

To a degree, yeah. Not extreme, but slightly, as though it's been out there for a while.

So in a funny sort of way the installation has gone from being a house to this strange place of contemplation.

It's not a house. It's not really a room. At first, when I took it out of the house, I thought what I'd do is make it look like it's the basement of MOCA, but that's not really going to happen either. It's a weird hybrid space.

But it seems much calmer to me now. The earlier version was much more theatrical—the mise-en-scène, the fact that you had to cross over a gangplank, and the implied danger of all that rushing water under your feet.

It should be much calmer, much simpler. I had described parameters for myself that were impossible to fill. I was sort of saying, "Here's the house, and I will reveal its dark mysteries to you or take you through them." And that was way too much. It became uninteresting. It became a burden in a way.

The thing that surprised me the most today is that even though you'd described the water pouring down the stairs, and I thought I understood it, when the water went on today, it was petrifying. The smell of it. The violence of it. I really was victimized by it to some degree.

It's a palpable relief when you unplug the pumps.

The tension is amazing. I can stand and watch a very highly propulsive fountain for an hour and not have anything problematic come to mind. But with the water on the wood on the stairway, you're back in someone's home. I hadn't realized how strongly the element of home and violation of home was going to work there.

I hope I don't lose it in the museum context, with the cement floor and those broad vistas. Whereas if I'd kept my original vision of a wood house and a stairway and the flood ...

Again, were you nervous about introducing the Madonna?

I am still, because I know that she's sacred. I tend not to think of
these things because I don't think of what the effect is going to be on
other people. I concentrate on what the effect is on me and what my
intentions are. So it was actually a surprise—it sounds naïve—but it
was a surprise when my assistant said to me, "Oh, you're going to get
Jerry Falwell going with this one." But now that I have more distance
on it, I understand that it is a very sacred object to people and they
really don't like it tampered within anyway. So I'm apprehensive about
that because I really don't like controversy. I don't like upsetting
people. It makes me very, very uncomfortable.

*But don't you feel like you have a greater claim than many to that particular
object just by virtue of its imposition on you as a child?*

Yeah, maybe. No. Everyone ... well, there are some millions of
Catholics. What would the world be like if we all went around reinter-
preting Mary? It would be kind of wild, wouldn't it?

*I guess part of what interests me is that at a certain point you could make
a determination between a devotional, let's say an enlightened, piece of ecclesiastical sculpture and a piece of kitsch. I guess it seems to me not to be so offensive
to actually ask for the reinterpretation of a form that's already been debased.
It's got to make it better.*

I don't think that my finished sculpture will have much relationship to kitsch sculptures. I don't think you'll remember that when you
see this. We also got NEA money for the catalogue. I have to talk to Paul
when he gets back,[26] but I think we should give it back. We haven't
gotten it yet, but I think we shouldn't take it because I think we're spit-
ting in the eye of a publicity machine, and I don't really want to be
part of that.

*Well, that misinterpretation is worse than anything that could be read into
the sculpture because then that becomes the dominant motif.*

I know, but I know I'm pushing that button to take government
money and then do something to the Virgin Mary. This is what drives

them wild. And then I think with the NEA in such a precarious place, it feels very irresponsible to do something like that when you know it's going to drive them crazy. I have no desire to be in a *Piss Christ* place.[27] I'd rather do a benefit print for the museum, let them raise the money that way, explain to the NEA. Make a deliberate choice not to enrage people. Because it's not my goal.

Was there an overriding desire of intent with this installation? It's the biggest thing you've ever done. It takes the work to a level of physical ambition that hasn't been visible before.

Yeah, it's getting the better of me also. No, truly it is. There are too many sorts of technical problems. That sounds shallow. It's not exactly that. It's too difficult. I'm finding it almost too difficult, and I'm unhappy a lot of the time because of that. But I've made this commitment to do this, and so I'm going to see it through and do it.

It has this funny half-consciousness, not of a full dream state, but of a dream state where you're trying to put yourself back to sleep and you construct a narrative that you can kind of take control of if you drift, so it doesn't go to a bad place. But at the same time you're beginning to lose control over it.

Yeah, I understand that state. It's not unlike being in the middle of the imagery. Certain things make sense, but then where are you when they don't?

INTERVIEW 4 (December 15–16, 1997)

RICHARD FLOOD: *I thought it would be good to talk about Los Angeles. Having seen so many potential ways to go with the piece in the working model, how did your editing process work?*

ROBERT GOBER: Some of it was technical; there were certain ideas that couldn't be accommodated in the museum due to either the amount of water or the amount of excavation.

At one point, in the working model, you would enter through a zipper. At another point there was the possibility of a window at the top of the stairs, and then there were a couple of different possibilities with the window itself: the idea of a bird outside or the water running over the lip of the window.

We went through a lot of visual ideas that didn't end up working out. What happens to me is I drag my old solutions with me when I have a new problem. That idea was a variation on the Dia prison window. The question was whether the water was coming from outside the building as in a biblical flood, or there was a water problem inside the building, but it was an idyllic day outside. And ultimately it didn't matter that much one way or the other; I decided not to use it.

In almost all of the material that's been generated around the show by writers, everybody talks about redemption being down below. Like this whole kind of reversal of stuff. Certainly, had the window been there, it would have been a more confused scenario.

It's true, although I ended up having a strong light come down the stairs on top of the water, kind of a heavenly light, which I was ambivalent about until the very last minute. Luckily I went away for a week right before the show opened, came back, and realized I needed it.

And did Jennifer Tipton do the lighting for this?[28]

She did. I would explain to her what I was imagining. She would have a conference with her technical assistant, Brian Haynsworth, and then he would arrange equipment for us to rent so that we could try it out in the studio ourselves. We'd fool around, then Jennifer would come in, a master of concision. She'd see what we'd done and make suggestions, and then maybe we'd have to rent something different, get gels or switch lights around. It progressed that way through the whole project. She was definitely responsible for achieving the look of sunlight underground. She gets you the stuff, leaves you alone to fool around with it, then gives great advice.

There was one element that I grew increasingly curious about when I was in the finished installation, which was your decision to double the two tide pools. What was the narrative behind that—that they both held these identical frozen moments?

Well, the show was laid out in a cross or cruciform arrangement. In a way, the open suitcases were the hands, palms up, left and right, except they were legs.

The other thing that was a constant in the writing about the piece—and I had very conflicted responses to this—was that almost inevitably in the opening paragraph or the second paragraph the writer would cite Bob Gober as an "openly gay artist."

Oh, this drives me crazy, although I guess it's interesting too. How would it read in a review of, say, Chuck Close's or Cindy Sherman's work if they were described as "openly heterosexual"? It would be bizarre. It is bizarre! Sometimes I think it's just an unconscious way of calling me a fag. But you know I've brought it on myself by bringing it up. I was naïve enough to believe that art was about human experience. But I've learned that the vast majority of people have not thought through these issues. And then there's that inane domino effect that seems to riddle arts writers.

Because it's on the record. Then they feel like they have to wrap it back in to keep the record going.

Oftentimes writers will ask me what they should read to understand my work, which seems a little crazy to me. It might help you write your piece, but it won't help you understand my work, I don't think.

Okay. I was curious what the consistency of the need to tell that story was.

Why do children taunt their peers? And where are the editors and the thinkers here? The subject is deep; the writing very often isn't. But you know, like most things, you get what you pay for. What do art writers get paid? Almost nothing, I'm told. You can't expect someone to turn themselves inside out for $200.

While there were references to baptism, references to cleansing, references to giving birth, I kept going back to the earlier piece you did about Robert Gober drowning in the swimming pool,[29] and I just wondered if there was some conscious thing about the perilousness of the infant's position over the water. For me it was totally benign. I wasn't thinking baptism, I was just thinking, "Isn't this bucolic?" What could be more beautiful than holding a baby over a pool that is all about giving life? That was complete unto itself. And then I thought, "Well, if there are all these other interpretations, could there be imminent peril there as well?"

It's an interesting thought.

Did you ever think about what period of time was being evoked in the piece at all?

Not really, no. But I think that it's always my time, the last forty-three years.

Somehow the suitcase, by the time I saw it in L.A., turned into a traveling salesman's suitcase. And in a way, when the bottom drops out of the case, there's this incredible fantasy that the kind of loneliness that a suitcase implies to me is fulfilled somehow with this memory or this projection into the future. I was obsessed about the Americanness of the piece. I know I keep doing this throughout the interview, but only an American author could have created this particular narrative. I really thought that when you got to the suitcase there was something so inherently lonely about an empty suitcase and … I realize I'm throwing it into a fictive context in asking you to respond to my fiction, but …

No, that's okay. I think we talked the last time about the retired circus family that used to live next door to us and how potent that was. And a lot of times I've wondered if I could make a worthwhile sculpture of a magician sawing a woman in half. But, for various reasons, I don't think it would be interesting or worthwhile. But as we're talking, I realize that maybe in a way I've made that sculpture by opening up a box and sawing myself in half or doubling myself. As I'm retelling it, it doesn't make as much sense as …

But it does make total sense. Because it's complete bifurcation both ways. Both horizontally and vertically.

Yeah. And a bit of a magic act too.

I guess the other thing was the stairway, which, in film and theater and in real life, is always this enormously evocative thing. Something is always lurking at the top of the stairs, or something is always going to come out to admonish the wrongdoers from the top of the stairs. Yet your staircase was so uninflected that it seems almost contradictory to the grandness of the mise-en-scène. Was that push-pull between domestic and ecclesiastical intentional?

I don't think that I worked with it all that rationally. I didn't need to; it's who I am.

I guess you anticipated a negative Catholic response to some degree or a negative conservative response.

Yes, because I felt it within myself as I was making the piece. My own startledness at what I was making and why I was doing it.

So it didn't come as a surprise when there was a negative—

No, it didn't come as a surprise. Although I didn't plan to create it. But it didn't actually come from people who experienced it firsthand. It came from the image being faxed around the country by the Catholic League for Religious and Civil Rights.

Because you never really saw it before it happened. Did it change for you in any way? Were there any surprises for you?

No, oddly enough, it was almost exactly as I had envisioned and built it in the maquette. More than anything, I was pleased that we had pulled it off. That was the surprise, when I was standing there watching people interact with it on the first night, when I realized that it was out of my mind and existed in the world.

Did you mind seeing people with it?

No, I loved it. Then I could let it go.

When everything was installed, did you in any way miss the fourth wall?

At first I did, because I couldn't get used to the intrusions from the peripheral light and the shadows of the people on the mezzanine but, ultimately, no, I don't think it mattered in an essential way to the show.

So the frontality of the thing was fine by you?

Yeah, in one way I think it worked. Because when you were in the deepest part of the show and you looked backward, you saw other people in the space going up and down the ramps, and sun reflected off windshields in the parking lot, and I think that was less clichéd than having a more chapel-like environment.

Because in the end it wasn't a chapel.

There's a feeling I have when I go into a church. The wonder of it. I always feel somehow as though I'm inside a miraculous human body when I'm in a stained-glass cathedral type of church, but then there's also a feeling after I sink down to my knees, that I am supposed to have an experience and I'm not quite up to it. So I think you avoid that at MOCA by opening up the front to the public. You're not supposed to have a culminating emotional experience necessarily.

And did your attitude toward the role played by the Madonna change at all when it was finished? Did her presence in the space hold any surprises for you?

We built her on the large sewer drain, but the drain was on dollies in the studio maybe six inches off the floor. So what surprised me was, when we installed the drain over the deep space of the brick shaftway, that suddenly she was floating. That was a surprise.

I guess part of what I found so surprising was actually how moved I was when I was there. What I thought was going to be a really strange tension around the central element of the Madonna and the culvert just never happened. And it wasn't that it didn't happen because I'd seen it before. Because when I had seen it before, I was experiencing it as something that was producing anxiety. But it was really very, very peaceful. Sincere is a funny word, but there was a sincerity about the religious aspects of the piece without sentimentalizing anything. Did you have an emotional or a spiritual goal with the piece?

That was a journey for me. And to circle back to your original question about how the imagery itself would change, grow, get discarded, that was the journey of my feelings through my relationship to these pieces. The heart of the show was the feeling that you got when you looked underground and saw the sunlight on the water. That was, to me, the emotional heart of the show. Is that what you mean?

Yeah. But I'm also curious if there was something about the nature of a personal religious experience: a personal sense of salvation or damnation that you wanted to at least offer as something to be thought about by the public.

It wasn't damnation. It was closer to salvation.

So that was an issue in there? The Madonna provided such a stable centerpiece for everything else, and it wasn't a violent center. It really gathered the forces of the room round it and made sense out of them.

It's kind of a contemporary burden that she has with the pipe.

For a lingering minute was the Madonna ever going to be conceived with the traditional garb, the blue mantle ...

Well, I thought it might be. First I wanted the garden statue aspect of it. I knew I was looking for that, but then I thought, well, what if I painted her blue and then sandblasted her, wore her way down. And I'd still like to try that; I just didn't get to it on this one.

Do you think the press information about being an ex-Catholic was in any way helpful to people looking at it, or was that also potentially a piece of information that would have been just as interesting to omit?

It was certainly very easy for people who disliked the piece to pick up on as a reason why I did it. That I needed to assault the Virgin because I was angry at the Church, which was not the case really. I was trying to get close to the Virgin. My mother had a sophisticated reading of the show. She told Daphne that she thought the whole piece was about me making a sculpture of my own birth. She didn't think the Virgin Mary was specifically the Virgin Mary. She thought she was perhaps a stand-in for motherhood. And then she had a hole in her stomach where the baby would have been. The coins had my birth-date. There was the man with the baby who was maybe giving birth. Those were her reasons.

All fairly compelling.

I think it's much more about the mystery of faith than organized religion.

Were you happy with the response?

I was. But, oddly enough, I was also removed because I was very satisfied with what I had created. But I was very gratified because I think that some people were moved by it. I think that's very rare, particularly when there's lots of stuff to think about; it's not that often that you're moved.

And of the writing around the show, did you think in the end Roberta [Smith]'s essay was the richest?[30] Not to make it a steeplechase. I just thought she hit a number of really interesting points.

Absolutely; for a newspaper, it was an extremely thoughtful piece. I felt that I learned a lot about Roberta from reading the article.

This was also, for you, the first really fully narrative piece in a way. Nothing prior to it had really willed the viewer into an entire environment.

Dia?

Not to the extent where there was a literal altar at the center holding every-thing together. Dia was a very holistic experience insofar as you were contained in an environment. The environment was very concentrated, providing an overall emotional ambience, but it wasn't a rite of passage. In this one you really had to deal with the Madonna first. Then you had to deal with the water coursing down the stairs. And by the time you got to the suitcases, you really needed the sense of hope that they provided. So I think it was structured very much in a way that was not like Dia, where the trail was much less marked down.

Yeah, well, it was a walk in the woods compared with a march down the aisle.

Speaking of a march down the aisle, I guess the other piece the Madonna really followed up on was the wedding gown.

I guess, with the hollowness at the center and then later by putting myself within the wedding gown, maybe similar to the pipe in the Virgin.

There was a remarkable continuity because the character had, in fact, existed before, only then the character was a different kind of void and the hollowness was not about reaching potential, but was really about a vacuum. Whereas this one was very much about the promise of fulfillment. In one of the first plans for the MOCA *installation, there was lathing, and two walls would be under construction.*

It was a house being built or being unbuilt.

Then the notion of the house disappeared, except for the stairway.

Yes, it did. Always in the house was the water underneath, but if you're in a house, water in the basement connotes a problem, if not a minor domestic catastrophe. All the symbols are dark. The metaphor of the house was too grand and too limiting at the same time—like I was somehow going to solve the mysteries of the house, which I found burdensome and ultimately thin. So that was part of the problem in that the metaphor was really too constraining.

Did the diapering of the baby fulfill a very specific goal?

The diapering was important, I think, to make clear that it was a nurturing relationship between the man and the baby. That the baby was loved and well cared for.

So it wasn't a deliberate masking of the child's sexuality. That makes it sound like a negative thing.

To degender the baby?

Yeah.

No. But one day I showed the piece to someone, and they gave a lascivious laugh and guessed that the man was buggering the baby. I never would have thought of that, so it also made it doubly important that the baby have a diaper on.

Do you feel a part of an artistic continuum?

Oh, I don't know how to answer that. I mean, obviously.

Well, there's always been the figurative element in your work, especially when figuration was at its most debased. Nobody was touching it really.

That's not really so. Because when I started, there was the whole Metro Pictures generation.[31] They pretty much had their foot in the door in terms of consciousness, but it was so different, so mediated by media.

And do you think the conch shell and the boy and the dog and the brains, with the Madonna, that you have to look at them in a new way?

Maybe. I don't know. I think I was just warming up with that work. I don't think it's ultimately that interesting.

Even with the materiality of those pieces, don't you feel a continuum with the Madonna?

Well, yeah. I mean, there is, but I don't know. It's not that interesting to me.

Then what were you trying do with them?

I was trying to make painting and sculpture at the same time, and I wasn't succeeding. And it wasn't until I found a way to combine the two that I began to be able to express myself.

You were seriously interested in painting?

Yeah, somehow I always grew up thinking I was a painter. I remember, as a kid, looking up at the clothes on the clothesline and deciding what I wanted to be. But it never made sense to me—painting. And it still doesn't a lot of times. I could never take the canvas and the paint for granted. And the only thing I ever really did was the *Slides of a Changing Painting*, where I was able to come up with a way to jettison the physical reality of painting and make painting just be an entertainment for your spirit and your mind.

Robert Gober: Sculpture + Drawing, ed. Richard Flood (Minneapolis: Walker Art Center, 1999), 9–31.

The Land of the Everlasting Hills

Trying to piece together the content and shifting contexts of Matthew Barney's *Cremaster 2* is rather like attempting to draw a map in the sand during a sirocco. Throughout the evolution of the film, Barney has ingested the teachings of the Church of the Latter Day Saints, the prophecies of the Book of Mormon, and the hagiography of Gary Gilmore, a Saint gone very wrong. He has merged his personal icon, Harry Houdini, with Gilmore's sponsor for immortality, Norman Mailer, and deposited them/him in the fin-de-siècle White City of Chicago's 1893 Columbia International Exposition. In *Cremaster 2* psychic scams and disciplined magic align and then explode into heavy-metal riffs and two-step syncopations. A queen bee releases a blizzard of drones and transubstantiates pollen into honey. Blood Atonement and rodeo rituals cohere in a schematic arena where destiny is a Brahma bull. *Cremaster 2*'s landscape is itself the fulfillment of a prophecy from Genesis that Joseph, son of Jacob, would inherit the land of the Everlasting Hills, which, in the teachings of Mormon, is interpreted as the Americas. *Cremaster 2*'s Everlasting Hills spread from the ice fields of Canada, along the crags of the Rocky Mountains, and onto the blasted terrain of Utah's Salt Flats. They both enable and consume the potential of the human characters who occupy them.

Trying to prioritize entries in Barney's syllabus is seductive but not particularly productive, as hierarchies keep mutating like the alien virus in a sci-fi movie. Hyperlinks are Hydra-headed, and the implication of narrative order is a mirage, albeit one that is formed with dimensional specificity. What may initially appear as a diminution of one's own associative experience can, in fact, be enhanced by the volatility of random possibilities; if it can be imagined, it can certainly be visualized and perhaps lived. The mesmeric power of Barney's parallel universe lies in its inevitable acceptance of an agenda that is ultimately human in its aspirations. It is never so alien as to shut the viewer out, nor so familiar as to make the viewer comfortable. Barney provides just enough of what we know to initiate a handshake, and more than enough of what we don't to suggest that a new millennium demands a new mythology. What follows is an exploration of just some of the source material utilized by Barney in creating this mythology.

QUESTION: What is the significance of the ten flags that are carried by the Highway Patrol in *Cremaster 2*?
I'm looking at the latest email from the Doctrinal Book of Mormon Answerman. It is in response to a question about the ten lost tribes and their distinguishing characteristics. So far, Answerman has been quite patient, but his most recent reply seems testy. "Well, they are lost, and it is not known in any specific detail what they have been doing." He offers the reassurance that "the Lord has had personal dealings with them over the past two thousand years" and that "Jesus Christ visited them shortly after His resurrection." A helpful, earlier email from a personal website had confirmed that there are, in fact, twelve tribes, two of which were never lost. The correspondent stated that the known tribes are those of Judah and Joseph: Judah's descendants being the Jewish nation; Joseph's being the Mormons.

But what of the lost tribes? Piecing together their story from a variety of Mormon-affiliated websites, I've learned that they're "sometimes referred to as the 'Lost Tribes' because they don't seem to be anywhere" and that "they were scattered to the 'North Country,' but over the years they seem to have either vanished or lost track of their ancestorship." Their names are Reuben, Naphtali, Issachar, Ephraim, Simeon, Dan, Gad, Asher, Manasseh, and Zebulun. Within the construct of Mormon teaching, the ultimate disposition of the tribes is reunification of all twelve. Implicit in that belief is the understanding that "Zion (the New Jerusalem) will be built upon the American continent; that Christ will reign personally upon the earth; and that the earth will be renewed and receive its paradisiacal glory."

QUESTION: Who is *Cremaster 2*'s antihero?
Encoded within the stream of information wafting in from the websites are miasmic breezes of racism, anti-Semitism, colonialism, and apocalyptic fever. Insular and cultish, the responses begin to form themselves into a millennial scenario that, in its dogmatic obduracy, is a celebration of predestined homogeneity. In a fairly logical way, the construct nicely accommodates the subject of a major coordinate on the *Cremaster 2* map, Gary Gilmore. In July 1976 Gilmore brutally, carelessly committed two murders on two successive days. He was on parole from a twelve-year sentence for armed robbery and had just broken up with his girlfriend, Nicole Baker. America was celebrating its Bicentennial, and the awfulness of the crimes in the middle of all that patriotic fervor caught and held national attention. The murders happened in Utah; Mormons murdered by a Mormon. What ultimately foregrounded Gilmore in the media was his demand for the right to execution. There had been no judicial executions in the United States for a decade, and Gilmore's refusal to enter an appeal set off a legal firestorm, as its outcome was likely to affect the fates of death-row inmates across the country. In the end, which came a short six months later, Gilmore was put to death by a firing squad. The mode of execution was his choice, and he entered into it in pursuit of the Mormon doctrine of Blood Atonement. Gilmore was a public relations nightmare for the Latter Day Saints, particularly because even as a Mormon murderer of Mormons, he lost none of his Church's baptismal privileges, including the guarantee of immortality. Through his self-willed Blood Atonement, Gilmore doubly ensured that he achieved the eternal glory that was his Mormon

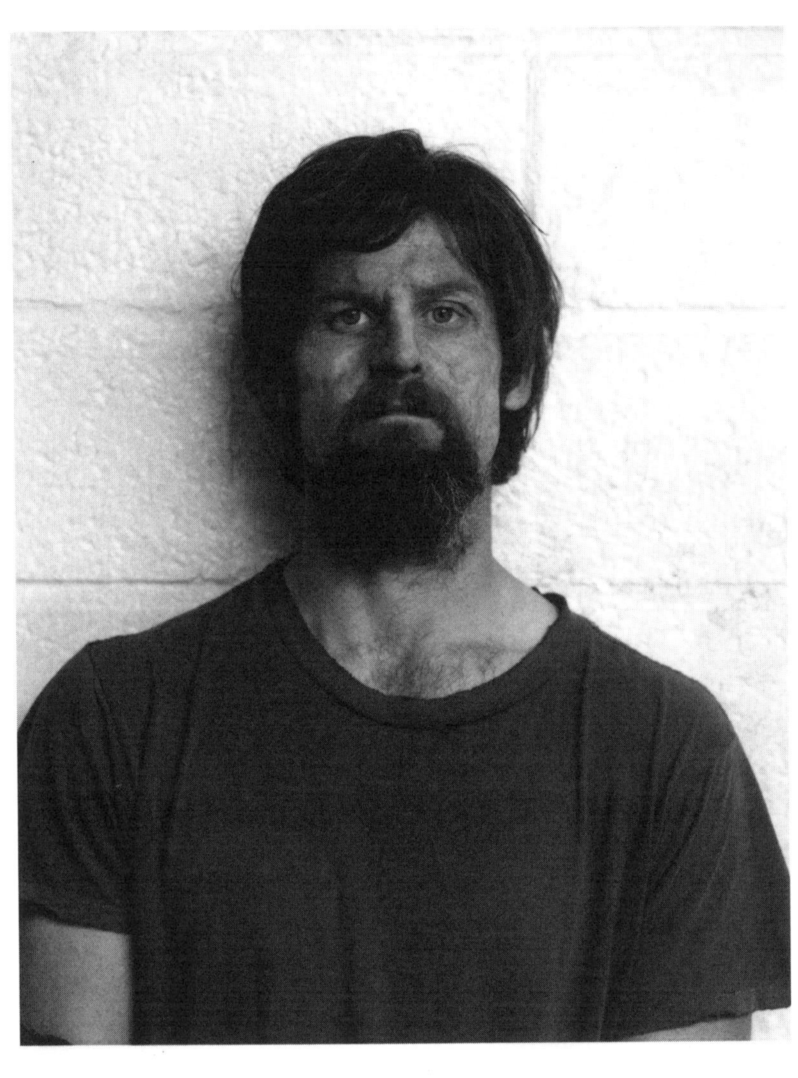

Matthew Barney, *Cremaster 2: Korihor*, 1999
Gelatin silver print in acrylic frame, 109.5 × 86 × 2.5 cm (43⅛ × 33⅞ × 1 in.)

birthright; it was the ultimate great escape.

The Gilmore played by Matthew Barney in *Cremaster 2* is both fact and fiction. Two gunshots and a quote ("This one's for me and this one's for Nicole") are as close as *Cremaster 2* gets to serving the historical record. The rest serves the artist and subsumes Gilmore into an anti-Bunyanesque, folkloric cipher. Yet, it is Gilmore's essential absence as a character that animates the events swirling around him and allows Barney's evocation of the topography of the Endless Hills to swallow his protagonist whole.

QUESTION: Was any material in Norman Mailer's *The Executioner's Song* crucial to *Cremaster 2*?

In 1979 Norman Mailer immortalized Gilmore in *The Executioner's Song*. Mailer's masterpiece defines *Cremaster 2*'s narrative little more than an olive defines a martini. Yet, contained in *The Executioner's Song* is a tale without which *Cremaster 2* could not exist. It occurs in chapter 19, entitled "Kin to the Magician," and introduces the possibility that Gary was the illegitimate grandson of Eric Weiss (a.k.a. Harry Houdini, a Jew and a descendant of Judah). According to Gilmore's paternal grandmother, the medium Fay Gilmore (a.k.a. Baby Fay and Fay La Foe), she had a liaison with the magician that resulted in an illegitimate child named Frank (eventually surnamed Gilmore, a.k.a. Seville, Sullivan, Kaufman, Coffman, and La Foe), who married Bessie Brown (a Mormon and a descendant of Joseph). While the story was as likely a vaudeville fantasy as not, Barney uses it as the key to his elliptical narrative, turning a hypothesis into a legend. According to Mailer's account, psychic Fay railed against Houdini while drawing anecdotally ever closer to him as a departed lover. It is the combination of Fay's dark, instinctive magic and Houdini's crystalline, theatrical magic that determines *Cremaster 2*'s coordinates for punishment and redemption.

QUESTION: Where do Harry Houdini and Baby Fay meet in *Cremaster 2*?
Cremaster 2 posits Chicago's Columbian Exposition of 1893 as an apt
meeting place for Harry and Fay. The Exposition was a federally
mandated celebration of the 400th anniversary of Columbus's discovery of the land of the Everlasting Hills, and Chicago vied for and won
the privilege of hosting it. John Root, a visionary architect, was named
the architectural codirector of the Exposition. He proposed a modernist
agenda that would celebrate a generation of heartland architects who
were raising a revolution against the prairie skyline. Unfortunately,
Root died before he could implement his vision, and the architectural
commissions to build went to a traditionalist elite imported from the
East Coast. They designed the Exposition's centerpiece, the White City,
and turned it into an architectural necropolis, a plaster-of-paris hymn
to a Beaux Arts pastiche. One of Chicago's greatest architects, Louis
Sullivan, knew that the White City was a sepulchral portent, and, writing of the Exposition's effect on its visitors, lamented: "They went away,
spreading again over the land, returning to their homes, each one of
them carrying in the soul the shadow of the white cloud.... They departed joyously, carriers of contagion, unaware that what they had beheld
and believed to be truth was to prove, in historic fact, an appalling
calamity."[1]

Did the Exposition's headliner, Harry Houdini, who spent much of
his career exposing psychics and spiritualists, see a parallel between the
nostalgic reinforcement offered by the architects of the White City and
those enemies of reason (like Fay) who preyed on the weak ones who
could not move into the future because they were mired in the past?

QUESTION: How does Barney's Baby Fay differ from Mailer's?
Brigham Young called his Mormon brethren the "industrious bees of
Deseret's hive," and *Cremaster 2*'s characters inhabit a succession of
customized honeycombs wherein they enact the rituals of birth, death,
and metamorphosis. Images of the hive are everywhere, and the film

contains a veritable congestion of bees. Fay is *Cremaster 2*'s Queen Bee and her subjects swarm at her command. In Barney's cinematic hive, Fay initiates the fertilization of her son's mate, and lives to challenge and tantalize her drones: Houdini, Frank, Gary. To mate, be driven from the hive, and die is the rule, but Fay's drones want to shuck their fate by exceeding the limit, by attempting transformations that will free them from the rule of the queen. Mating, murder, and magic name the roads they follow in pursuit of their goal. Yet, in the end, the politics of the hive are as predetermined as they are indifferent. Gorged on royal jelly, fertile beyond imagining, arbiter of all order, the queen exists to tempt the drones to annihilation. This she does in what that most sensual of beekeepers, Maurice Maeterlinck, in his *Life of the Bee*, calls the "nuptial flight," during which drone and queen unite in "the hostile madness of love." Once the coupling is finished, the queen "descends from the azure heights and returns to the hive, trailing behind her, like an oriflamme, the unfolded entrails of her lover." It is then, after "the male has given her all he possessed, and much more than she requires," that the queen luxuriates in the drone's "seminal liquid where millions of germs are floating, which until her last day, will issue one by one, as the eggs pass by, and in the obscurity of her body accomplish the mysterious union of the male and female element, whence the worker-bees are born."[2] Fay, in her terrible duality, is *Cremaster 2*'s protean, invincible center.

QUESTION: What landscape is being mapped in *Cremaster 2*?
The landscape of *Cremaster 2* stretches from Jasper, Canada, to Wendover, Utah. It encompasses the pristine Athabasca Glacier, which dominates the Columbia ice field and is known as "the mother of rivers" because its "nourishment zone" resides on the Continental Divide and flows north to the Arctic Ocean. From the ice fields, navigating against the glacial advance, the film races down the spine of the Rockies to the bone-white remains of a prehistoric lake, the Bonneville Salt Flats.

It is a landscape that understands infinite liquidity and absolute dehydration. It is not an accident that places Fay and Houdini in the fertile vastness of glaciers and Gary in the fragile ecology of a dead lake. Gilmore's terrain is as blasted as the chances he's run out of, while Fay and Houdini occupy a zone that is epic in its potential for metamorphosis.

Matthew Barney: Cremaster 2 (Minneapolis: Walker Art Center, 1999), unpaginated.

Openings: Francesco Vezzoli

*The surroundings become a museum of the soul, an archive of its experiences;
it reads in them its own history, and is perennially conscious of itself; the
surroundings are the resonance chamber where its strings render their
authentic vibration. And just as many pieces of furniture are like moulds of
the human body, empty forms waiting to receive it ... so finally the whole
room or apartment becomes a mould of the spirit, the case without which the
soul would feel like a snail without its shell.... The ultimate meaning of a
harmoniously decorated house is, as we have hinted, to mirror man, but to
mirror him in his ideal being; it is an exaltation of the self.*

MARIO PRAZ, *AN ILLUSTRATED HISTORY OF FURNISHING FROM THE
RENAISSANCE TO THE 20TH CENTURY*, 1964

The work of Francesco Vezzoli is essentially digressive, so let me begin
with an illustrative digression of my own.

Mario Praz (1896–1982) was one of those glittering Renaissance
minds who nowadays seem to exist only in the imaginations of other
writers. His interests were prolix and his prose, in its lavish conversational ambience, was more Walter Pater than Walter Benjamin. Yet
buried in the gorgeousness of his words is a direct, acerbic intelligence
that is an odd blend of the Age of Reason and the Machine Age. He left
behind an avalanche of books (*The Hero in Eclipse in Victorian Fiction*,
Machiavelli and the Elizabethans, and *Mnemosyne: The Parallel Between
Literature and the Visual Arts*, to name but three), and his extraordinary
appreciation for the decorative arts is now memorialized in Rome's
Museo Mario Praz, where his myriad collections are housed in an

environment that visually parallels his 1964 decorative sermon. If all of this sounds a bit precious, it is. But the preciousness is fueled by passion and its aim is ever to persuade.

Praz provided Luchino Visconti with the inspiration for his elegiac twilight film *Conversation Piece/Gruppo di famiglia in un interno* (1974), in which an aging aesthetician meets, accepts, and affects the future. An autumnal Burt Lancaster plays the character modeled on Praz and a Lamborghini-sleek Silvana Mangano embodies everything that threatens his "mould of the spirit." The film's title (whether in English or Italian) pays homage to Praz's 1971 book *Conversation Pieces: A Survey of the Informal Group Portrait in Europe and America*. Improbably, the Visconti film, Praz, and Mangano are all sweetly interwoven in Francesco Vezzoli's absurdly compelling video project *An Embroidered Trilogy*.

Each segment of the trilogy was realized (somewhat indifferently) by a different director, and each is a chain of intertextual digressions. The first, *OK, the Praz Is Right!* (1997), is the work of John Maybury (completed the year before the release of his film about Francis Bacon, *Love Is the Devil*) and features Iva Zanicchi, the hostess of an Italian game show called *OK! The Price Is Right*, who earnestly lip-synchs her way through a pop song while posturing in a room in the Museo Mario Praz. An impassive Vezzoli sits on a sofa embroidered by Praz while stitching a portrait of the author on his embroidery hoop. What is in no way apparent is the fact that Zanicchi, as a young singer, vocalized on a song featured in *Conversation Piece*.

The second segment, *Il sogno di Venere* (1998), was shot by Lina Wertmüller (director of *Love and Anarchy*, *Swept Away*, and *Seven Beauties*, all of which featured Giancarlo Giannini, the star of Visconti's last film, *The Innocent* [1976]). The setting of the video is divided between the house of Suso Cecchi D'Amico (one of *Conversation Piece*'s screenwriters) and a Roman nightclub, Officina. It features the actress Franca Valeri (a comedic interpreter of the kind of bourgeois women played with ruthless self-loathing by Mangano). Valeri is first seen reclining in

Vaselined serenity on a couch embroidered by Mangano and, later, grotesquely voguing to a Kraftwerk recording while Vezzoli, astride a dormant motorcycle, works on an embroidered portrait of Mangano.

The third segment, *The End (teleteatro)* (1999), was filmed by noted cinematographer Carlo Di Palma and stars Valentina Cortese (the epitome of a clichéd Italian diva in François Truffaut's *Day for Night* [1973]), who was, over a decade earlier, Mangano's costar in Richard Fleischer's weird non-epic epic *Barabbas* (1962). Shot in Cortese's operatically decorated Milanese apartment, *The End* documents the actress delivering the lyrics from the Beatles' "Help!" as if they were a soliloquy from *Orlando Furioso*. After pummeling an already literally bruised Vezzoli (sitting impassively with his embroidery hoop), she careens through the apartment in a muscatel ball gown devouring every overripe piece of decor in her wake. It's a performance that cannot possibly have been directed, and its ambiguous *verismo* is truly disturbing. What's particularly creepy about *The End* is that it's never remotely clear who is in on the joke or, for that matter, if there's a joke to be in on.

Vezzoli's more recent project, *A Love Trilogy: Self-Portrait with Marisa Berenson as Edith Piaf* (1999), is less complicated than its predecessor if far better made. The soundtrack is Pop Lite Piaf, and that's okay. Marisa Berenson is still as gorgeous as she was in *Barry Lyndon* (1975), and that's comforting. Her gowns are all Valentino couture, and that's glamorous. Vezzoli appears for a moment as a groom left standing at the altar, so while he's still modestly in his project, he nevertheless remains politely in the shadow of his diva. Berenson disciplines herself to cry and lip-synch to Piaf so she's invested enough to show she cares about Vezzoli's vision. Clearly a lot of phone calls were made to obtain the gowns, get the hair and makeup people, and arrange for the luxe locations. Yet the result is a bit like catching a whiff of perfume lingering in an empty elevator. You're left craving the kind of loony, morbidly chic anomie that informed Richard Avedon's memorable TV spots for Calvin Klein's Eternity. The brilliance of Avedon's commercials lay in the ambiguity of his motivation: Is he knowingly or naïvely superficial? That question also animates Vezzoli's *Embroidered Trilogy* but, unlike Avedon, the product he's pitching is more ambiguous. I think it is a nostalgia for the kind of overripe glamour that, say, Ross Hunter poured into his Lana Turner vehicles (like *Portrait in Black* [1960]). The virtue of the *Embroidered* project—in which the artist appears improbably ensconced in the lairs of aging divas—lay in the transgressive promise of violating the wall between life and art. The flaw of the over-art-directed *Love* project is that the wall remains all too firmly in place as lovely tableaux drift by like swans on a placid lake.

Vezzoli isn't alone in his obsession with iconic divas and cinema legends. In Great Britain, Douglas Gordon has been deconstructing and recontextualizing the work of Alfred Hitchcock and Martin Scorsese, among others. In America, T. J. Wilcox has created a charming cycle of films that embroider together such disparate historical/film/ fashion icons as Marie Antoinette, Norma Shearer, and Kate Moss. In France, Pierre Huyghe has arranged complex cinematic portraits (both tender and caustic) of the woman who dubbed Snow White's voice into French for Disney and of the German actor Bruno Ganz. All of these artists are sampling and reclaiming the past, to rearrange and inhabit its contours with their own sensibility.

Let us return to Praz, but for "furnishings" read "cultural signifiers": "In general patricians who inherit splendid furnishings from ancestors move among them naturally and, even if they care for their inheritance, they never hesitate to mix the modern and the antique, odd chairs and signed pieces, with an aloofness that [the] author of *The Courtier* would have approved. But the true enthusiast of furnishing is like the herbalist who selects each flower, gathers, assorts, harmonizes, and never tires of seeking perfection." Vezzoli, like Wilcox and Huyghe, is a "true enthusiast," and his instinctive arrangement of cultural vagaries would, I think, have been endorsed, if with a raised eyebrow, by the progressively embraceable Praz. Truly, the Praz is right!

Artforum 38, no. 7 (March 2000): 120–21.

Gentlemen Callers:
Alice Neel and the Art World

Andy Warhol had the twentieth-century portrait down pat. Warhol knew that everybody wants to be a product, to have a recognizable presence, a perfected façade, in the supermarket of celebrity. Why look bad in your portrait, especially when you are paying for it? Why be interpreted when all you want is to be celebrated? Why let an artist's bad attitude frustrate your longing for a blemish-free immortality? Why spend hours, days, weeks sitting in discomfort for an artist who is going to get you all wrong? Why take a chance in a McDonald's world when you can simply approve a Polaroid and get on with your life? There is no reason whatsoever to take time out of your already overcommitted schedule only to be compromised by someone else's inability to articulate graphically the wonder that is you.

Warhol knew that unflattering portraits are usually pictures of people who cannot afford the flattering ones. Portraits are traditionally meant to commemorate and celebrate heads of state, leaders of society, and princes of the church. If a portrait does not contribute to the stratification of the society that maintains the strata, isn't it a variant of genre painting? If the artist isn't commissioned by the sitter, can the result ever really be called a portrait? Isn't it something else, something to do more with the compulsion of the artist than with the aspirations of the sitter or the society that the sitter represents? Portraits are serious things: they are emblematic of degrees of inclusion and purpose in a meritocracy where placement and achievement exist in nervous harmony. Portraits are not meant to rock the boat. Yes, they can be subversive. Goya knew all about that. (But Goya also knew that the trappings of authority, properly portrayed, could strengthen a weak chin and communicate its otherwise quivering manifestation of privilege.) It is extremely difficult to find a career built on portraits that does anything, however brilliantly, other than gild the civic and societal lilies of the era. Occasionally a vivid, prescient crank like Thomas Eakins springs up and unerringly finds the moth nesting in his sitter's gown, but Eakins was a lonely pathologist operating in an amphitheater filled with cosmetic surgeons like John Singer Sargent. While Eakins could be seen as the progenitor of a new kind of analytic portraiture, his legacy was shared by relatively few artists. One of those few was, eventually, Alice Neel.

Neel's beginnings, influenced as they were by the editorially driven agenda of the Works Projects Administration (WPA), are archetypally of the period. The faces that stare out of her relentlessly urban mise-en-scènes from the 1930s are depictions of both the puppets and the puppet masters, individualized just enough to carry a message but not enough to bare a psyche. Gradually, fueled by politics and circumstance, Neel began to look more closely into the faces of those who shared her ideals and those who might profit from them. In Greenwich Village and later in Spanish Harlem, she created an album of Americans who were both fighting for change and overwhelmed by the enormity of the battle. Still, it was not until the arrival of the tie-dyed sixties that Neel really immersed herself in the radical possibilities of portraiture and commenced on a body of work that would bring her renown, if not fame, and security, if not affluence. The irony is that these late pictures were devoted, in large part, to a succession of nervously, provisionally fleshed-out psyches from the New York art world. It is tempting to hypothesize that a greatness was unleashed in Neel's art because, for the first time, she was painting people who did not matter to her, but that is too glib a response. The difference between society's children and society's darlings was not really the issue. Neel was truly interested in people, and in the 1960s she was painting people whose goals were parallel to her own. In these paintings she was searching for herself as much as for the essential oil of her sitters. It was in this attempt to find a reflection of her own gravitas in others that she began to draw close to the anxious greatness that defines the portraits of Eakins. Both Neel and Eakins reveled in a truth that the slave can never tell the master: we are all, in essence, the same.

The majority of the people Neel painted from 1960 onward bore little or no outward resemblance to those who had preceded them on her canvases. She had been away from the downtown art scene since 1938, when she moved to Spanish Harlem, and she was starved for collegial conversation. In 1955 she began to make forays into the world of dueling aesthetics by attending meetings at the Abstract Artists Club, which brought her into proximity for the first time with a mainstream avant-garde. Here she could meet her intended peers and practice the language of inclusion; she could learn the rules of the coven. Then, momentously, in 1958 she entered therapy for what she described as "nervous disturbances" and which she later attributed to undiagnosed "heart arrest."[1] The peculiarly specific phrase "heart arrest" could also be interpreted as a quite apt description of the emotional life of a woman approaching the age of sixty, her two sons mature, her last love affair dissolving, and facing the realization of how much has been sacrificed to make her art and the awful lack of recognition that that art commands.

Neel credits her therapist with having "inspired" her to "call up Frank O'Hara."[2] She had met the critic at the Abstract Artists Club, and he had visited her studio in Spanish Harlem; he was also a curator at the Museum of Modem Art, a respected poet, and an ingenuously manipulative muse and strategist for a number of artists. He was the first in a platoon of art-world-affiliated males that Neel would paint. These were men who, by granting her permission to paint them, allowed her to look at them closely in a way that was not driven by sexuality, politics, or "otherness." While Neel produced a number of paintings of women in the art world, they somehow seem less opinionated.

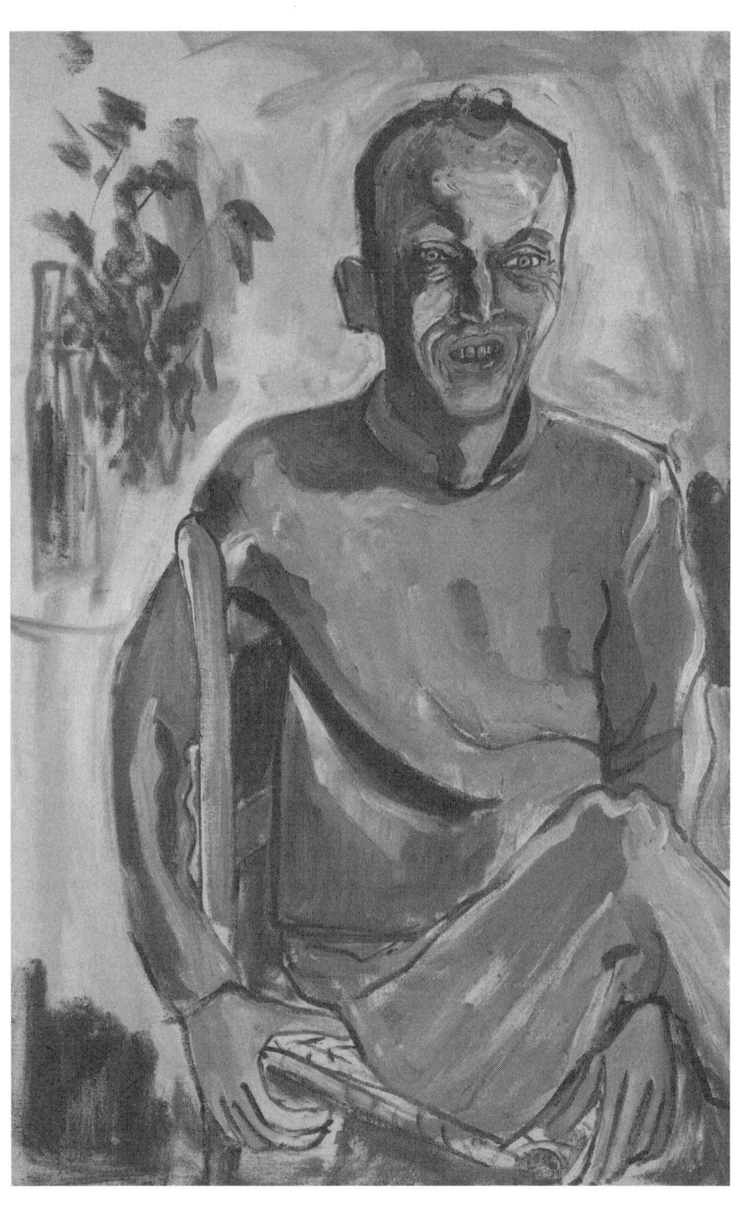

Alice Neel, *Frank O'Hara No. 2*, 1960
Oil on canvas, 96.5 × 61 cm (38 × 24 in.)

246

There are marvelous, revelatory portraits of women, like those of Linda Nochlin, Sari Dienes, and Ellen Johnson, but they tend to be the exceptions. Perhaps it was harder for Neel to really look at the women, and perhaps she was less interested in how they were looking at her. Maybe men had already taken up so much of her life—as lovers, husbands, and sons—that simply having them passively, noncombatively available for scrutiny was a luxury that allowed her to work with greater vigor. There is also the possibility that having shouldered so many traditionally male responsibilities for so long, she found it easier to identify with the more naked agendas of the men and their willingness to be defined by a pose. Then, too, Neel was in her maturity and, while still capable of shocking candor, was more like a grand old auntie whose eccentricities were capable of fueling her sitters' bravado. Her sexually libertarian past and analytically realist present gave permission to both gay and straight men to assume within the sanctuary of her studio whatever identities they wanted. The chemistry did not always work, but it frequently produced moments of startling mutual clarity—moments when one can almost catch Neel's ambition, anxiety, and defiance in the eyes of her sitters.

When O'Hara showed up to pose for Neel in 1960 he had already been painted by Philip Guston, Grace Hartigan, Jane Freilicher, Fairfield Porter, Alex Katz, and, most notoriously, Larry Rivers.[3] While not a virgin sitter, he was a kind of holy innocent, and Neel's first portrait of him, achieved over five sessions,[4] shows him in gorgeously romantic profile, rather like a young pharaoh. He stares liquidly into a milky light, a vase of Whitmanesque lilacs behind his head. In this first portrait O'Hara is all poet and muse; the curator is nowhere to be found. He is very much a passive vessel to be admired. Neel finished the portrait on his fifth visit and asked him if she could do a second. *Frank O'Hara, No. 2* (1960) was completed in a day, and in it, I suspect, Neel paints the curator missing in its predecessor. O'Hara's pose has been yanked from profile to frontal view. His hands, out of the frame in the first painting, are carelessly rendered clutching his chair as if he is a patient in a waiting room. The lilacs are now dead, and the gently directed light of the first painting has become an assault. An odd, almost doodled brushstroke on O'Hara's high forehead twists into a pair of little horns. His *maybe* smile is a rictus that could as easily signal terror as pleasure. It is a cruel portrait, which Neel claimed "expressed his troubled life more than the first."[5] Perhaps, but one cannot help but wonder what transpired between the first sitting and the last to result in such a violently assaultive representation. Comparing the two paintings offers an experience akin to what Oscar Wilde had in store for his readers when he sent Dorian Gray racing to the attic to see the portrait of what he had become. While a champion of abstraction, O'Hara was no enemy of representation. Yet he never included Neel in an exhibition, nor did he, as a critic, ever write about her work. Something must have gone horribly awry between sitting one and sitting five to inspire Neel's aggressive, apparently spontaneous flaying of the poet's flesh from the curator's skull. Neel's laconic summation of the episode was that "the second *Frank O'Hara* was my first reproduction in *Art News*."[6]

In 1962 Neel moved out of Spanish Harlem to an apartment at 300 West 107th Street (close to Columbia University), where she would live out the rest of her life. Having left Spanish Harlem, she never really looked back. When asked in 1984 about the decades spent painting her Harlem neighbors, Neel responded: "Of course, it was foolish to paint them because that doesn't get you anywhere in the art world. Painting the decadent intellectuals, the real world, that's what you'll get noticed for. That's not why I painted them, but nevertheless it's more apt to get you somewhere than painting unknown Spanish people."[7] Having been set adrift by a Cuban husband and a Puerto Rican lover, she was perhaps seeing herself as a victim of *machismo*. But the new people in Neel's life, the "decadent intellectuals," were just as ghettoized as their predecessors, and she knew it. They were simply plugged into a program of public assistance that both she and they knew better how to exploit. The iconic realism with which she imbued her neighbors in Spanish Harlem is only rarely present in her meditations on her white artistic peers, but that does not mean that the heroicism of the previous decades is gone; it is simply reconstituted. The battle is the same: to individualize those fighting for a future in a society that is only marginally aware of its need for their contributions. The eccentric dignity Neel conferred on her sitters in the best of her art-world portraits attests to this. It is probably not simply wishful thinking to read her remark concerning "unknown Spanish people" as a defiant, ironic aside born of the belated Warholian realization that to paint the celebrated ensures celebrity. Ultimately, Neel painted very few people who could (or would) substantively alter her material reality, and it is unlikely that this was ever really a motivating factor in her choice of subjects.

After disposing of O'Hara, Neel steered a clearer course. While she did not cater to her sitters, she never again subjected them to quite the Wildean punishment she had inflicted on O'Hara. An early curatorial champion, Hubert Crehan, for example, is depicted as a working-class stiff. Crehan, who had previously organized a survey of Neel's work at Reed College in Oregon, was also the first critic to look exclusively at her portraits, which he did in 1962 in an issue of *Art News*.[8] Walter Gutman, a patron of the arts and producer of the 1959 film *Pull My Daisy* (in which Neel achieved a high degree of visibility by appearing with such Beat luminaries as Allen Ginsberg and Gregory Corso), is portrayed as a benign *capo*, more avuncular than powerful. Ginsberg later appears (1966) in one of Neel's most ill-conceived portraits, which manages to look like Haight Ashbury poster art without the graphic sophistication that posters were achieving during the dawning of the Age of Aquarius.

Characteristically, Neel did not do terribly well when she was trying to pass as a contemporary; her real skill was as a cultural anthropologist eagerly exhuming the all too recent present-past of yesterday.

The horrible costumes of the sixties lend her portraits from this period the awful accurateness of Goya's court portraits, where the physiognomy of the sitter is often subsumed by the specificity of the sitter's costume. In Neel's sixties portraits it is easier to *see* those men who managed to wander through the peacock fantasy of the period without succumbing to its lure.

Robert Smithson, painted in 1962, is an all-American assemblage of raking angles. Neel referred to Smithson as "wolf boy,"[9] and indeed, she paints him with a look of feral intensity. One arm supports his head, while the other pulls over a leg to rest on his knee. An untamed cowlick darts from his hair and suggests a youthfulness that insinuates that the intensity of his expression might just as easily be that of a self-absorbed adolescent as an adult visionary. There is a similar ambiguity in the set of his lips, which are drawn up toward a smile that could simply be a motor response to the knit of his brow. In 1962 Smithson was a twenty-four-year-old painter and eight years away from *Spiral Jetty*, which would change the course of contemporary sculpture. To Neel, he represented another generation, and she invests him with a seriousness that, more than in any of her other art-world portraits, harks back to the days when the measure of a man was part and parcel of his politics. Her portrait of Smithson is very much like what one expects might have resulted had the WPA assigned her the task of painting the young Abraham Lincoln.

Henry Geldzahler sat for Neel in 1967, shortly after he had been named curator of twentieth-century art at the Metropolitan Museum of Art. Like Frank O'Hara, Geldzahler was a professional sitter. Unlike O'Hara, he came without a profile. Short and pudgy, he was a studied power broker with a carefully constructed public façade. That he agreed to sit for Neel is not surprising; that he posed so affectlessly is. Why he was posing in an apartment on West 107th Street is not a mystery. There was a stir around Neel's portraits, and Geldzahler liked being inside a stir. There was also a stir around Geldzahler's planned exhibition,

New York Painting and Sculpture, 1940–1970, and Neel wanted to be validated by being included. He could have done it, but he did not. Neel reported that in response to her request to be included, "He looked straight into my eyes and answered, 'Oh, so you want to be a *professional*?'"[10]

Given the tensions that must have been roiling on both sides of the canvas, the painting is remarkably benign. Geldzahler does look a little petulant, but he was staring down the barrel of a motherly, gossipy gun. For her part, Neel went through the mechanics of the picture with some energy. She accords his fat little face all the honor she would an apple in a practiced still life and accommodates a pose that certainly evolved from Geldzahler's effort to keep his tummy tucked in. Neel utilized her remarkable digital vocabulary to lend a sort of hysteria to his right hand, which twists against nature into a compositional mannerism that recalls the excesses of El Greco and the shortcuts of Goya in dealing with their sitters' extremities. Neel consistently signaled her subjects' comfort, or lack thereof, in their hands, but Geldzahler's hand is remarkable in its inability to settle into the overall composition; it is looking for a way out of the picture. Perhaps Geldzahler bored her and knew it, or perhaps it was the reverse.

Whatever the reality, the portrait is fascinating in its perverse dual depiction of power and weakness. Neel did not lionize her prey. Rather, she depicts Geldzahler as a truculent child who has, perhaps ill-advisedly, gotten himself exactly where he wanted to be and is not having the fun he thought he would. Curiously, in the end that works for both artist and model: she gets wiser, and he gets younger. It is interesting that the last extended interview with Neel about her art was conducted by Geldzahler for Andy Warhol's magazine *Interview* (published postmortem in January 1985). So while they may not have gotten exactly what they wanted from the portrait, they twice paired to share the same stage.

Refugees from Warhol's Factory also came to Neel seeking sanctuary. In 1970 Jackie Curtis and Ritta Redd became the gender-bending subjects of one of Neel's most moving portraits. Curtis was one of Warhol's "superstars," a transvestite with incredible screen presence, and Ritta Redd was his boyfriend of the moment. Huddled together like Hansel and Gretel in the presence of the witch, these two boys with transgendered dreams sit as if awaiting a court verdict. Curtis, on the right, is all Joan Crawford attitude: "Go on, coppers, throw the book at me!" Redd is all Brandon De Wilde sensitivity: "Come back, Shane!" They are among a number of true political and sexual revolutionaries (including Abdul Rahman, Kate Millett, Bella Abzug, and Annie Sprinkle) painted by Neel from the 1960s through the early 1980s, and her compassion informs the painting without ever overwhelming it. Both sitters wear stripes, and while it may have been serendipity, the reference to prison garb is obvious and scary. Jackie's shoulder pads hint at an idealized Hollywood pantheon of femme fatales who inevitably fall for the wrong palooka and, if they are lucky, take a bullet in the gut. Redd is a little more complicated. Part Tom Sawyer and part Little Lord Fauntleroy, he is the personification of knowing innocence. Even his awkwardly introverted feet seem oddly available to the advance of Jackie's insinuatingly positioned right foot, with its open-toed high heel and torn black stocking revealing a curiously aggressive big toe. It is one of those wonderful pictures by Neel that somehow gets much bigger than the subject ostensibly being portrayed. It is as if Neel knew that this relationship would end badly—was even forecasting that eventuality—but was totally committed to portraying all the theatrical possibilities of the moment.

David Bourdon and Gregory Battcock, both critics, were another gay couple who sat for Neel that year. While they occupy the same picture frame, Neel essentially maps out two different paintings, and therein lies the work's edgy merit. Bourdon is all elegant composure in a business suit and tie. He is neatly coifed, and his languidly dripping fingers sign "refined sensibility." Battcock is a tousled, unshaven, hungover mess perched on the edge of a daybed. He is stripped down to a sleeveless T-shirt, yellow briefs, and red socks. While the two men's bodies turn toward each other, both stare resolutely at Neel. A hairbreadth separates their knees, but between those knees runs an invisible line that ruptures the picture. In its assignment of power through pose, it is a devastatingly unnerving portrait of a relationship that has gone irrevocably wrong.

The most riveting portrait that Neel would paint of anyone in the art world was, ironically, of Andy Warhol, who arranged to sit for her in 1970. The Factory days were long over in the wake of Valerie Solanis's attempt on his life, but Warhol was still the most famous artist in America, and Neel knew it. She had some kind words for him: "As a person, Andy is very nice"; but she also resented him enormously: "As an art-world personality, he represents a certain pollution of this era. I think he's the greatest advertiser living, not a great portrait painter."[11] Nonetheless, what they created together is one of Neel's masterworks. It had to have been an act of incredible faith for Warhol, who was notoriously shy about his body, to have removed his shirt to reveal to her what it had become after he was shot. He was thirty years Neel's junior and still deeply attached to his own reclusive mother. In the garrulous, gossipy presence of Neel, he may well have found, for a moment, another mother to whom he could expose his vulnerability. Whether one knows the sitter is Warhol or not, the painting is painful to look at. Only Warhol's closed eyes give permission to linger on what, one suspects, he himself refused to see. Part of the painting's power is that Warhol is not only shutting us out, he is shutting himself in.

For Neel, suffering had usually been reflected in the eyes, as in *T. B. Harlem* (1940), or *Fuller Brush Man* (1965). When she sat for Robert Mapplethorpe in 1984 for her own extraordinary portrait, she reportedly asked to be photographed with her eyes closed so that she could see what she would look like when she was dead.[12] Aside from an early portrait of John Rothschild (*John* [1933]) and that of the corpse of her father (*Dead Father* [1946]), it is hard to find a painting in which Neel does not use the sitter's eyes as a point of entry into the picture, but she forgoes the device in the Warhol portrait. The almost complete absence of color in the composition—a wash of blue behind the upper torso, a wash of tobacco behind the calves and feet—also serves to isolate Warhol, both emotionally and physically. The awkward relationship of his body with the sketched-in couch on which it sort of sits signals that the body occupies a zone in which context means nothing. The only color that does not serve to foreground the figure is a pull of urine yellow off to the side, which in its creepy suggestion of incontinence further distances Warhol from any whiff of idealization. Neel gave all her attention to the face, which is almost beautiful, and the liquid flow of flesh below it. The girdle that stops that flow punctuates the painting, and the eye wanders down past the lap to the brilliantly unresolved mess of the hands and onto the oddly, beautifully painted shoes. The torso is all sour cream, against which the delicate pink nipples become a scary reminder of the potential for sensuality that has been leeched from the rest of Warhol's body. It is a painting that hovers dangerously between cruelty and compassion, and Neel never again attained quite its level of terrible, transformational intensity. It is difficult to imagine what Warhol thought of the painting, but he kept the pages of *Interview* open to Neel's voice and her work.

Jackie Curtis returned to Neel in 1972, and again she more than rose to the occasion. In *Jackie Curtis as a Boy*, Neel taps into a complicated psychosexual theater of impersonation. The fact that the phrase "as a boy" was added to the title indicates that the artist wanted to eliminate any sense of normalcy from the outset. Whether the portrait is of a girl or a transgendered male posing as a boy, it was clearly important to Neel that "posing" was the issue. In the painting Curtis looks as suspicious as he had two years earlier, but now Neel has placed him in a chair rather than on a couch, which confines his body language and forces a more organized pose. Curtis is wearing a red turtleneck T-shirt under a baseball flannel that drapes untucked over a pair of blue jeans.

His legs are crossed, and one hand plays over his thigh while the other holds the arm of the chair. He is any mother's son. But wait, the amplitude of his thigh is wrong: the crossed leg is pressed too tightly and rides too high over the knee. The hand on the chair clutches it too tensely, and the face, divided by a snaky S-curve, looks as if one side is covered in five o'clock shadow while the other is completely hairless. What begins to be revealed is an extremely complex portrait about multiple identities and multiple dreams in which Neel reclaims a lost boy but is also aware of what the boy has been lost to: his dream of becoming the dangerous other. Here, at last, is the safe Jackie, but Neel, like all mothers, knows that "safe" is purchased at enormous risk when the child is too eager to fulfill the parent's fantasy.

In 1972 another caller arrived at Neel's door. John Perreault, a young critic and curator who was organizing the exhibition *The Male Nude* at the gallery of New York's School of Visual Arts, wanted to include Neel's notorious but seldom seen portrait of *Joe Gould* (1933). Neel's version of what followed differs from Perreault's own. As she recalled, "I said: 'Isn't it a shame that I'm going to show something I painted forty years ago, but I don't have a male nude now, because you know, both my sons are married and working.'... He said: 'Well, you can always paint me.' So I immediately got a canvas out."[13] This was not her lover Kenneth Doolittle passed out in a tumescent stupor. This was an ambitious young curator who was surrendering willingly to Neel's libidinous eye. By the time Perreault arrived at Neel's door she was already legendary for asking people to pose in the nude. Not many acquiesced, which is unfortunate considering the clothing of the period and the occasionally awful editorial statement it makes about the person wearing it.

Freed of the need to sort out the wardrobe, Neel lavished all her attention on depicting Perreault as a sentient animal. But he is not an innocent creature in a forest glade. He is clearly not relaxed; he is definitely posing. It almost appears as if he is being tipped out of the daybed on which he reclines in an effort to display his genitals to maximum advantage. The positioning of his legs—one up, one down, both crooked at the knee—creates a peculiar starfish shape out of the sheeting, which interestingly complicates the composition. Neel was obviously happy to be painting body hair and used it as a kind of electric calligraphy to animate the lolling body. Strokes of green on the chest and a blush of the same on the thigh and in the beard could hint at the temporality of the flesh, but here they add a kind of sensuality, a hint of the forest encroaching on the painting. Perreault's face, surrounded by bacchic curls, is curiously noncommittal albeit alert. He seems to be locked into direct eye contact with the painter, and whether it is a stare-down or a transmission of energy is unclear. Whatever the dynamic, the result is definitely more than a nude: it is a nude of John Perreault. Knowing it was destined to be shown in the context of *Joe Gould*, Neel gave it her best. It does not have the raucous totemic bite of its predecessor, but it was a declaration that she was still a player and, given the opportunity, still had the skill to shock. In the case of *John Perreault*, both the artist and her subject also received what they wished for. He got a new, instantly notorious painting for his show and the cachet of being its subject, while she was represented in his exhibition in the way that she wanted to be. It makes one wonder what might have happened had she been able to sweet-talk Henry Geldzahler out of his pants.

Still in 1972 the superrealist sculptor Duane Hanson came to sit before Neel's insatiable easel. The result is a very strange, idiosyncratic painting. Seated in a hardback chair (kinder for a quick sketch than for a longer study), Hanson is a cacophony of mismatched reds. Hair, turtleneck, fur collar, greatcoat, pants—all are at war with one another. The samurai-like armor of the clothing does little to dwarf the enormity of his head, and the entire composition feels as if it has been devised simply to give that head a resting place. There is a pathetic ostentation in Hanson's gaudy raiment, for which his face seems to beg forgiveness. It is one of Neel's more melancholy portraits, with Hanson's

beseeching smile and crinkled eyes, framed by teased-up hair and
frontier-style chin whiskers, fighting to establish his humanity. The
whole effect is of an outsider who has seriously misjudged the dress
code for the party to which he received a last-minute invitation.

A year later, in 1973, Neel found time to revisit her past through a
portrait of her old friend Raphael Soyer and his brother Moses. Raphael
Soyer was a realist painter whose career paralleled Neel's, but without
the abysmal lows and heady highs. A Russian immigrant, Soyer had
known Neel forever through their shared commitment to socialist
politics and representational painting. Moses, also a painter, apparently approached Neel and said, "If you intend to paint us you should,
because none of us will live forever."[14] The portrait that resulted, with
the two old survivors seated at the end of Neel's daybed, is truly elegiac.
Mortality hangs heavily over the painting, in which Raphael is the
skeptic and Moses the believer. Characteristically, Neel separates the
brothers, as if she is the interviewing officer at the scene of a crime.
Moses, looking like he is awaiting notice of the end, stares straight
ahead. Raphael, perhaps in avoidance, looks down. Biographies aside,
it is a very beautiful painting, filled with a shared understanding about
transience. There was nothing to be gained by painting the brothers,
except perhaps to testify that they had arrived, had endured, and were
ready to pass on.

In 1974 Neel painted one of her most forgettable portraits. Its
subject is Jack Baur, then director emeritus of the Whitney Museum
of American Art, the museum that had just given Neel the retrospective
she had craved. Neel was thrilled, but the exhibition was hastily organized and did not include a catalogue. What should have been a triumph
turned into a quietly debated controversy. Both friends (like Lawrence
Alloway) and enemies (like Hilton Kramer) had scarcely a kind word
for the show. Alloway blamed the curator; Kramer blamed the artist.
But Neel was happy and seemingly wafted above it all. Part of the problem, and also a virtue, of the retrospective was that it was somewhat

prompted by the growing criticism of museums as enemies of women artists. Vocal feminist critics, curators, and academics were no longer content to sit back and allow themselves and the artists they advocated to take a backseat to the men. As Neel was increasingly, albeit ambiguously, cast as a prototypical feminist, showcasing her work must have seemed like a quick and easy way to silence the women. The result was an ill-conceived production that saw a truckload of her portraits sharing the museum's limited space with *The Flowering of American Folk Art* and an exhibition to honor the now-deceased Frank O'Hara (*Frank O'Hara: Poet Among Painters*).

Neel was not unaware of the debt she owed to the feminist movement (although she would never have called it a "debt") and happily coasted on its growing momentum by hitting the lecture circuit and sharing her indomitable history with women across the country. Nor did she leave these women out of her work. The 1970s saw a legion of art-world women arriving at West 107th Street to have themselves and their contributions commemorated. Among them were Irene Peslikis, founder of Redstocking Artists (depicted as *Marxist Girl* [1972]); Cindy Nemser, cofounder of the *Feminist Art Journal*, who posed nude with her husband, Chuck, also an editor of the journal; Linda Nochlin, feminist art historian, depicted with her daughter, Daisy; Bella Abzug, feminist politician and author; Ellen Johnson, curator and art historian; and Mary D. Garrard, art historian and second president of the Women's Caucus for Art. The feminist writer Kate Millett arrived via a photograph supplied by *Time* magazine for a portrait Neel would paint for its cover (August 13, 1970). These women all took part, either directly or indirectly, in staging the Second Coming of Alice Neel. They were repaid, at worst, by weirdly Valkyrian documentation (*Bella Abzug* [1976]) or, at best, by provocative divination (*Mary D. Garrard* [1977]). Some, like Ellen Johnson, even got a portrait that was as peculiarly, eccentrically individual as its subject.

In the late 1970s and early 1980s Neel's production slowed down. She managed to generate a few tender portraits of art-world men, like the Fluxus artist Geoffrey Hendricks and his partner Brian Busack, and the French video artist Michel Auder. The year before her death, in 1983, she painted a heartbreaking portrait of the art historian and critic Meyer Schapiro. She had first painted Schapiro in 1947, in a deliberately naïve style that recalls the work of her WPA days. And yet, examine the eyes: they are big enough to really *see*. Look at the lips: they are parted to ease on the deluge of words that wants to spill out. Look at the hands: they are trying to say what words cannot. Then fast-forward to 1983, and there he is in Neel's barrel-backed chair. It is not one of Neel's great portraits, but it is an inspired depiction. Perhaps a photograph could have produced the same emotional effect, but a photograph, with all of its chemical verisimilitude, has yet to achieve the expressiveness of paint. Schapiro is diminished, but there is an eloquence in what has been lost. His face is eagerly awaiting the punch line that Neel has suspended in order to sustain his perfect expression. He is waiting for her to finish a story that will have no ending. In Neel's late portrait of Meyer Schapiro, one sees a sitter and an artist in perfect alignment. It is a beautiful painting, not because it is beautifully painted but because it is beautifully conceived. That is the wonder of Neel's artistry. Unlike most of Warhol's portraits, Neel's depiction of Schapiro is not flattery but rather painting, and it reveals all the virtues and flaws of which the medium is capable. Even more than Neel's audacious nude self-portrait, painted in 1980 at the age of eighty, her portrait of Schapiro is an illumination of all the wisdom and peril of old age. In her imaging of Meyer Schapiro, Neel achieved the ultimate self-portrait. Look into his, or their, eyes. They have seen the world.

Alice Neel, ed. Ann Temkin (Philadelphia: Philadelphia Museum of Art, 2000), 53–65.

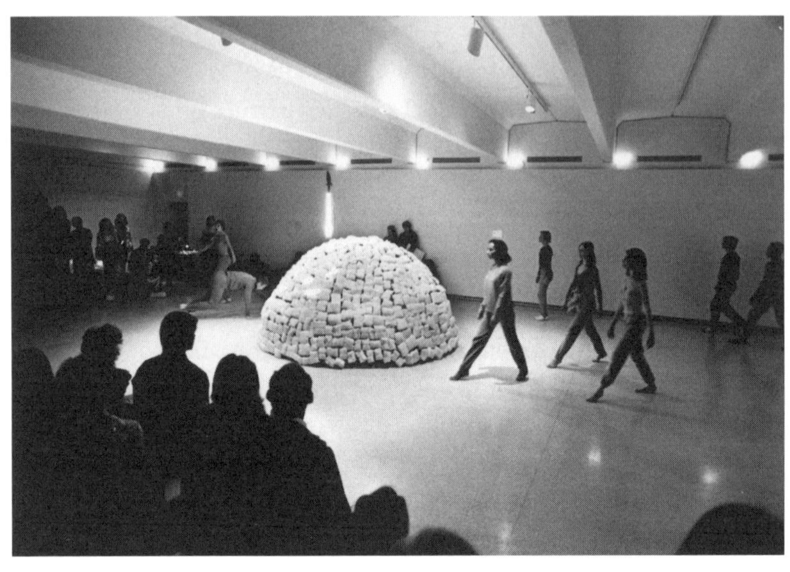

Merce Cunningham Dance Company performing *Canfield* in the exhibition
Mario Merz, Walker Art Center, Minneapolis, 1972
Photograph by James Klosty

260

Introduction: Zero to Infinity

(with Frances Morris)

The phrase *arte povera* first appeared in a text authored by a twenty-seven-year-old art critic named Germano Celant to accompany his exhibition *Arte povera e IM Spazio* at Genoa's Galleria La Bertesca in September 1967. It occurred in the text's last sentence, which also concludes Celant's discussion of a work by Emilio Prini, a young Genovese artist who had never before exhibited. Prini was one of six artists selected by Celant to populate what he called "the real terrain of Arte Povera"; the others were Alighiero Boetti, Luciano Fabro, Jannis Kounellis, Giulio Paolini, and Pino Pascali.[1] All but Prini had a diversity of exhibited work behind them, but at that moment, in the autumn of 1967, all shared a crystalline understanding of the marriage of concept and materials.[2]

Two months later, in the November–December issue of *Flash Art*, Celant issued a manifesto that would forever link him to Arte Povera (and a group of artists who exemplified his ideals of artistic production at the time). In the article "Arte Povera: Notes for a Guerrilla War," there is a brief analysis of a work by Fabro that captures the essence of the larger discussion: "We are conditioned in such a way that we are not able to see a floor, a corner, or an everyday space. Fabro suggests a rediscovery of the floor, the corner, or the beam that joins the floor and ceiling of a room. He is not concerned with satisfying the system. He wants to dissect it."[3] Celant also used the essay to expand his field of artists. To the six selected for the Genoa exhibition, he added another six: Giovanni Anselmo, Piero Gilardi, Mario Merz, Gianni Piacentino, Michelangelo Pistoletto, and Gilberto Zorio. (Over the next four years, four additional artists would intermittently occupy the terrain of Arte Povera as well: Pier Paolo Calzolari, Mario Ceroli, Marisa Merz, and Giuseppe Penone.)[4]

Supporting Celant's efforts to identify, if not define, a new generation of Italian artists was a remarkable infrastructure composed of journals, critics, curators, and dealers. In addition to publications such as *Domus* and *Flash Art*, there were *Bit*, *Data*, and NAC (*Notiziario arte contemporanea*), based in Milan, and *Marcatrè* and *Qui arte contemporanea*, based in Rome. The critic and protofeminist Carla Lanzi was forcefully recasting the traditional relationship between artist and critic to create a more synchronous, porous continuum. In her critical masterwork, *Autoritratto* (Self-portrait; 1969), Lanzi wove together the voices of two generations of Italian artists with her own to achieve an intellectual density that might best be described as orchestral. *Con temp l'azione*, an exhibition curated by Daniela Palazzoli, brought together three Turinese commercial galleries, literally uniting them with a map of thread running through the city's streets. In response to the new artistic practice, the dealers Gian Enzo Sperone and Fabio Sargentini moved from traditional gallery spaces to challenging, industrially scaled environments.[5] The collector Marcello Rumma organized and sponsored a trio of annual exhibitions in Amalfi; the final one, curated by Celant in 1968, truly sought to dismantle the barricades between art and life. As far from the centers of artistic productivity and commerce as Italy may have seemed at the time, it was a remarkably energized and volatile creative environment.[6]

In June of 1970 Celant curated his epic, contextualizing exhibition *Conceptual Art, Arte Povera, Land Art* at Turin's Galleria Civica d'Arte.[7] By then many of the artists associated with Arte Povera had already embarked on an ambitious international itinerary. In 1969 they were well represented in the influential group exhibitions *Op losse schroeven: Situaties en cryptostructuren* (On loose screws: Situations and cryptostructures), organized by Wim Beeren for the Stedelijk in Amsterdam, and *Live in Your Head: When Attitudes Become Form*, organized by Harald Szeemann, which debuted at the Kunsthalle Bern and subsequently traveled to Germany and Great Britain. In the United States, Pistoletto had been the subject of a solo exhibition at the Walker Art Center in Minneapolis as early as 1966; in 1969 Zorio appeared in group exhibitions at both the Leo Castelli Gallery (with Anselmo) and the Solomon R. Guggenheim Museum in New York. In May of 1970 Fabro, Kounellis, Mario Merz, Pistoletto, and Zorio were represented in *Between Man and Matter*, an exhibition curated by Yusuke Nakahara, which toured the cities of Tokyo, Nagoya, and Fukuoka. A month before Celant's exhibition opened in Turin, Jean-Christophe Ammann curated *Processi di pensiero visualizzati: Junge italienische Avantgarde* (Visualized thought processes: The young Italian avant-garde) at the Kunstmuseum Luzern, which focused almost exclusively on the Arte Povera impulse.

Clearly, Celant's manifesto had turned into something big enough to cast a shadow. Then, with *Conceptual Art, Arte Povera, Land Art*, he married his creation to the world. Paternal duties discharged, he was ready to move on, to leave Arte Povera to the historical past. It was, after all, not only the beginning of a new decade but also the end of one of the most tumultuous of the century. In retrospect, Celant stated: "Certainly influenced by the position of Carla Lanzi, who in those years had advocated the search for a private and personal identity, I told the artists that I was fed up with the label—which left little room for other languages, such as music and dance, architecture and design—and I believed it important to deal with their work individually, at this point." By the time that all of the artists whose surnames started with *P* (other than Pascali, who had died after a motorcycle accident in 1968) were represented in Kynaston McShine's legendary exhibition *Information*, at the Museum of Modern Art in New York, in September 1970, Arte Povera was hooked up to a respirator. In May 1971 Celant pulled the plug: "When the Munich Kunstraum organized their 1971 exhibition [*Arte Povera: 13 italienische Künstler*], I requested that the title of the show should not be 'Arte Povera,' but the names of the individual artists. My request was not accepted by the director, or by the [artists], so I decided to take a stand. I wrote a catalogue essay (which also appeared in *Domus*) in which I asserted that the label 'Arte Povera' must go, so that each artist could make the most of his own singularity."[8]

The organizers of the Munich exhibition also attempted to enlarge the Arte Povera field by adding three artists not previously included in the roster: Gino De Dominicis, Vettor Pisani, and Salvo. Thus, while Celant was attempting to put an end to it, others were advancing his former position and attempting to expand its construct. Ten of Celant's *famiglia* of artists were included. Despite this minor meddling with the selection of artists (and, of course, the disregard for Celant's wishes as to the exhibition's title), it remains singularly impressive that, even in the heart of Bavaria, Celant's creation was honored in his own language; it had not been translated into *Arme Kunst* but remained carapaced in its subtly untranslatable Italian.

For Celant, however, it was clearly time to move on; Arte Povera was no longer action itself, as he had envisioned, but rather an echoing chain of completed actions. Ironically, the Munich exhibition was the most dematerialized, anti-object manifestation of Arte Povera yet realized. Of the thirteen artists, only six showed three-dimensional work. Another six contributed either photographic documentation of previous work or photographs of completed actions; one, Prini, although present during installation, exhibited nothing. Clearly, this does not sound like a group of children intent on defiling the values of the father. Nonetheless, the self-referential historicization of artistic practice and the fetishization of the photographic document in the Munich exhibition were symptoms of the kind of passive malaise more often found in an older organism.

Over the next thirteen years Arte Povera wafted through the art world like a scent without a source. Then, suddenly, in 1984 it was spectacularly back at Turin's most glamorous architectural eccentricity, the

Mole Antonelliana. The reappearance was an extravaganza orchestrated by Celant, bearing a title, *Coerenza in coerenza* (Coherence in coherence), which, in its vagueness, completely sidestepped any issues of past politics or present familial tensions. Twelve artists were invited to participate, and with this invitation the chisel bit into the stone of history. One no longer had to worry about where to place Ceroli, Gilardi, Piacentino, or Prini; they were eliminated from the resurrection. Writing on the exhibition, Celant stated, "When I used the term 'Arte Povera' once more some fifteen years later it had become historical, and seen from the right perspective, it worked once again as a 'conflict' for the art of the 1980s and its return to the order of the day."[9] (Here it is helpful to recall that the art of the early to mid-1980s was, in Italy—and in the marketing centers of New York, Cologne, and Paris—something called the Transavanguardia, which was the brainchild of Achille Bonito Oliva, a curator and critic from southern Italy, who had populated his movement exclusively with Italian narrative painters of a new generation.) Celant's exhibition at the Mole has to be seen as more than a sentimental reunion. What he installed was literally a skyscraper of provocation and a reclamation of lost intellectual property. *Coerenza in coerenza* was a bravura manifestation of a new version of Arte Povera in which the curator and artists collaborated to produce an exhibition that might best be labeled environmental theater.

In January 1985 another incarnation of the exhibition (now flatly but historically titled *Del Arte Povera a 1985* [From Arte Povera to 1985]) opened at the Palacio de Cristal and Palacio de Velázquez in Madrid. Here (most notably in the exquisite Beaux-Arts conservatory in the Retiro gardens), Celant installed something that was toe-curlingly beautiful but as wildly overaestheticized as Marlene Dietrich in Josef von Sternberg's *Blonde Venus*. In its transcendent second coming, Arte Povera was perhaps becoming too cosmetically enhanced to allow for a glimpse of its original, highly individual, rigorously articulated, liberatingly ugly bone structure.

The last of the trilogy of exhibitions took place at P.S. 1, the Institute for Art and Urban Resources, Long Island City, New York, in October 1985. Like the two prior presentations, it mixed work from more than twenty years, combining the old and the new in relationships that challenged and invigorated (and occasionally obfuscated) any art-historical narrative. *The Knot: Arte Povera at P.S. 1*, as the exhibition was titled, seemingly exploded out of nowhere and changed everything. New York was then in the throes of a prolonged flirtation with inter-national painting. Suddenly the appearance of all that Italian sculptural muscle made the painting look as if it should be parked on a fainting couch.

A fascinating caveat in Alanna Heiss's preface to the catalogue more than hints at the tensions that surrounded the exhibition and, by exten-sion, the selection of works in it. It is worth quoting because it lays bare the ultimate dilemma of Arte Povera, its artists, and its creator.

Although presented as a group, these artists, in fact, do not represent one. Their divergent interests and pursuits make them more dissimilar than similar. Of course, through sharing mutual exhibition experiences, they know each other. Some are, indeed, friends. But it would be a serious error to regard these twelve artists as a tight group dedicated to proselytizing the message of *arte povera*.

I suspect that several of them would deny the appropriateness of their inclusion in this or any other group defining a movement. Several would, most likely, assure you that they do not understand the meaning of the term *arte povera*. The problem of categorizing artists in any movement is genuine; the same thematic inadequacies pursue Pop Art and Minimal Art.

For instance, there are artists not represented in this exhibition who might be considered by some critics as historically relevant, impossible to omit. To *arte povera* enthusiasts, the presence of some might be considered tangential. The obvious and primary reasons why these artists are included in this exhibition is simply because they were invited to participate by the curator.[10]

There is a lot going on in these paragraphs. First, there is a denial of any group identity or aesthetic kinship among the exhibiting artists. Then there is the distancing between some of those artists and Arte Povera, as well as the suggestion that "*arte povera* enthusiasts" might take issue with the selection of artists. Finally there is the conclusion, which quite clearly states that an invitation from Celant is all the artists have in common. It sounds more like the setup for a country house mystery than an exhibition, but it does accurately mirror the classic psychological conflict of wanting to be included while resenting the need for inclusion. It also explains the exhibition's occasionally confusing conflation of old and new work in which the historical context (*Arte Povera at P.S. 1*) could be perceived as being in conflict with the contemporary exhibition (*The Knot*).

So, eighteen years after Arte Povera's first incarnation in Genoa, the twelve artists were together again. And where were they? They were at P.S. 1 in Long Island City, across the East River from Manhattan. They had come from a conservatory in Madrid and an architectural folly in Turin. To a number of the artists (and their dealers), they might as well have been back in Genoa. Everything that would have signified a definitive end to marginality and regionalism (or exoticism) lay on the other side of the river, at the Museum of Modern Art or, next best, the Guggenheim Museum.

While much was made of the appropriateness of P.S. 1's idiosyncratic architecture for the work, it was hard to ignore that the artists were, at midcareer, occupying an alternative space. Why? Was it because they were again united in the service of Arte Povera? Aside from Heiss's distancing preface, the only voice in the catalogue belongs to Celant, who, while recontextualizing, was still providing the context. Although it was an enormously influential exhibition that caught the imagination of several generations of non-Italian artists, *The Knot* begged as many questions as it answered. That the exhibition was essentially twelve mini-retrospectives further confused what was truly original, what was adaptive reuse, what was installation, and what was arrangement.

Now, as we write, another fifteen years have passed, and the influence of the artists associated with Arte Povera continues to grow and inform the cultural landscape. So too does the label Arte Povera continue to exoticize the work and problematize its assimilation into the canon of modernism. Arte Povera appears, in its origins, related most overtly to conceptualism and minimalism, but while there are superficial parallels with those tendencies, it is also inherently Italian. There is a quotational fluidity in Arte Povera that allows absolute compositional simplicity to coexist harmoniously with cultural citation. The radical early work remains stunningly fresh and, in its reductivist rigor, still almost shockingly ahead of its time. Yet it is also work that has no fear of narrative implication, cultural inflection, or humanist discourse. Understanding Arte Povera's essential difference from any parallel zeitgeist is key to understanding its importance to the art of our time. To experience the breadth and depth of that contribution, it is necessary to start at the beginning; that is the intent of the present exhibition.

Reflecting on *When Attitudes Become Form*, Charles Harrison, who organized its showing at London's Institute of Contemporary Arts in September 1969, recalls more than twenty descriptive labels paraded at the time for the new international tendency documented in the exhibition.[11] Arte Povera stands apart from the rest, both in its stubbornly foreign character and in its incapacity to suggest stylistic or formal traits, as do many of the other contemporary terms cited by Harrison, such as anti-form, earthworks, systems art, land art, and organic matter art. Unlike these other terms, Arte Povera suggests both cultural specificity and conceptual breadth, emerging from a distinctly Italian context but encompassing more than a formal or stylistic approach.

To revisit Arte Povera as a national school, within the short time frame from its genesis in the early 1960s to its dissolution almost a decade later, is therefore to allow more complex, local readings to emerge. Within these local readings many voices and dialogues can be heard: dialogues with a preceding generation of Italian artists as well as with the artists' peers abroad, and also dialogues with materials and processes, with the physical and metaphysical dimensions of life, and with history, the history of art, and the history of ideas.

Arte Povera has always resisted translation and been equally resistant to definition. Even Celant often found it easier to frame its meanings within a series of negations. And just as he never settled on a fixed quota of artists for the group, so he continually restaged its rhetoric in key texts that punctuate its history. At first, he trumpeted Arte Povera's transgressive political dimension in the manifesto-like "Arte Povera: Notes for a Guerrilla War" (1967), then he moved the agenda along in his 1969 book *Art Povera: Conceptual, Actual or Impossible Art?*, in which he repositioned the Italian artists within an international context of extreme individualism and experimentation outside all systems and institutions. The book was published simultaneously in Italian and English, with the *e* dropped, oddly, from Arte Povera in the title of the English version.

Subtitles are designed to elucidate. Celant's 1969 subtitle proposed, in an interrogative manner, a wider international geography for his selection of artists. For the present exhibition *Zero to Infinity* was chosen as the main title to denote a field of radical, unbounded experimentation, while the subtitle—*Arte Povera 1962–1972*—locates this within a tight geographic sphere bounded by Rome, Turin, Genoa, and Milan. In its reference to Roland Barthes's notion of "degree zero," the title also evokes a laboratory situation in which speculative research dominated the agenda.[12] Consciousness of the fact that these artists were operating on the margins of the known, working toward unforeseen ends, is conveyed in the multiple ways zero and infinity—as symbols, images, words, and concepts—figure in their art of the time.

Zero to Infinity defines a situation in which young Italian artists of the early 1960s were able to work in a free and speculative way. The slate had, of course, as Carolyn Christov-Bakargiev argues,[13] been wiped clean by an immediately preceding generation of Italian artists, foremost among them Alberto Burri, Lucio Fontana, and Piero Manzoni, each of whom contributed to a reconsideration of the relationship between art and life and of the role of the object. Arte Povera thereby emerged out of, as much as in opposition to, indigenous Italian art. This development in Italy paralleled a broader international tendency (in the United States, the trajectory was through Pop art to minimalism and conceptual art) in which the supremacy of painting was challenged from both the theoretical side and the practical side as artists found in sculpture an extraordinarily rich field of exploration.

In Italy dissemination of the antirationalist writings of American philosopher John Dewey, as well as the widely read and discussed writings of Umberto Eco, were among key sources validating, while not theorizing, new approaches. As Corrina Criticos explains,[14] Dewey and Eco endorsed experimentation, complexity, and diversity, underwriting an art made without preconceptions (zero) and without the limitations of ideological or theoretical systems (infinity). This open and fluid approach did not deny history, but rather allowed artists to occupy a position from which history, including the history of painting, could be renegotiated.

The lack of a programmatic theoretical base allowed the artists to respond with ease to more cerebral approaches abroad. But however close the encounter, they refused to speak the same language. The gulf with minimalism was apparent. While American minimalist artists explored new forms and materials for obviously formal and symbolic reasons, in Arte Povera the relationship between form and material is always elegant but rarely straightforward. That the basic cube provided so many of them (Boetti, Fabro, Paolini, Pascali, and Pistoletto) with a relevant formal device—rendered as an infinite cube of air by Pistoletto, as a wall-slung cube of earth by Pascali, or as an inhabitable man-sized three-dimensional canvas by Fabro—demonstrates how this eclecticism might engage in an eloquent and occasionally humorous dialogue with more systematically restrained practices.

Underlying this experimental approach was an insatiable appetite for new materials and a restless desire to explore new processes. Art could be made from anything: living things, products of the earth, and industrially produced materials, as well as immaterial substances such as moisture, sound, and energy. Art could be made in any way. It could be painted, handcrafted, industrially produced, gestured, spoken, written, acted, filmed, dreamed. It might exist as an object for time immemorial or as a momentary, time-based action. Indeed, few of the artists in *Zero to Infinity* limited their practice to the production of discrete objects.

Zero is a beginning, the starting point in a process. For Mario Merz it precedes the starting point of the Fibonacci series, a recursive number sequence, just as the concept of infinity posits a continuously advancing endpoint. The Fibonacci sequence is derived from a mathematical problem involving the pattern of reproduction in rabbits, published in the early thirteenth century by the Italian mathematician Leonardo of Pisa. In the nineteenth century, scientists began to discover similar patterns in nature; for example, in the spirals of sunflower heads, in pinecones, and in animal horns. From around 1970 Merz employed the sequence as a metaphor, not only for systems of proliferation in nature but also for other patterns in life. He was enchanted by the infinite variety of numbers, and his exploration of the Fibonacci sequence opened up a new way of working consonant with his passion for the mysterious interconnectedness of the natural and the man-made, which found resonance in his earlier work in the primary architectural structure of the igloo.

Beginnings in time, evoking the point at which growth occurs, like the center of a ripple when a pebble is thrown into a pond, also inform

Giuseppe Penone's work, starting with his first experiments in natural determination. In his extensive photographic series documenting the surface of his body, zero is the point from which the whorls of the fingerprint unfurl, denoting our uniqueness as individuals and remaining throughout our lives. In his series of *Alberi* (Trees), Penone inverted Merz's exploration of proliferation or growth, progressively stripping back the layers of wood from around the knots evident in the flat planes of a machine-cut plank to reveal the younger natural core beneath, literally returning the man-made to nature.

For Pier Paolo Calzolari, zero is the point at which moisture freezes, a point suspended in time, the moment of epiphany. Calzolari began making ice works in 1967–68, employing an electrical refrigerating device to frost the surfaces of a number of his works. Working also with lead, mercury, and neon, as well as living materials such as moss and tobacco leaves, he was fascinated by states of contrast and metamorphosis. The endless interconnectedness of beginnings and endings is evoked in his *Zerorose* (1970), both an utterance and an image on the gallery wall. Infinity is literally figured by Calzolari as an intertwining symbol of tobacco leaves with lead in an endless dialogue between naturally occurring materials and their transformed state.

The early practices of many of the artists seem to function as starting points, rigorously pared-down experiments in which simple "what if?" questions are posed without preconceptions. Many of Alighiero Boetti's early Arte Povera works came from primary investigations of shapes and materials: stacking strips of wood into a Plexiglas cube, layering hundreds of identical paper doilies to create a vertical column, massing bundles of kindling sticks into a thick and richly colored carpet. Each work seems to derive density, mass, and strength from multiple, fragile components. Interested in ordinary and everyday materials and humble repeated gestures such as stacking, layering, weaving, and tracing, Boetti created an extraordinarily rich body of work with the simplest of means. This rigorous reductionism found its own endpoint, its own zero degree, in the large iron-framed glass window he made in 1969, *Niente da vedere, niente da nascondere* (Nothing to see, nothing to hide). Placed against the gallery wall, it bore no traces of craft or artistry and framed nothing, in an absolute reversal of the notion of painting as a window onto the world.

The conceptual rigor of Boetti's endeavors is matched by the very different early work of Luciano Fabro, whose experiments in glass and steel also addressed primary questions of the perception and nature of geometry and space. In *Buco* (Hole; 1963), Fabro employed a sheet of glass obscured with both transparent and reflective elements to demonstrate that perception involved both direct sensation and mediated experience: in viewing the work, it is impossible to look through the glass without simultaneously seeing what is reflected. He went on during 1967 and 1968 to make a series of works, each of which is subtitled *Tautologia* (Tautology), including *Pavimento–tautologia* (Floor–tautology; 1967). These are simple formal or conceptual propositions that draw attention to nothing so much as themselves, inverting the logic of representation. Fabro's increasingly eclectic investigations of different materials, both impoverished and astonishingly sumptuous, always began with the substance itself and its properties, including its physical, historical, and social dimensions. He employed the banalized "boot" form of the Italian landmass, for example, as a template on which to stage a series of enigmatic and compelling conversations between different materials.

Piero Gilardi, the most self-consciously political of the artists associated with Arte Povera, undertook a different kind of speculative research. His *Tappeti natura* (Nature carpets) were highly realistic simulations of natural surfaces made of synthetic materials. They were designed for mass consumption, being made "on the roll" and available for sale by the square meter.

Many of the works produced at this time were small-scale or ephemeral, like Gilardi's almost Franciscan *Pettine e sandali* (Comb and sandals;

1967). There were few of the grand gestures with which we now asso-ciate the later practices of many of these artists. That Marisa Merz's eclectic works (tiny knitted shoes and words; a live conversation, trans-mitted from the cockpit of a light aircraft; a strangely intestinal hang-ing work installed at the Galleria Sperone and later at the Piper Club in Turin in 1967) were even noticed alongside the more declamatory practices of Jannis Kounellis or of her husband, Mario Merz, testifies to a situation in which the democracy afforded materials was extended to include the scope or scale of projects. It also testifies to the compel-ling and poetic aura of Marisa Merz's work. Her ephemeral performance at Ostia Lido in 1968, recorded in photographs by Claudio Abate, in-volved laying rolled blankets bound in wire along the beach facing the incoming tide. The gesture evoked, through metaphor, the mysterious conductive and insulating properties of materials, the shelter of the domestic realm, and the enigmatic and ultimately consuming power of nature.[15]

Emilio Prini, who produced some of the most conceptual and de-materialized work associated with Arte Povera, was absorbed in experi-ments with space and time, in a quest to reconnect aesthetic experience with a durational experience of lived time. In *L'USA usa* (The USA uses; 1969), a tape recorder continuously recorded its own sound until it broke down, while in a work in progress of the previous year, a camera was used continuously until it rendered itself inoperable. From early on, Prini was as concerned with exploring hypothetical projects as he was with realizing finished work, and the erasing of work or the covering of its traces was often more important than its production. In 1967–68 he made a series of *Ipotesi d'azione* (Hypothetical actions), which existed only as written lists. He also made a series of actual physical gestures, or *Azioni tipo* (Typical actions), which he recorded photographically. Subsequent installations of these vast photographs, however, strewn or stacked on the floor and held down by lead weights, might obscure as much as reveal them. Interested in the moment of action and percep-

274

tion, Prini made a number of works, including *Asta curbata* (Bent pole; 1967), in which the viewer's attention is directed away from the idea of a work of art to an awareness of the basic dimensions of space, and thus to experience itself.

For others, such as Gilberto Zorio, infinity was rooted in the alchemical, elemental, and metamorphic power of materials and their mercurial effect on one another, whether they are chemicals reacting to moisture or substances or phenomena—including, for example, sound—transformed through an encounter with another. For Giovanni Anselmo the mysterious force fields that influence the rising of the sun, our earthbound weight, and our verticality gave rise to works of extreme formal intensity exploring the magnetic pull of our environment or the energy locked inside inert matter or invested in materials through the actions of man. In Anselmo's work infinity could evoke the endless passage of time, inscribed in a block of granite or demonstrated in a projected beam of light.

Infinite, also, seemed the potential for inventing new strategies. Witness the chameleon-like practices of a number of key artists. In his short career Pino Pascali managed to produce at least half a dozen highly distinctive and equally compelling bodies of work. Michelangelo Pistoletto's conceptually coherent passage from painting to sculpture via his mirror paintings and Plexiglas tableaux finally erupted onto the home ground of Arte Povera with his *Oggetti in meno* (Minus objects), a series of independent, self-contained propositions, hand-built objects made from materials without value, such as cardboard and newspaper. Many of these works enter into dialogue with Pop, while ultimately denying its transatlantic language. Each artist—with the exception of Paolini, whose adherence to a singular quest is unique and remarkable in this context—developed a "signature" style slowly, and the landscape is littered with parallel and intersecting paths as artists such as Boetti and Pistoletto worked apparently in conversation with each other.

Art in general and painting in particular make up the subject and content of Giulio Paolini's work. His art draws our attention to the material properties of painting, its systems for representing space through perspective, its two-dimensional nature, and its power to generate meaning through representation. An exploration of the nature of painting also underlies the early work of Jannis Kounellis. After making large canvases featuring letters and numbers, elementary symbols that might have been taken from billboards and street signs, Kounellis moved away from the constraints and conventions of mark-making on a flat surface, producing paintings from discarded coal sacks stretched over bed frames. By 1967 he had begun working with installation, assemblage, sculpture, and performance, employing elements such as music, fire, and live animals. This expansive vocabulary allowed him to range very widely in his work, exploring mythology and history as well as the contemporary and the everyday.

Zero to Infinity begins with the earliest experimental works from this group. It ends not only as Celant abandoned Arte Povera to champion more radical modes of experimentation but also as mature styles became evident and a generation crystallized into individuals. When Szeemann organized Documenta 5 in 1972, he included many of the artists he had first brought to prominence in *When Attitudes Become Form*. The informal, experimental, and collegial atmosphere that underpinned the sprawling, fascinating, energized 1969 exhibition had given way to discrete bodies of work, shown under the subtitle "Individual Mythologies." Many of the artists had found dealers, and most were locked into solo exhibition strategies. Some had developed what would become lasting signature styles. Three decades later, it is understandably with some reluctance that a number of senior practitioners have endorsed this exhibition's return to zero, forgoing as it does their individual histories in favor of an examination of the laboratory period in which they emerged as artists. Growing out of an enormously fertile postwar culture and nurtured by an active and ambitious network of curators, dealers, and critics, Arte Povera propelled Italy with lightning speed from the periphery to the center of an increasingly international art scene. If one examines the trajectory of its early years, it becomes clear that Arte Povera can no longer be understood as a term denoting impoverishment, either of materials or process. Instead it denotes the possibility, which these artists grasped, of making art without theory and beyond convention, from zero to infinity.

Zero to Infinity: Arte Povera 1962–1972, ed. Richard Flood and Frances Morris (Minneapolis: Walker Art Center; London: Tate Modern, 2001), 9–20.

Tear Me Apart, One Letter at a Time

Collage has been kicking around for centuries. It has most often fallen into the category of anecdotal, perhaps as a sentimental *billet-doux* or maidenly remembrance. In the early twentieth century, collage found a new life as something torn and cut from newspapers, magazines, cigarette packages, theater programs, posters, and musical scores. The results were no less anecdotal, but the subject matter (whether abstract or figurative) became elevated as it served to liberate compositional formats (Pablo Picasso) and political realities (John Heartfield). Collage gradually became identified with such artistic practices as cubism, dada, and surrealism. Its strong graphic presence bled into the world of design, where its influence grew and flowed into architecture, literature, and music. The creation of collage is one of this and the last century's great popular, international pastimes. Anyone can make it and most do.

As a mass phenomenon, collage coincided with the rise of radio and, later, television. The world has gradually been transformed into a series of nonlinear opportunities dominated by sound, motion, and space. Traveling through this expanded landscape of moving images, audio alternatives, and the insistently transformative internet can be a delirious safari: eBay fire sales, fast breaking news, YouTube provocations, celebrity sex tapes, beheadings, Wikipedia entries, and Al Jazeera headlines. On the highways of the world, radio stations manically switch between rock anthems, bully pulpits, psychotic phone-ins, and traffic and weather reports. iPods are embedded with collages that keep the public on its treadmills and Exercycles, riding on buses and jogging out of Shady Rest into the sunset. The most basic playground for contemporary collage is the human body where tattoos of crucifixes vie for space with Maori totems, and Our Lady of Guadalupe rises from roiling oceans brimming with raging dragons and busty mermaids. In literature, William Burroughs, the master of the cut-up, has been followed by wild boys from Iran, Chile, and Japan who mold hip-hop and rap into word tornados that spin across the globe.

The future of collage feels secure. Newspapers and websites are filled with juxtapositions and extreme abutments that simmer with tension. Attempts to interlink patches of boldface type result in a sort of cultural Tourette syndrome. Nothing really lines up; there are no helpful parallels to be discovered. Everything is whacked together in fragments that temporarily cohere but cannot hold fast. The density of the information becomes puzzlingly abstract while understanding takes a backseat to the aesthetics of arrangement. Headlines appear pasted together like ransom notes and truth is taken hostage. Images are edited, manipulated, scrambled, and reassembled to serve a multiplicity of motives. In a plague of plagiarism and autobiographical invention, the value of authorship grows weak as truth is woven into a collage of fiction and preassigned fact. The creative highs that come from a construction of fractures create a public of junkies who simply become another element in the field. We are all changing parts in the *respirant* collage.

Collage: The Unmonumental Picture (New York: New Museum, 2007), 8–9.

Not About Mel Gibson

The dismal drum of Huichilobos sounded again, accompanied by conches, horns, and trumpet-like instruments. It was a terrifying sound, and when we looked at the tall cue from which it came we saw our comrades who had been captured in Cortes' defeat being dragged up the steps to be sacrificed. When they had hauled them up to a small platform in front of the shrine where they kept their accursed idols we saw them put plumes on the heads of many of them; and then they made them dance with a sort of fan in front of Huichilobos. Then after they had danced the papas laid them down on their backs on some narrow stones of sacrifice and, cutting open their chests, drew out their palpitating hearts which they offered to the idols before them. Then they kicked the bodies down the steps, and the Indian butchers who were waiting below cut off their arms and legs and flayed their faces, which they afterwards prepared like glove leather, with their beards on, and kept them for their drunken festivals. Then they ate their flesh with a sauce of peppers and tomatoes.

BERNAL DÍAZ, *THE CONQUEST OF NEW SPAIN*

I blame it all on Mel Gibson. The American continent would be free of human sacrifice and ritual cannibalism if he hadn't dreamed it up for *Apocalypto*. Things wouldn't be out of control in the Middle East if he hadn't started flinging the guilt and violence around in *The Passion of the Christ*. Think about it—America would be free of the Bush presidency if Gibson hadn't repelled the British in *The Patriot*. He won the pivotal battle of Ia Drang in Vietnam for *We Were Soldiers*, and was around for the fall of Sukarno in *The Year of Living Dangerously*. Sure, he performed one act of decency when he bestowed freedom on the Scots in *Brave-heart*, but that hardly compensates for his psychotic invention of bad history.

Bad history is that which evolves from tampering with, denying, or replacing the tentatively real with something else that is probably less real. Gibson's bad history is part of a much larger conspiracy whereby the public is seduced into a narcotizing dysfunction that strips away its fragile ability to fully separate the life it is living from its mediated life as an audience member. In the twenty-first century, everything exists simultaneously in an unending tumble cycle. Society is victimized by the nonemphatic fluidity with which the media cuts from Britney Spears's money shots to the Iraqi quagmire, from a crippled global environment to pandemics drifting around the world like tumbleweed, from genocide in Darfur to famine in North Korea, from rising crimes against children to *American Idol*, from the spread of AIDS to Madonna's deus-ex-machina version of adoption. Reality is a collage composed of whatever grabs our attention, and the competition is limitless. People lunge heedlessly into traffic with the *Survivor* soundtrack playing on their iPod. Others sit in restaurants alone with their mobiles or stalk the web in search of meaning. People want their distractions instantly and use their ears and mouths as sockets. Even television is prospering because it has learned how to graft the identities of the creatures it broadcasts onto those who view it. The real and the doppelgänger coexist; that's the twenty-first century's Manichaean malady.

I solemnly swear that all the houses and stockades in the lake were full of heads and corpses. We could not walk without treading on the bodies and heads of dead Indians. I have read about the destruction of Jerusalem, but I do not think the mortality was greater than here in Mexico, where most of the warriors who had crowded in from all the provinces and subject towns had died. As I have said, the dry land and the stockades were piled with corpses. Indeed the stench was so bad that no one could endure it, and for that reason each of us captains returned to his camp after Guatemoc's capture; even Cortes was ill from the odours which assailed his nostrils and from headaches during those days in Tlatelolco.

BERNAL DÍAZ, THE CONQUEST OF NEW SPAIN

I blame Mel Gibson's father, Hutton Gibson, for spreading bad history from the pulpit by calling the Holocaust a "fiction." Iranian president Mahmoud Ahmadinejad has also tried to erase from memory the millions of Jews and Gypsies and gays and other inconvenient people murdered during WWII. Together, as Catholic and Muslim fundamentalists, they show how the power of prayer can obliterate memory. Mr. Gibson and President Ahmadinejad are simply examples of apocalyptic minimalists, and they exist quite nicely with the maximalists, such as those diviners who conjured Iraq's weapons of mass destruction to populate a strategy leading to war. Our world is very much like the empire of cosmetic surgery: remove the offending nose and add the pillowed lips to live the dream life behind the fantasy face. As the twenty-first century moves forward, it is being forced to barrel through masses of relative "truths," which only last as long as they are convenient. Because the public is willing to exist in a state of dangerous distraction, the inherent need for truth atrophies, and "truth" becomes an oratorical device, a sound bite, a lie. Such is the kingdom of the West.

Then there is the rest of the world. Obviously, Mel is out there seeping into Mongolia and Rwanda and Afghanistan and Haiti. No nation is strong enough to withstand the lure of unnecessary abundance, and Mel is a part of that. The ability to pause and reflect has been leveled by distracting dissonance in the West. It has disappeared elsewhere as well because life permits only immediate reactions or total closure. The statistics tell some of the story—as many as 655,000 civilian deaths in Iraq since the US-led coalition initiative began, over 300,000 deaths from AIDS in South Africa in 2005, some 400,000 killed in the Darfur genocide and another 2,000,000 displaced—but they don't tell of the huge suffocating weight that is the sum of these numbers, a weight that is capable of crushing what we understand as civilization. Of course, these numbers are always going to be discounted and denied by those who embrace bad history and shove the statistics into an editorial meat grinder. The political disregard of difficult facts is the major generator of dangerous assumptions. One of the first auguries of the twenty-first century was the destruction of the giant sixth-century Buddhas of Bamiyan in Afghanistan. As part of a rampage of cultural disremembering, the Taliban blew them up to rid the nation of its non-Islamic past. In the rubble of the exploded Buddhas is the century's first invitation to its ongoing orgy of bad history.

Humanism does not consist in saying: "No animal could have done what we have done," but in declaring: "We have refused what the beast within us willed to do, and we wish to discover Man wherever we discover that which seeks to crush him to the dust."

ANDRÉ MALRAUX, *THE VOICES OF SILENCE*

Making art in the early twenty-first century is just the same as making art in any other century, except for the money that coats everything like ash. It is accompanied by the creation of artist hierarchies where vanity and insecurity go hand in hand like the opposing strains of a Labradoodle. It is a nervous time, and artists respond to that. Some are clinging to nostalgia as if it were an antidote to SARS, some to technique, which has become the varnished mausoleum for "masterpieces." And nowadays there are masterpieces everywhere, racing into the marketplace like sperm to the womb. Paintings are, of course, where the masterpieces are most frequently identified, but they are also found in highly produced moving-image works, digitized photography, drawings, the lately rehabilitated art of collage, and occasionally sculpture, particularly if there are fabrication costs. (Not so long ago, it used to be enough for something to be "fabulous" or "brilliant.") What is good in an age of maximal distraction is that there is no time wasted waiting for a masterpiece to achieve connoisseurial consensus. Some blowhard just pronounces it so, and that's that. Well, maybe it helps if there is a carefully choreographed auction where a manipulated record is set and an art world riff on bad history commences as dollars, euros, yen, and rupees confirm the status of a masterpiece. But, really, the appellation has replaced the reality.

While the masterpiece syndrome is understandable in a time of acute instability, it does not respond to its time, just the market. Our time demands the anti-masterpiece. Things that are cobbled together, pushed and prodded into a state of suspended animation feel right. Stubby, brutish forms that know something of the world in which they are made tell the contemporary story. Works that appear hurled into uncomfortable, anxious relationships run parallel to life. Objects with knots of nerve endings reaching out to find a brain mirror the fugue states of everyday consciousness. The world is beset by volatility; objects that suggest something akin to an honest response to life help frame the questions that animate the culture. Life is also composed of grace notes, and when those notes become art, they lift our spirits through the modesty of their rendering. The materials used by many of today's artists are redeemed from the rubbish heap and are Franciscan in their simplicity. Extravagant gestures have given way to a handshake or a hug (maybe even a shrug). The best of the work defies a simple knee-jerk response because it tends to be conversational, it wants to slow the passer-by down for a chat. The work is not about delivering last words or winning a debate but about questioning everything from its formal properties to its place in the world.

ALBERT P. RYDER, QUOTED IN LLOYD GOODRICH, *ALBERT P. RYDER*

Beyond the masterpiece, there lies nothing but freedom. And, as we
learned from Kris Kristofferson, "Freedom's just another word for
nothing left to lose." Sculpture is one of the final frontiers for the artist
who truly wants to tempt fate—the artist who prefers to utilize the
carrot rather than chase it. From the very beginning, sculpture has
always rubbed shoulders with the real. Its association with religion and
personification has given it a totemic presence that complicates space
and viewer perception much more than any other medium. Sculpture
can often enhance or destabilize the received primacy of painting,
but the reverse is highly unlikely. In times of siege and flight, paintings
can be rolled or folded or disappeared in less conventional ways, as
suggested by Carolee Schneemann's literally stunning performance
Interior Scroll (1975). In the smoke of battle, sculpture is likely to be used
as a weapon, melted down, chopped up, sold for scrap, or simply hidden
in plain sight by virtue of its nature.

In the twenty-first century, the most genuinely new sculpture
appears in the guise of a Cold War agent subverting the situation behind
the Cor-Ten curtain. Outside of the white box, today's most innovative,
essential sculpture is testing all the limits. One of its strongest characteristics is the inherent ability to camouflage itself from any formal
hierarchy. Traditional sculptural materials (e.g., wood, marble, bronze,
steel) have sustained a long residency in the realm of the approved, the
salable, and the competitive. In its letter of agreement with the market,
the traditional can be Brobdingnagian, glitteringly reflective, seam-
lessly undulant, seductively touchable, purposefully haughty. However,
formalism and traditionalism have become elite and moribund, like

jewel-freighted dowagers struggling from the porte cochere to the limo, they are not in step with the pace of our time. What is immediately contemporary is sculpture that does its best to insinuate itself into the texture of the world. There isn't time or distance enough to perpetuate monuments. We live in a world of half-gestures where there is no definitive stance and the sands shift incessantly over a desert of evidential truth. Sculpture is now that thing that jams its foot in a door and scurries around looking for a comfortable corner from where the new becomes the inevitable. No absolutes are reliable and no hierarchies are consistent, so that which seems most a part of the world in its freshness, rawness, and anxiety trumps the autopsies of the acceptable and the negotiable. Sculpture is the medium that knows best how to live in the present and find the future.

Unmonumental: The Object in the 21st Century (London: Phaidon; New York: New Museum, 2007), 10–13.

Wool Gathering

Now he's against his own for.
For him the word is the way.
Yet there is no door.
Thus he saves all keys and compares them,
one is the same like the rest;
the rest are different like the one.
This one will open no door and let him in.
Inside he will receive words alien to thought...
GREGORY CORSO, FROM "AIR IS TO GO"[1]

There is a jazz/beat/punk rhythm in Christopher Wool's work, the constant sound of snapping fingers, the kind you hear from fans at the end of a Miles Davis drone or what comes tap-tapping out of a Gregory Corso poem. There's a fragmented consistency that is shadowboxing throughout his career, a consistency of dueling familiars, not quite a divided self so much as a self united by Pentecostal voices.

ACCEPTED INFORMATION
Materials:
stencils, paint rollers, tapestry rollers, silkscreens, spray paint on canvas, paper, aluminum
+ language, graffiti, transmittable viruses

The Shaker-like simplicity in the roll call of Wool's materials is suc-
cinctly in keeping with the burly elegance of the work. Here there are
no fetish props to accessorize a stage set of an artist's studio. All of it
has the economy of a commercial signage studio, which is appropriate
insofar as signs (and portents) are what the artist deals in.

NOTES ON THE WORK:

> *Visions! omens! hallucinations! miracles! ecstasies! gone down the*
> *American river!*
> *Dreams! adorations! illuminations! religions! the whole boatload of*
> *sensitive bullshit!*
> ALLEN GINSBERG, FROM "HOWL"[2]

Wool hasn't left much of the American angst and anger out of his art.
The terse staccato of his language—rushing between noir wiseguys,
Burma Shave teasers, punk rants, Lenny Bruce riffs, and zen smack
downs—is a mad, imploded sampler of rage, denial, and brutal pragmatism. Vowel-less paintings composed of letters such as "TRBL" and
"DRNK" are streamlined reminders of national and personal avoidance,
sandpapering away the content to achieve the narcotic that Martha
Rosler long ago termed "disinformation." Similarly, a phrase painting
like *HELTER HELTER* (1988) sidesteps the bloody sludge of Tate/
LaBianca in favor of something slightly more horrible, an innocent
phrase trailing intestinal miles of associative gore.

ACCEPTED ART HISTORICAL CONTEXT
Jackson Pollock, Andy Warhol
+ Kazuo Shiraga, León Ferrari, Cy Twombly

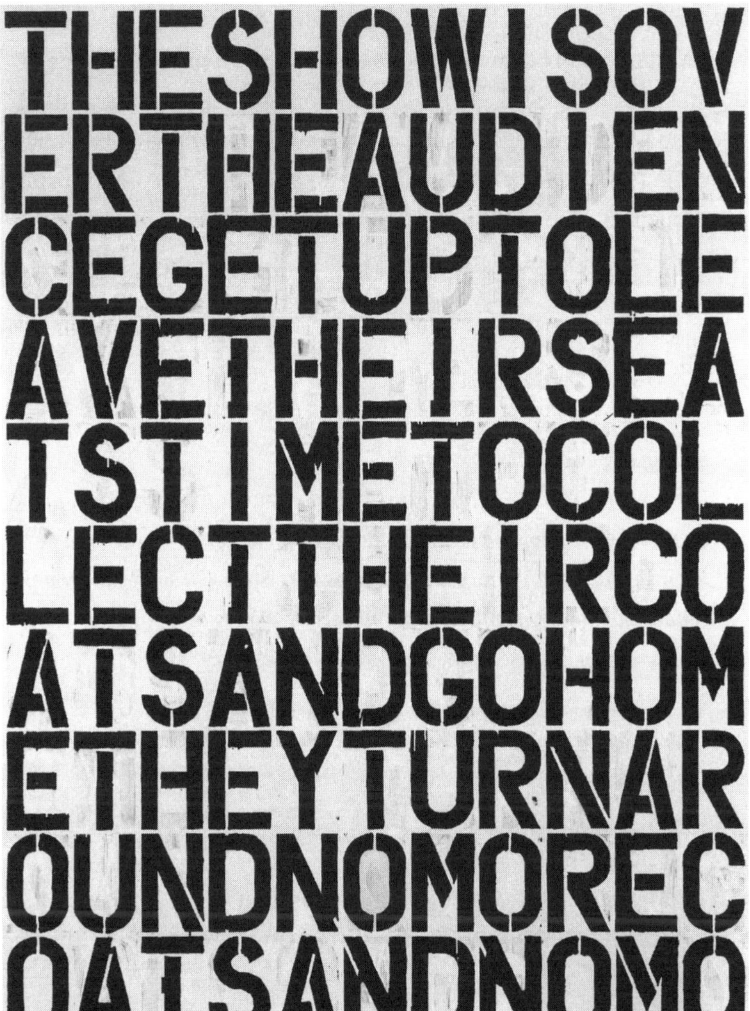

Christopher Wool, *Untitled*, 1990–91
Enamel on aluminum, 274.3 × 182.9 cm (108 × 72 in.)

It's very easy, very comforting to pare down Wool's heritage. Pollock and Warhol are great predecessors. For American painting, it really doesn't get better. Still, there's a lot of focused Gutai chaos, a lot of neo-concrete's anxious formalism (especially as expressed by Ferrari, Argentina's Mad Max of art making), and a caviar dollop of atmospheric gorgeousness. The thing is that heritage is one thing and sensibility is another.

NOTES ON THE AESTHETIC:

> *First of all, what is the Beautiful?*
> *For Schelling it is the infinite expressing itself in the finite; for Reid, an occult quality; for Jouffroy, an indestructible fact; for de Maistre, what is agreeable to virtue; for Père André, what conforms to reason.... In short the primary condition of the Beautiful is unity in variety, that is the principle.*
>
> GUSTAVE FLAUBERT, FROM *BOUVARD AND PÉCUCHET*[3]

Or, what is ugly? It, too, is beautiful if reasoned properly.

ACCEPTED PEER GROUP

Richard Prince, Sherrie Levine, Cindy Sherman
+ Sigmar Polke, Rudolf Stingel (an interesting three-person exhibition)

A meditation on Polke:

> *The light from outside struck against the leaves of black latticework.*
> *Tree-shapes, hummocks, swirls, vague animals were traced in their diaphanous thickness; and the light came in, frightening and yet peaceful, as it must be behind the sun, in the bleak spaces of future creations. He tried to banish from his thoughts every form, every symbol and name of the Gods, the better*

GUSTAVE FLAUBERT, *SALAMMBÔ*[4]

There is a ravishing prodigality in Polke's work that seems very much
at odds with the pinched syllabus of contemporary painting. His
passions embrace history, astrology, mathematics, the mineral kingdom, and—quite seriously—alchemy. His is an outsize talent for these
times. Flaubert was such a talent, as was Walt Whitman, Orson Welles,
Roberto Bolaño. Polke uses transparent polyesters like Salome used
veils—for art, seduction, and empowerment. Unlike Polke, Wool is not
a romantic dramatist but a choreographer of barometric pressure, and
both men are united in their climatic intensity and pursuit of the transformative accident. As Dr. Watson might posit, "There is more here
than meets the eye."

On making a great work of art:

*Danton: Last night I had this dream: I was fishing. I caught an eel. As the
fish I had caught flapped on the wood dock, my hook slipped out of its
mouth. This made me very upset. Surprisingly, when I put my hook back into
its seemingly smiling therefore sly mouth, the fish readily accepted it. (The
audience beginning to see Robespierre and his men advancing on Danton
realizes Danton's faster and faster closer to his death, at the point of punk
ecstasy, in the daylight.)*

KATHY ACKER, *IMPLOSION*[5]

A similar pistol-whipping of genres makes Acker and Wool a kind
of latter-day, time-inappropriate Ginger and Fred (Masina and

Mastroianni) in their thrill at confounding expectations. Without fail, just as you are about to get comfortable (think you've found the rhythm), they pull back, re-arm, and blast those expectations to smithereens. Still, what they produce is recognizable, a facsimile of the accepted. It is also obdurately oppositional. Sure it reads … looks like prose or a picture … it just isn't exactly either. It's another version of *Predator* (1987) in which the pixels keep forming and reforming, a portrait emerging from an oil slick.

THOSE IN FAVOR OF PUNK ECSTATICS
Thomas Crow, Ann Goldstein, Richard Hell, Jim Lewis, Greil Marcus, Friedrich Meschede, Glenn O'Brien, Marga Paz, and Jerry Saltz

> *I don't want my work to feel all sweat-soaked and tortured. I'd like to be like a crooner, effortless seeming, smooth. That doesn't mean it actually is easy. And it doesn't mean you don't have backbone, or even aggression. Like Frank Sinatra. Or Miles Davis, maybe. It's like magic. I want my things to just appear. Not be painted. Just appear.*
>
> RICHARD HELL INTERVIEWS HIMSELF AS WOOL, FROM "BEING CHRISTOPHER WOOL"[6]

THOSE NOT IN FAVOR OF PUNK ECSTATICS
Dave Hickey, Christopher Knight

> *Actually hanging a painting by Christopher Wool in a museum … is like reprinting one of Andy's Marilyns in Photoplay. It seems at once redundant and oddly dissonant—like the weird tang of a chicken omelet—the kunsthalle being the chicken, in this case, and Wool's painting the egg.*
>
> DAVE HICKEY ON WOOL'S RETROSPECTIVE, FROM A 1998 REVIEW IN *ARTFORUM*[7]

Needless to say, I reject Hickey's troubled analogy.

The first time I was really aware of work by Christopher Wool was in a now legendary exhibition at 303 Gallery in 1988. It was a collaboration with Robert Gober and included *APOCALYPSE NOW* (1988), arguably one of Wool's most important paintings ("SELL THE HOUSE, SELL THE CAR, SELL THE KIDS"). It was probably the painting of the year, and one of the most emblematic pictures in the recession to come that would humble the art world the following year. It offered such a simple, reductive solution for moving on that it became a kind of late-eighties mantra. Wool has kept that edge over the years, slamming down the insults ("IF YOU DON'T LIKE IT YOU CAN GET THE FUCK OUT OF MY HOUSE"), the rapturous asides ("YOU MAKE ME"), the waking nightmares ("THE SHOW IS OVER THE AUDIENCE GET UP TO LEAVE THEIR SEATS TIME TO COLLECT THEIR COATS AND GO HOME THEY TURN AROUND NO MORE COATS AND NO MORE HOME"), and the very American lament ("PLEASE PLEASE PLEASE").

As Wool has gradually pulled away from language, he has moved ever closer to paintings that slip further and further into the void. There is a real menace that comes with the fog and the rot and the glimpses of graffiti hanging in the air like satanic versions of the northern lights. Dense and suffocating, the pictures are as much about the deadening of sound as the obstruction of clarity. There is no penetrating the gelid soup and there are no criteria for trusting one's deadened senses. There are also those surfaces that bear the violent evidence of splatter forensics. Even the rare smear of color is symptomatic of bruising or mold. However, there is also something exquisite going on in these paintings. Looking at them is much like riding a ferry as it cuts through the mist rising off the water. The foreground is opaque and yet filled with incident. The slow slosh of the water fills your head and the erased destination becomes one with the fog. These are paintings that know their time, paintings that understand that subject matter—like dreams of tomorrow or news of the day—is no longer describable.

Parkett, no. 83 (2008): 138–43.

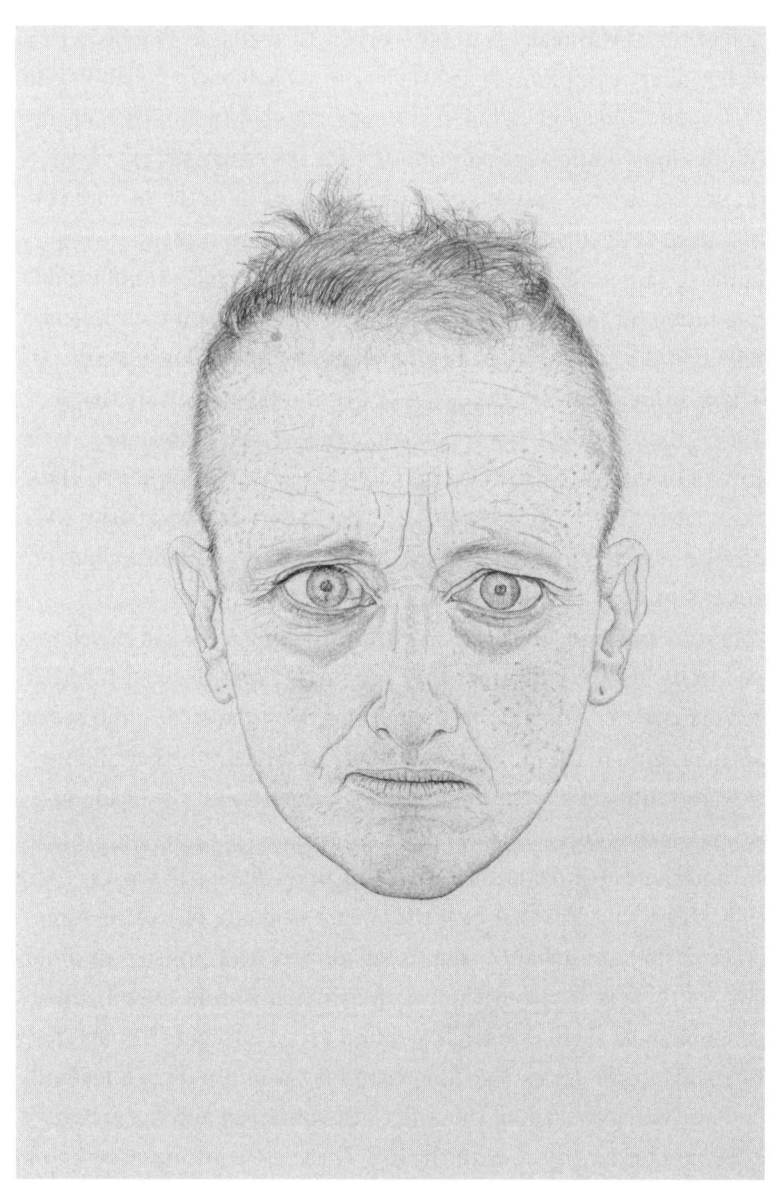

Michael Landy, *Self-Portrait*, 2007–8
Pencil on paper (one of twelve portraits), 70 × 50 cm (27½ × 19¾ in.)

294

Sitting: Michael Landy

When I arrive at Michael Landy's Bethnal Green studio, we sit and
chat over coffee in the entry room. It is a minimalist combination of
kitchen, dining, and social space. There's a compact wall of kitchen,
a blonde table, and matching bench. It's a totally spare environment,
but not a swoony, John Pawson kind of spareness; it's simply efficient.
Sitting there, I experience a degree of anxiety for what is to come that
keeps me talking, having a second cup of coffee, delaying the move
to the studio. It's not alarm exactly, just an anxious awareness of the
unknown. I've only had my portrait done once before—when I was
around eight years old. It was a pastel by a nice lady who had gained
a modicum of fame doing portraits representing the children of the
United Nations in their native dress. I wore a yellow shirt and blazer
that must have been the native dress of suburban New Jersey. Michael
was being as nice as the lady, and I decided to be a man, get up, and
do what I'm there for.

Michael's studio is a clean, rectangular cube. It contains an easel,
a bench matching the one in the entry, and an adjustable tub chair
on wheels. There is a concrete floor, some lighting equipment, many
boxes of meticulously sharpened HB pencils, and, leaning against the
wall, a framed self-portrait of the artist. Above, slanted opaque skylights
provide illumination. Far across the room sits a large table covered
with drawings under glassine paper.

Michael doesn't push (it's not an *On Chesil Beach* sort of deadly awk-
wardness) and I willingly submit to the process. Michael sits on the
bench, I on the chair. He looks at me quite intently. I feign an attitude

of remove, but my resolve cracks rather quickly. I feel that it's incumbent on me to take charge of a conversational gambit. We gossip about some of his previous sitters. Michael's anecdotes are funny, wicked even, until I notice that they are also directed at my restless babbling. Oh well then, okay, I'll shut up.

Next I'm directed into a pose and I go itchy—all over my body. I need to blow my nose. I'm getting a cramp in my calf. I need to take off my shoes. Jeez, the studio floor is cold. Michael rolls me closer to him, slams my knees between his, and looks at me more keenly than previously. I want to please him, to lose myself in the pose. I begin to feel as if the pose and I are one. But then Michael makes a funny movement with his head. I'm confused. Is he doing an exercise, some version of a Kathacali head rotation? He looks vividly alert, eyes bulging—a rebus monkey seeing someone stealing its fruit. Then his hand reaches out—in slow motion. The palm makes contact with my head and gently reunites me with the pose.

We both smile nervously, but I know that something has changed. He's taken control. On the face of it, my acceptance of his prompt seems only fair if we're going to accomplish this thing together. I attempt to wrap myself in passivity while, of course, keeping my pose dynamic. Occasionally, he adjusts the set of his head on his neck to great effect. If I slip out of the pose, all Michael does is move his hand like a lavishly negligent conductor and I correct it instantly. (Do I imagine a barely audible clucking noise?) Eventually, we break for lunch and are joined by Michael's partner, Gillian Wearing. The conversation allows me to catch up on a larger number of people that I see only rarely, a number of whom have already been drawn by Michael.

When we go back into the studio, I ask to see the other portraits and Michael shifts through them removing and replacing the glassine. The eyes are what unify the agenda. People I know look almost haunted. Their faces are expressionless, but that doesn't mean that they lack character. Occasionally, in rendering the hair, there is an allowance for whimsy, but more often not; the portraits possess the melancholic gravity of people suspended in time, drained of initiative, travelers waiting for a flight that will never leave the runway. I remember the first drawings in what would become this initiative. They are of Michael's father and they are literally stunning. They transcend the requirements of the genre and offer a depth of expression that touches on mortality. When I first saw them, the words spoken by Linda Loman about her beleaguered husband, Willy, in *Death of a Salesman* came back to me: "attention must be paid." These paternal portraits, along with Michael's self-portraits, are masterpieces of purpose and gesture. Clearly, the act of documenting one's self and one's parent raises the stakes enormously as it must also accommodate the motives of love and pride. Regardless of the end of my journey in the studio, I'm humbled to be in the Landy men's company.

We resume and Michael pulls our work area back toward the wall, trying to keep the ascending light even. I'm convinced I've got my role in place and sit as still as possible. Gradually, something that sounds like a car driving over an empty plastic bottle works its way into my consciousness. It's not happening at regular intervals but often enough to become anticipated. I think one of us mentions it, but I'm floating down a river of oblivion and the sound of the bottle, cries of children, men yelling are all somewhere far away on the shore. Michael's warned me about dozing off so I will myself into this suspended state. I wish I had looked at my face in the bathroom mirror during the lunch break. Michael is staring hard again. His head is bobbling and he outlines an oval of air with both hands as if framing his advancing face. Occasionally, as he has done throughout the day, he changes pencils, sometimes holding three as he works. Now and again, I am aware of him drawing; it's a restful sound, like leaves scattering in the breeze. At other times, I hear him erasing and wonder what has killed the rhythm of pencil on paper.

I ask for a break and go to the bathroom mirror to see whom

Michael is looking at. It's the face of a stranger, barely formed, a caul stretched tightly over it. It's a face hovering just below the surface of the water. What is he drawing? When I go back into the studio, I go over to look at his self-portrait and really stare it down. I don't think it's the face I've been looking at during the sitting. As I resume my pose, I am determined to give Michael the same level of attention as I am receiving. It's dangerous because I keep slipping into his pores and veins, aspects of the face but not the face itself.

Two markers in Michael's physiognomy begin to pull me in. The first is the intense vertical formation of wrinkles that fan out above his nose, between his eyes. These wrinkles are in his self-portrait but the depth of their incision is not. The four vertical slices begin to look as deeply carved as those belonging to Abraham Lincoln on Mount Rushmore. I can almost hear Strauss's *Thus Spake Zarathustra* crashing away as they emerge and cohere. The other marker is the shape of Michael's mouth. Again, his self-portrait is gloriously, self-critically accurate but, with my sitter, I am also seeing a kind of ghost mouth. Closed, the lips resemble a horizontal leaf shape. But peeping out above his top lip, almost as if in a tracing, is the upper half of a cupid's bow. It changes the face entirely, sweetening it up and adding a tiny girlish distraction. But it's elusive. A turn of the head, an adjustment in his expression, and it disappears. Yet, once seen, it remains in the mind's eye.

Finally, there are the artist's eyes surrounded by scimitars of downy flesh. The eyes themselves are the kind of sea blue that one glimpses in advertisements for high-end resorts. Once abstracted, the face is extremely difficult to reassemble. I wonder if this ever happens to Michael. Does he become so addled with one feature or another that he simply loses the face of his sitter as I do his? While Michael cleans up, I have the opportunity to look at my portrait, but I don't. Tomorrow, I'll be back for the second session and I'll see it then.

The next morning, I return to the studio. We work, converse, eat, and drink coffee. The scenario for the day is a mirror image of the day before but the energy of confrontation is absent. Later, I seem to remember that we both understood simultaneously when the session was over; there was a little pop, an exhalation of purpose. Michael seems tired and I sense that there is something wrong with the picture; I don't push to see it. Only when Gillian wanders in and starts looking at it (then me), do I want to see what Michael has made. It's an enormously delicate portrait of someone who could be me—or not. I'm no longer certain I know what I look like, so I'm not comfortable passing judgment. Michael thinks that something may have gone wrong early on as regards the shape of the head. We don't linger over it. I do know that I've been changed by the sittings. They've left me with an acute need to look hard at the faces I care about, to really see them for the first time. It's quite remarkable, almost joyous, to know that something I thought I understood remains a lovely chain of mysteries. It also dawns on me that Michael's journey is about embracing these mysteries, not solving them.

Michael Landy: Everything Must Go! (London: Ridinghouse, 2008), 396–97.

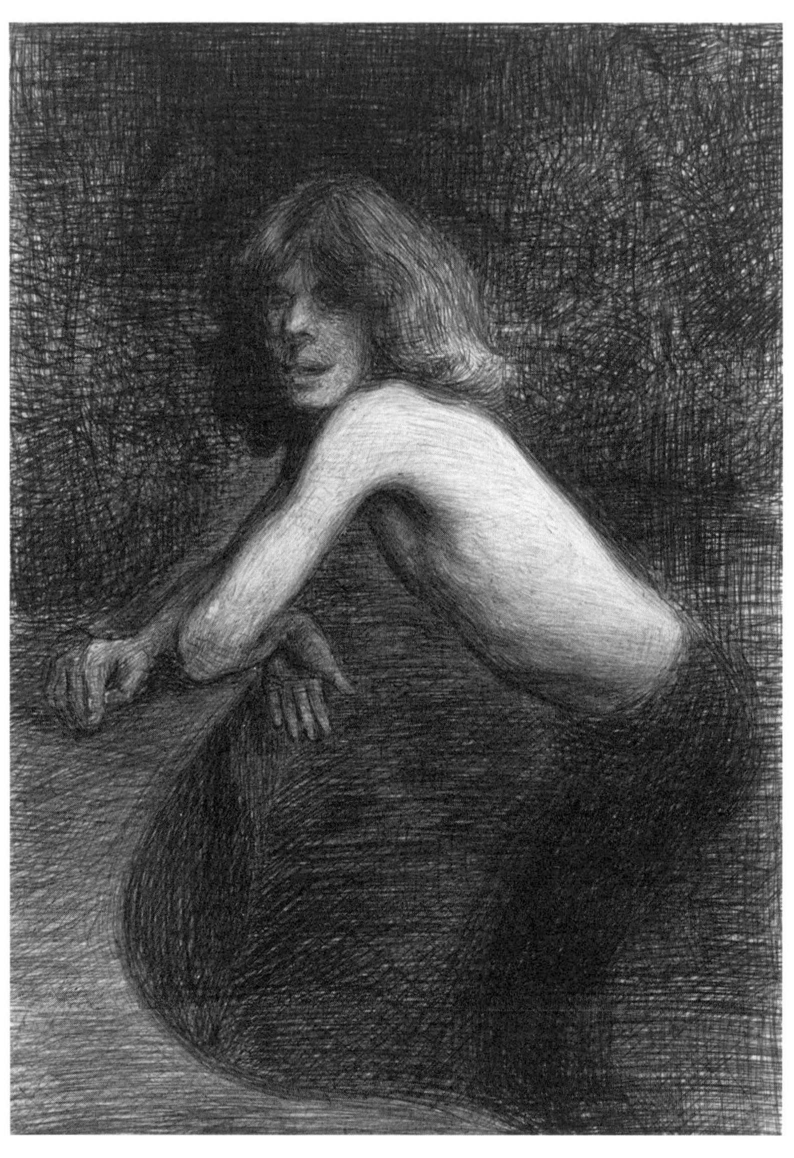

Steven Shearer, *Moonlight*, 2005
Ballpoint pen on paper, 33.7 × 24.8 cm (13¼ × 9¾ in.)

49° 16' N: Steven Shearer

Steven Shearer is a collector and cataloguer of great style and substance. He is active in those markets where the devil might well be expected as a prime competitor. Shearer is collecting souls as they surface in the fantasies of myriad adolescents. They are the kids mastering their air-guitar poses and they are the kids who made it out of the basement and onto the concert circuit (if only the pre-show at the local tractor pull). Their names rarely signify their identity; more often it is the hair or the pose that defines them and provides them with a legion of brothers. These kids inhabit Shearer's world by the hundreds, each of them absorbed into the oversoul of musky adolescent anonymity. To be sure, individual faces peep out, but it's more like portraits of entrées on a laminated menu. It's as if Shearer is playing the role of a karmic detective, sorting through the legion of the lost and putting them in a holding pen until they are able or worthy to move on to their next level of existence. Kids are obviously transitional by their nature, but Shearer offers an alternative; he will freeze them in the agony and ecstasy of their hormonal ascendance. Not unexpectedly, he has also frozen himself in a state of suspended adolescent endeavor, including in his work pictures of himself with his guitars in the basement of his parents' suburban house. Perhaps it's a way of holding on to the past or maybe it's a warning to himself to find another room, another pose well outside of the picture.

The adolescents roam through Shearer's heroically scaled "accumulations" in which uncountable numbers of jpeg portraits form huge public gatherings like thematic raves. The boys also appear in his "longhair" drawings and paintings where the artist's love of the media he is working in (silverpoint, crayon, ballpoint pen, oils) provides both more and less information about the subjects. Certain muses dominate. Leif Garrett is to Shearer what Celine Dion was to Caesar's Palace: the main event. Many accumulations are devoted to Garrett in his sixteen-year-old prime as an overstyled and underdressed pop icon looking like the identically coiffed younger brother of Farrah Fawcett (whose career was simultaneously spiking as she played the bubble-headed Jill Munroe on *Charlie's Angels*). Looking at Garrett is scanning a roadmap of exploitation. As he ages in Shearer's accumulations, he becomes ever more unavailable to the camera, relying on a couple of standard poses with eyes that register like a motel vacancy sign. What ultimately makes the ex-singer/actor such a Shearer superstar is that he becomes a tragedy of uninflected banality. Garrett's career ended with a sudden finality shortly before his eighteenth birthday as the result of drunken car crash that turned his passenger into a paraplegic. Yet, in Shearer's aspic accumulations, he remains a golden product for mass consumption.

Over the past two years, Shearer has created a number of oil portraits of someone who looks very much like Garrett; the face also bears an oil-slick resemblance to the artist. Unlike Dorian Gray, Shearer is taking the portrait out of the attic and confronting it in public. The most romantic painting, *As a Boy* (2006), has an almost Pre-Raphaelite look to it, like a study for an androgynous page recycled from a Rossetti painting. But wait; is it as simple as that? Is the smile more self-aware than it first appears? What is that look of complicity passing between the sitter and the painter? *As a Boy* also shares a similarly ambiguous smile with Leonardo's *John the Baptist,* in which it is commonly assumed that the Baptist has been transformed by the incubus of Bacchus and, rather than announcing the Christ, is asking us to return to the pagan grove. Still, there is a mirrorlike directness in the subject's face that further suggests a time-traveling self-portrait. The Leif depicted in *Wave* (2006–7) could easily spring from a medieval bestiary, so strangely is he poised between animal and boy. An arm caught in frantic motion could be either welcoming or defensive. The subject's dark, predatory face sinks into a head of ash-blond hair that could easily have been arranged by a gum-cracking hairdresser at the Mall of America. The iridescent, slightly simian silver-gold beard and mustache appear to be pulling the loose adolescent body back into a dark and predatory place. The vegetable skin and feral face imply something dangerously out of balance, like the mythical stories of boys raised by wolves and their usually heartbreaking fates.

Another portrait of Leif, *Boy with Orange and Green Face* (2007), portrays its subject at the end of a long toll road. The boy is sated, narcotized, and available. He has nothing left to experience in his secondhand, over-the-shoulder pose. This version of Leif could easily depict a barstool habitué of Vancouver's Downtown Eastside (a.k.a. the Low Track), which is a festering ten-block nightmare where everything is for sale and nothing is forever, where used condoms and needles are as common as cigarette butts. It's dangerous and wide open; it's a perfect destination for kids who don't know where to go other than hell. *Boy with Orange and Green Face* is a painting of the void and the voided. It is as much about a state of existence as it is a portrait. It is impossible to ignore and impossible to come to grips with.

While some of the longhairs are apparent portraits (particularly the drawings), others are stylized types in demand of no model. In these paintings and drawings, hair cascades like waterfalls suffused with an internal light. The hair is a marvelous vehicle for Shearer to revel in a kind of electric abstraction but it also provides a hiding place for the boys who wear it. There is a brooding melancholy that puts these isolated subjects in a detailed but constantly morphing interior: sometimes a café, then a railway carriage, perhaps a confessional, maybe a bordello parlor. The faces, when seen, have a self-contained emotional silence. Whatever supplementary drama occurs in the longhairs happens in the strange, forward hunch of the boys. It is a posture that suggests helplessness and withdrawal as the shoulders attempt to form an inward arc. Recent work in the series, featuring a Medici-style profile with a great large nose, is a combination of Shearer's beloved inspiration, Edvard Munch, and the early Picasso of *The Absinthe Drinker*, whose subject perfectly foretells the defensive posture of the longhairs. In a painting such as *Guys and Dolls* (2006), a pastel palette and symbolist fantasies lend an antic freedom to the more Spanish schemes of the longhairs. Only two paintings out of the series, *PoCo Trail* (2006) and *Forest* (2006–7), open up to a panoramic landscape where lone longhairs contemplate the experience that lies ahead: a straight road or a forest hugging the road's perimeter. The crackling, ember-red colors of the landscape create a molten environment where choice is inevitably a mortal decision. Nonetheless, paintings about alternatives are a remarkable notation in Shearer's universe of grave givens.

Before the portraits, there were the "laminates." In them, there is no delight in painting, no seduction, no whispers of Fauves or symbolists. The laminates are utterly straightforward and formulaic: C-prints scissored from their original context and slapped onto large, brilliantly colored canvases. There is no oil painting precedent here, no hues that can be traced back prior to the 1960s; the pictures are literally skindeep. The laminates are also resolutely post-Pop. Superficially, they promise the same kind of hard-candy delights as pictures by the grand inheritor of posh Pop, Jeff Koons. However, the laminates don't deliver a joyous gloss; they're scrappy and have a disturbing, almost evidentiary edge to them. Part of their snarkiness can be attributed to the ill-fitting match between photo finish and canvas but, more important, the subject matter has everything to do with style and self-presentation as manifestations of class. There is no editorial stance, as that was what Shearer found already in place on the internet. Haircuts, posturing, arrangements of possessions all suggest a suburban empire where history is accidental and identity is based on repetition. Just as Shearer's hometown, Port Coquitlam, maintains a website that urges one to be "Bear Aware" and read up on "Beaver Management," its history has now been irrevocably co-opted by Robert W. Pickton, a pig farmer and Canada's most prolific mass murderer. Places and people with no fixed identity are always dangerously vulnerable to history being imposed on them. This is also true when Shearer offers a stereo set, accessorized by African-style knickknacks, for laminate contemplation, or gives star treatment to a black Mustang listing on a flat tire with most of its grill scissored away by the artist. The laminates have no depth and no artifice, yet the best are both utterly brutal and as mysteriously creepy as a stalker.

The terse, decisive editing of the laminate images leads directly to an intense, unbroken chant that seethes just below the surface of the images. It has its own Rosetta Stone and resultant sacred writings. Sourcing hundreds of internet sites, Shearer composed an exhaustive "list" of metal bands, with dates of their recordings, releases, and performances. This archive in turn provided the elemental source for the artist's "poems," which are theatrically scatological incantations that act as the insinuating scripts for Shearer's metal epiphany. The list, for example, unearths bands with the name "Holocaust" from Canada, Poland, Finland, Spain, Sweden, the UK, Brazil, Honduras, and Germany. Once you have the list, the poems are created by using the band names, the titles for individual cuts, and a sympathetic creation of new imagery, new black magic. Shearer governs his poems with a system of rules that keeps their production formalized and their language as hysterically over-the-top as possible. The poems are pushed to a maniacal, eruptive, declamatory madness that stops just short of becoming howlingly funny. In creating the poems, Shearer is walking the same razor's edge that Jack Nicholson did in Stanley Kubrick's *The Shining* (1980), wherein the line between horror and hilarity is barely discernable, as in PRISONS OF FOUL FLESH / SUCK MY UNHOLY VOMIT / CONSUMED IN EVIL OBSCURITY / GUTTED WITCHFUCKING HELL / etc.

As long as you don't stop chanting, it keeps on feeding the hunger.

Satan first slithered into Shearer's work in his earliest sculpture, *Activity Cell with Warlock Bass Guitar* (2007). The design of the structure was adapted from a book from the late 1960s called *Teenagers' Rooms*, which advocated the penal panopticon design in which prisoners are under constant surveillance. The *Activity Cell* is an iconic demonstration of the power of minimalist design with honey-finished ply supporting a canopy of Howard Johnson blue and containing a room upholstered in tomato-red fabric. It's a great-looking environment until you become aware of the fact that the space is created for surveillance. Then, too, there is the highly desirable Warlock guitar lying in the center of the cell, like catnip for anyone who knows the power of the instrument. Washed up in the cell, the Warlock resembles a satanic hero deprived of his powers and destiny. The Warlock also suggests that the teens using the *Activity Cell* are as likely to find themselves in a world of ever-shrinking opportunity as they are of following into the future of the suburbanized Warlock. It is amazing that so much of Shearer's work lies in the cradle of the *Cell*. Here is a home for the isolated and the anal, the longhairs and the monsters, the iconic and the democratic, the political and the gothic, the stoned and the free.

Double Album: Daniel Guzmán with Steven Shearer, ed. Richard Flood (New York: New Museum, 2008), 20–24.

Animating the Essence: Marisa Merz

I've known Marisa and Mario Merz for thirty-some years and was really changed by both of them: changed in the way I look at art and changed in the way I think about art and its possibilities. I remember the very first show I saw that Marisa was in—it was an enormous show in Berlin, in an exhibition hall that had been an old train station. It was before the wall came down, and the show was filled with Europe's and America's most vigorous, muscular male artists. In one isolated spot within this exhibition, there was a plinth and on that plinth was one of Marisa's little mute handfuls of a head. It was absolutely the most revealing work in the entire exhibition. It was a message that humanity comes first, it was a message that even though the eyes of the head couldn't see that thought was what was going to keep us together, thought would, in the end, be the most important contribution that creatures like us could give. So from the very beginning, with Marisa, it was her heads, whether they were drawn or painted or molded, that captivated me and gave me a lifelong interest in what she does.

Another occasion I saw her work was in one of the Documentas, and again it was an exhibition very, very heavy on male artists, primarily European and American. It was a very aspirational show, and there were a lot of wonderful things in it: huge paintings, amazing enormous sculptures, very heroic. And you turned a corner and went into a little room, almost like a vestibule; it was completely silent in the center of all this bombast. What you found there was a beautiful little wax fountain, and the fountain had a tiny spout of water coming up. It was no bigger than a span of two hands; the walls banked up and then, pinched into the wax, were four canoelike indentations. It was that simple, that serene. And all of the noise from the outside stopped. You were in this chamber, this chapel of contemplation, and I thought, "This woman has saved my life in two exhibitions. Twice she has taught me the meaning of silence and twice she has taught me the meaning of peace."

In 2003 the Winterthur Museum in Switzerland and the Gladstone Gallery in New York had on show an incredible suite of drawings by Marisa. When I first saw them, I was really moved because it was like looking at … you know, in old movies in the States, the actress Bette Davis was always smoking and the smoke rings would begin to do these magical things for the camera, particularly in black-and-white film. There's always this exquisite sense of romance, and I think, for many people, part of the reason they have such difficulty giving up smoking is because of cinema, the history of smoking in cinema, where everyone's always gorgeous, nobody dies of cancer, and passed cigarettes are the highest moment of romantic interaction. But with these drawings, I thought there was something so extraordinarily otherworldly about them as well—they're almost disappearing and reappearing before your eyes. This is a skill in drawing that is incredibly difficult to achieve. When you look at drawings like these, you're looking at pure spirit but you also see that spirit on flesh, so there's substance as well. As I've said, they're coming together and then they're coming apart, like smoke.

Before we depart from these, I would like you to look at the mouths, because in Marisa's work there is a role of the magic triangle. In her sculpture, in her drawings, in most manifestations of what she's doing, this magic triangle—the triad, the trinity—is a Cabalistic sign, and it always appears. It's the eyes, it's the mouths; sometimes even when the mouth is at its most luscious and welcoming, it's in the form of a beak, so it can bite you as easily as it can kiss you. You never see the tongue, but one wonders what the tongue would look like if you were to see it. Would it be forked or would it be round and luscious? I think, with

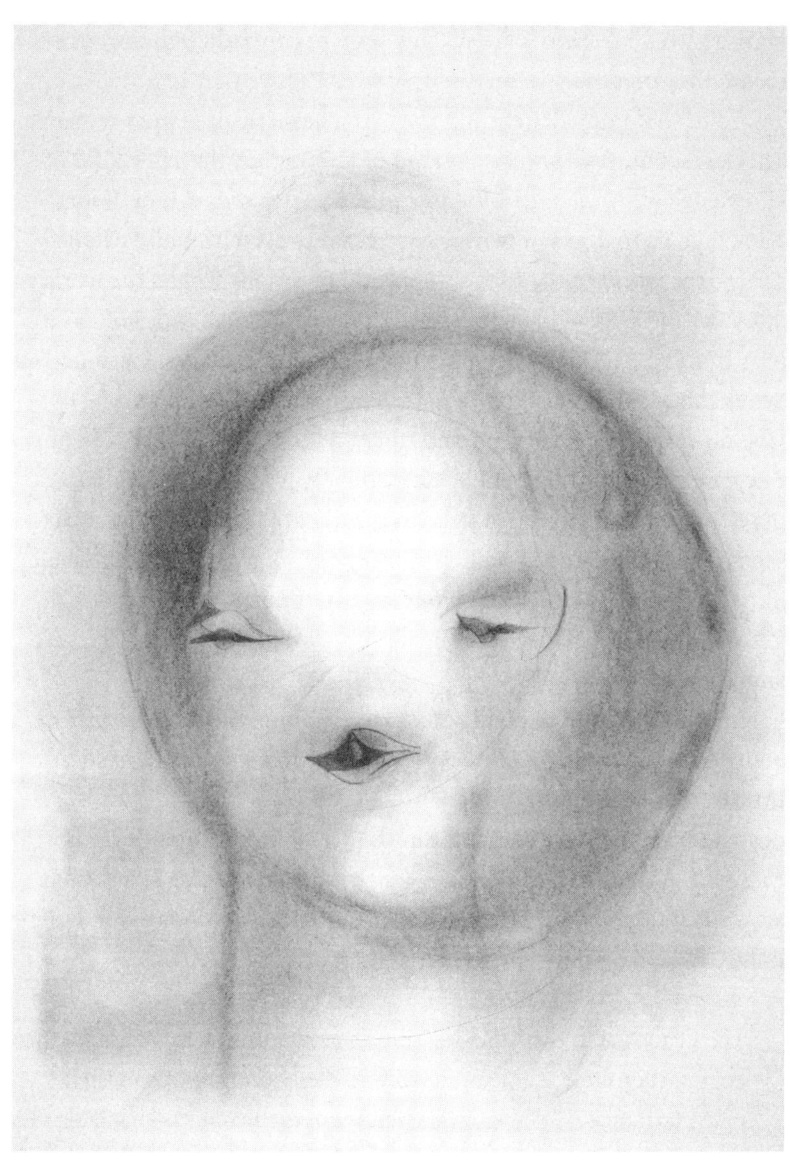

Marisa Merz, *Untitled*, 2003
Pencil and charcoal on paper, 100 × 70 cm (39⅜ × 27½ in.)

Marisa's women, there is always this state of contradiction they exist in: are they predatory or are they passive? Passive they're not—we can get rid of that immediately. But they aren't exactly predatory either. They are women with a certain kind of knowledge, the same kind of knowledge we would attribute to a priestess or a seer or a pythoness. They take us to another world that Marisa deals with quite extensively—the world of the exotic, the world of Scheherazade, the world of Byzantine icons—and that's the world we meet in a series of paintings from 2006. There are women who enchant to survive, just as Scheherazade did. They're women from the harems, women who control; no victims of any caliph, they're going to survive on their own. They are hieratic—as I've said before, they're priestesses. I would propose that these are a race of women the likes of which we have never seen before: they are self-sufficient, they are alien, and they are whole unto themselves. They need no one nor anything. They need no male affirmation and they need no female sisterhood of approval. They are simply complete.

In the exhibition at Fondazione Merz, among the most surprising and wonderfully exciting I've ever seen, the drawings are flanked by little heads of clay; both the drawings of the women and the heads (gender aside) are really of the same family. I've written at length about these little heads in the catalogue for the *Arte Povera 2011* exhibitions across Italy curated by Germano Celant. Because that book is in Italian only, I'd like to end here with my original text:

The heads could easily be described as mute, but that is missing the energy they emit. There is actually an element of horror in their epic numbness, like a paralysis that renders the mouth incapable of expressing what it wants to say, needs to say. The latter is at the core of the tension that accompanies the head. Yet there is a voluptuousness in their quiet, a fullness that is beyond vexation. The positioning of the heads is various: some sit facing directly ahead, some rise from a column of a neck, some tilt up, others loll back staring up as if their necks were too weak to support their head. All possess an embryonic blindness that recalls the sightless prophets who populate ancient history, particularly the ambisexual Tiresias. The state of blindness that Merz visits upon her heads is also perhaps a reflection of her own apartness, of a willful selectivity that feeds her isolate spirit. The mouths of the heads differ, from a simple gash to something more fully rendered through a delicate pinch of clay. The ambisexuality mentioned previously is present in the heads: they are not male, they are not female, but they're definitely human, and their aspiration is in their fashioning. These are votives, and as such, they are the representation of a vow or a wish that is emblematic of humanity. In Merz's apartment, there is a room that is filled with one of Mario's iron-and-glass spiral tables. There's only space enough to navigate around the edge of the table. On it and below it are things so incidental that they could have blown in through the window or been temporarily placed in a moment of careless housekeeping. What makes the room so memorable, so charged, is the presence of many heads in various states of finish. By finish, I don't mean completion, but rather that which differentiates a fact and a thought. All are intensely individual, something that their atypical proximity emphasizes, and each has its own intensity. Part of the dynamic lies in the play of light and shadow over their surfaces: Is there a flicker under an eyelid? Are the lips parted? It's an unforgettable environment, one that is meditative but far from silent as the spiral uncoils and the heads draw a collective breath.

Marisa Merz (Turin: Hopefulmonster, 2012), 12–19.

Both of Him

In 1951 Kim Jones was living in a Southern California commuter community for Los Angeles. It was one of thousands of towns spread out across the United States that had been waiting for the troops returning home from World War II. The houses were wishfully middle-class with new cars in driveways and televisions enshrined in the living rooms. *Catcher in the Rye*, the classic novel of American adolescent angst, made its debut. The comedy series *I Love Lucy* drove television sales up and up. L. Ron Hubbard published his first book on Scientology, unleashing the cult's first dose of indoctrination. Coast-to-coast telephone service was a brand new luxury. The stain of segregation was still in place, ignored by the white majority, but there were stirrings. The past was still very close, as noted by President Harry Truman's announcement that the state of war with Germany had just ended. The future was knocking on the door as the Cold War claimed its first prisoners, Ethel and Julius Rosenberg, who were sentenced to death (and executed three years later) for espionage. The United States' involvement in the Korean War was recruiting another generation of soldiers (36,516 would ultimately not come home) to be whisked into a conflict that would end with the division of a country into two, just as it would in Vietnam, where American advisors were already working with the French in their collapsing colonial empire.

In 1951, when Kim Jones was seven years old, he was diagnosed with Perthes disease. Perthes is caused by the loss (or increase) of bone mass and a compromised delivery of blood to the femur. Its primary victims are prepubescent males and its treatment calls for hospitalization, traction, braces, use of a wheelchair, and physical therapy. For Jones the rehabilitation took three years and kept him in a state of social isolation, removed from family and school for extensive periods of time. When he finally entered fifth grade, he knew all about being alone on his own. Around this time, Jones began avidly drawing cartoons (inspired by the Disney comics that he loved) and creating battle maps across which he deployed hundreds of troops and tanks in a never-ending panorama of war. Talking about his drawings, Jones said: "Most of them are cartoons but some are those early war drawings—a little world that I could control. That's why children build those worlds, because everyone else is in charge. It's the one place where they're actually in charge."[1]

In 1966 the United States was mired in the Vietnam "conflict" (the US government never declared it as a war to its citizens or described it as such to Congress). The American presence had gone on for years but, in 1965, 100,000 troops were sent to Vietnam and, in 1966, another 100,000 were deployed. The war was no longer invisible and an anti-war movement grew in strength in the United States. At the time, Jones was enrolled at Chouinard Art Institute but decided to enlist in the US Marines and was sent to Vietnam on a tour of duty that would last just over a year. He delivered mail between bases under circumstances that were exceedingly dangerous and lived in nightmarish camps where the burning of marauding rats was commonplace. He got out two months prior to the launch of the Tet Offensive, which fully revealed the true horror of the war stateside. Back home, Jones finished his degree at Chouinard (which, that year, became the California Institute of the Arts) and was accepted in the graduate program at the Otis Art Institute of Los Angeles County (now Otis College of Art and Design).

After completing his MFA in 1973, Jones started exploring himself through drawings, sculpture, installations, and performance. His materials were as simple as possible—mud, sticks, string, pantyhose, chicken wire, foam rubber; he also began documenting performances through photography. Some of the sculptures he crafted might be seen as extensions of the camouflage of war but also the braces he had been confined in during the Perthes episode. The sculpture also turned into costumes for the performances and was worn in his installations. Gradually, a persona began to emerge—Mudman—who persists through the entirety of Jones's career. Mudman is a unique artistic creation but it is also a doppelgänger—the paranormal self. Like a medieval sin-eater, Mudman could also be seen as a creature absorbing the evils of the world through the penance he seems to be enacting in tasks of endurance and self-mortification.

At 6 a.m. on the morning of his thirty-second birthday (January 26, 1976), Jones started walking the length of Wilshire Boulevard, a sixteen-mile stretch from downtown Los Angeles to Ocean Avenue in Santa Monica, just short of the Pacific Ocean. He was stripped down and covered in mud. Pantyhose were pulled over his head to conceal his face. Strapped to his shoulders was a cagelike structure made of bits and pieces of twigs, string, and foam rubber that rose up and away from his body. Jones was clearly camouflaged but, in that urban setting, from what was not at all clear. As the walk stretched out before him, Jones fielded questions from fellow travelers in a polite if opaque demeanor. There were incidents along the way—a gas station attendant refused to allow him to use the bathroom (he pissed down his leg), police refused to let him stop and rest—but they were minor and nonthreatening on the part of Jones or those he encountered. Twelve hours had passed when he arrived at his destination. He repeated the journey in early February, reversing the walk from Santa Monica to One Wilshire Boulevard.

The walk could be seen as a simple endurance performance or the official introduction of a new performance identity. But there were other references that couldn't be dismissed, and one of them was of the Christ, burdened by the cross, on his final walk to Golgotha, where he would be crucified for the sins of man. One can also run through the index of James Frazer's *Golden Bough* and find names like Dionysus, Attis, and Osiris, all of whom share characteristics of Mudman. As an alter ego, Mudman serves his creator very well through his folkloric resonance. The character is, in fact, something that we carry with us in our unconscious. First glimpsed, it is strange more for an unexpected context than its alien presence. Mudman has the power to be remembered and accepted like something from a dream.

The dream soon turned into a nightmare. Jones's next performance, in February 1976, would put everything he had done thus far in his career on the line. He was invited to perform at the Union Gallery on the campus of California State University, Los Angeles. When he arrived, he transformed himself into Mudman while reading a prepared text on the creature he'd just become. Then he removed a cloth from a cage he'd earlier placed on the floor. Inside the now visible cage were three rats, which Jones/Mudman doused in lighter fluid and set on fire. The trapped rats became frenzied, screaming and thrashing in pain. If the fire seemed in danger of dying down, he would light it again and again until the rats were incinerated. What added to the horror was that, as the vermin burned, Jones/Mudman knelt by the cage and screamed along with them, joining them in their agony. It would take two years before Jones was able to perform again. Mudman had killed and would have to atone.

The rehabilitation of Mudman was, of course, not a concession to conformity nor was it a smooth passage. It was more of a quiet period (1978–81) followed by a gradual escalation of the undigested rage that had led to *Rat Piece*. Initially, Jones returned to the use of Mudman as a photo opportunity. Many of the persona's images were circulated in the newly launched magazine *High Performance*, where pages were also given over to Chris Burden, Paul McCarthy, Bruce Nauman, and other artists pushing the limits of action and identity. The most iconic image from that time was Mudman perched high on a telephone pole, which also caught the look of the low-budget sci-fi movies that were popular at the time. Other photographs had Mudman posed as an anarchic warrior from the future/past striding through the desert or silhouetted before the sky. All of these photographs were safely contained as memory aids but had none of the frisson of live confrontation. That is until Jones and Paul McCarthy were substitute teaching for Barbara T. Smith at the University of California, Irvine. McCarthy decided to make a penis painting and Jones performed *Cut Piece*. Jones was dressed in a loincloth and boots with pantyhose pulled over his face under a helmet of foam and sticks; there was no layer of mud, just the artist's skin. The action consisted of the artist cutting himself twenty-seven times with a razor blade—up his right leg, across his chest, and down to his left foot. After the cutting, he attempted a self-portrait in pencil and then pressed his bleeding body against the paper. He then asked someone to turn out the lights and sank to the floor where he started saying the phrase "Get out of my room," taking it from a murmur to a convulsive scream, which marked the end of the action. What Jones had achieved was a strange transubstantiation where the blood transformed into a painting, not wine. It is one of a number of Jones's performances where Catholic ritual is utilized and, in its suggestion that Jones is atoning for the sins of the world, again proposes Mudman as an avatar for Christ.

In the early 1980s Jones began a transition from Los Angeles to New York. Leaving behind his West Coast support structure and vehement critics, the artist arrived less well known and somewhat less angry. While he kept Mudman alive, the persona became less frightening, less unpredictable. Mudman became well known on West Broadway, which was then the absolute center of the New York art world. In the raucous street theater of Lower Manhattan, Mudman seemed a ghost from the past as well as a reminder of a cultural malaise that stayed with the country in the wake of Vietnam. There was a quiet dignity—oddly a sense of peacefulness—that emanated from the persona, which made the character even more perplexing.

As Jones slowly made his way into the arena of commercial galleries, his drawings and sculpture became part of his larger identity. The War Maps, which he had been creating since adolescence, were noticed for their sheer visceral bravura but also as frozen animations. With surging topographies, filled with battling armies (indicated by an X and a dot), the war campaigns were seen as if under a haze of drifting smoke, which was occasioned by Jones's constant erasures as he moved the campaign around the paper or, in some instances, directly on the walls. Jones is known to keep a drawing in progress for decades, returning to it when the need arose. Another body of drawings enters a world of teeming fantasy, like fairy tales from the devil's diary. They are nothing on the order of the brooding War Maps and show an exquisite facility that is a seductive combination of Goya and Daumier. Mudman also inhabits this world but doesn't dominate it; he turns up as a quester—a traveler looking for answers in a world bereft of them. The third body of Jones's drawings makes use of photographs of the artist in the Mudman guise. In them, Mudman goes about his day—posing, drawing, walking. Strange growths expand into environments, the harness reaches enormous proportions; it's a world in constant mutation.

Jones is a singular artist. He has had his alter ego with him for the length of his career. That alter ego never strays and remains the heart and soul of Jones's program. Mudman doesn't seek conversation or give interviews; he doesn't attempt to explain his relationship with Jones; that's up to Jones. One is a force, the other activates the force. In voodoo, it's called "mounting the horse" when the houngan priest takes possession of the spirit force. Jones has mounted the horse time and again. He has harnessed fury and beauty; he has unleashed terror and joy. Are he and Mudman one? No. Are they a couple? Yes.

Inauguration of MMCA Seoul: Connecting_Unfolding, ed. Eunju Choi (Seoul: National Museum of Modern and Contemporary Art, 2014), 37–39.

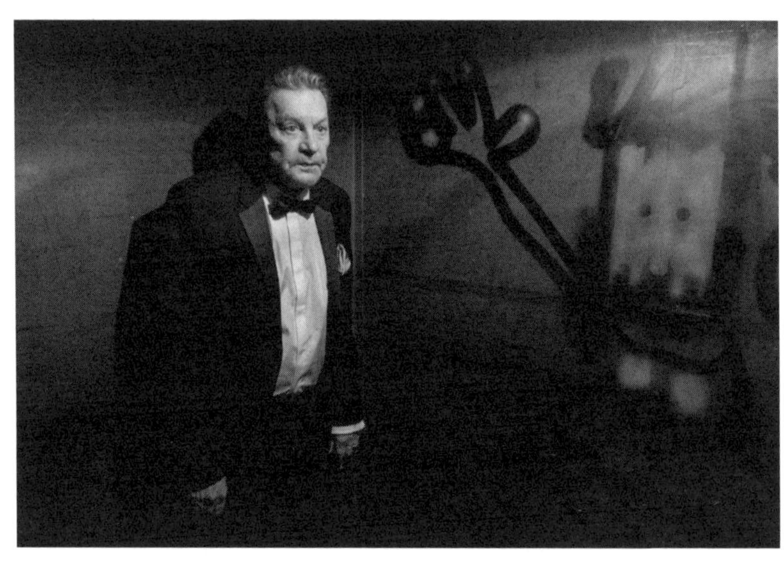

Helmut Berger with graffiti, Vienna, 2014
Photograph by Bryan Adams

Francesco Vezzoli:
The Kiss (Let's Play "Dynasty"!)

Helmut Berger was twenty years old when he met Luchino Visconti.
He was a bourgeois Austrian kid and had been bouncing around
Europe for two years before ending up in Rome. He was also beautiful,
and it wasn't long before Visconti gave him a role in a Silvana Mangano
vehicle called *The Witches* (*Le streghe*, 1967), an episodic film in which he
was billed under the name Helmut Steinbergher, a variation on his
given name, Steinberger. He has only minutes on-screen as a house-
boy, seen carrying luggage and serving dinner, but the camera never
loses sight of him, as if he is melded to the director's peripheral vision.
His next appearance in a Visconti film changed everything and gave
him the career that lasts to this day. The role was Martin von Essenbeck,
the seriously mad scion of a German industrial dynasty, and the film
was *The Damned* (*La caduta degli dei*, 1969).

In *The Damned*, Berger makes his debut performing a skit honoring/
ridiculing his grandfather's birthday. He vamps as Marlene Dietrich in
the *Blue Angel* (*Der blaue Engel*, 1930), only to be cut short by news that
the Reichstag is burning in Berlin. During the course of the film, his
perversities grow at a furious pace until, finally, after raping/seducing
his Oedipal mother, he ends the film as a triumphant SS officer reigning
over the family's steelworks. Along the way, he becomes the incarnation
of pure, incandescent evil. The steady escalation of the character's
awfulness could have gone horribly wrong, but Berger nails it brilliantly.

With his silky, almost amphibian good looks and strangulated peacock voice, the character is unforgettable and stingingly unique.

In 1972 Visconti's *Ludwig* was released. It is an epic of such singular extravagance that it perfectly matches that of its subject, Ludwig II of Bavaria. The part was bespoke fitted for Berger. He brilliantly captures the neurotic splendor of this ruler who could not stop building palaces, funding Richard Wagner's operas, torturing himself to keep his homosexuality at bay, or falling in love with his mirror image, Elisabeth of Austria (played by Romy Schneider).

Visconti and Berger's last collaboration was *Conversation Piece* (*Gruppo di famiglia in un interno*), in 1974. Burt Lancaster plays the film's protagonist, "The Professor" (a.k.a. Mario Praz), an aging, agoraphobic aesthete dragged into the real world by a flatulently vulgar, somewhat sinister industrialist family and their unwilling pet, a pansexual anarchist gigolo played by Berger. The role of the dreadful, marauding mother is given to Mangano, Visconti's favorite actress (as she was for Pier Paolo Pasolini; curiously, both directors were inclined to use her in an almost Kabuki-like way, her stylized wigs and makeup elevating the Byzantine sobriety of her presence to a state of autoerotic paralysis).

The Lancaster character is based on Mario Praz, an intellectual and author who specialized in the epicene and the morbid, and the Professor's apartment is an homage to Praz's home in Rome (now a notable decorative arts museum), but adapted to Visconti's theatrical taste. The intellectual waywardness of the film follows the Professor's psychic renewal as a duet with the anarchist's marriage of violence and feral, seductive vitality. In its depiction of the growing intimacy between the existentially careless boy and the emotionally calcified man, it is tempting to see the film as a reflection of the twelve-year-long relationship between Berger and Visconti. Visconti died two years after the release of *Conversation Piece* (at the age of sixty-nine), leaving Berger, as he expressed it, "a thirty-two-year-old widow."

In 2000 Francesco Vezzoli made a short film called *The Kiss (Let's Play "Dynasty"!)*. The star of the film is Helmut Berger, and he is a mess, bloated and thick-tongued. At last the actor's disturbing nasal voice seems appropriate to the persona. Even before the first word is uttered, *The Kiss* looks like a cautionary tale—a sort of parody of the story of Dorian Gray (a role once played by Berger in his glistening twenties). The film begins with the soundtrack of the television series *Dynasty* blaring and the camera rushing through a fabulously overwrought apartment (filled with an auction-load of Ludwig II of Bavaria's furniture), past tables lined with Vezzoli's framed portrait embroideries, and coming to a sudden stop in front of molten-gold draperies. The awful, tinny *Dallas* theme finishes, the curtains part, and Berger is revealed sitting on a chaise embroidering a portrait of Brad Davis, the star of Rainer Werner Fassbinder's last film, *Querelle* (1982). (Sick with AIDS, Davis committed suicide in 1991.) On the soundtrack, the mindless ditty that tinkles maniacally throughout Fassbinder's sublime apache of artifice plays on and on, with Jeanne Moreau endlessly croaking Oscar Wilde's phrase "each man kills the thing he loves" to a hurdy-gurdy beat. Berger tosses his needlepoint aside and rises. (A flickering television plays a scene from *Dynasty*.) He enters a secret room through a bookcase (an important, parallel destination for the Professor's encounters with sex and politics in *Conversation Piece*), and there encounters Vezzoli, sitting lightly draped with a piece of rope. Berger tosses the rope aside. (Why? Ten years earlier Berger, as a Vatican accountant, was found hanging from a bridge in *The Godfather: Part III*. Perhaps.) He then proceeds to a sofa, picks up a script, and begins to read lines spoken by Alexis Carrington (Joan Collins) in *Dynasty*. "I'm the bitch!" he happily announces. (Stop! Why is he the bitch? Oh, wait, he played a character on *Dynasty* for nine episodes in 1983–84. Yeah, that's the connection.) Vezzoli responds as Steven Carrington, Alexis's gay son (or occasionally gay son, depending on the tolerance of the series's advertisers). You notice that both performers are wearing Kardashian jackets, horrible and totally in the spirit of Collins's haute, louche, big-shouldered *Dynasty* costumes. They quarrel, and, prodded by Alexis/Helmut, Steven/Francesco responds, "My virginity is gone." Enraged, Berger has his one Friedrich/Ludwig/Konrad moment and brays, "Gone? Like mine? Where? In the ear, in the nose?" (A flickering television plays a scene from *Dynasty*.) Berger tears up the script, careens into another room, and, after turning off a third television playing *Dynasty*, sinks into a couch and stares desolately at the camera. (The end.)

AN ANXIETY

After all is said and done, I hope Berger is okay with Vezzoli's movie. He has been in tons of them, a lot of which are really bad (or fabulously awful, like my favorite, *Salon Kitty* of 1976, directed by Tinto Brass). Based on his bio, it appears that Berger stopped making qualitative choices a while back, but he is definitely a workhorse and, though the roles seem to be slowly drying up, he is still getting parts. I wonder whom he sees in the mirror. There must be mornings when he sees the golden boy in Vittorio De Sica's *The Garden of the Finzi-Continis* (*Il giardino dei Finzi Contini*, 1970) or Elizabeth Taylor's lover in director Larry Peerce's *Ash Wednesday* (1973) or Glenda Jackson's more convincing lover in Joseph Losey's *The Romantic Englishwoman* (1975). He was a gorgeous man, and that has all melted away into wrinkles and jowls. (Through the cruelty of art, he had a preview of aging courtesy of the prosthetics he wore at the end of *Ludwig*.) Perhaps great beauties assess their looks rigorously and adapt like tennis pros who no longer compete. He always seemed to enjoy his looks, using them like some actors use their hands. I would like to think that his curiosity and need to perform brought him into Vezzoli's universe of fandom, and I hope that he had fun doing the gig and that the soulful stare at the film's end was just him acting.

EARLY WORK

A big part of the charm of Vezzoli's early films is how many personal passions he crammed into them. They are like suitcases filled to bursting. You can feel his wild enthusiasm to celebrate everything that he embraced. The films often have an amateurish quality (even though the first three were shot by known directors), because they are meant to appear quite conventional; they don't really want to look all that different from what they reference. There is a lot of hammy acting and playing dress-up, but with what appears to be real sincerity. These are not "art" films, because they glory in what they reference—they want to be what they reference. They are the creations of an outrageous fan, and they work best when the maker's sincerity overwhelms the irony, resulting in lovely acts of innocence.

Francesco Vezzoli, ed. Cristiana Perrella (New York: Rizzoli International, 2016), 39–40.

Paul Thek: Real Misunderstanding

1 Ingmar Bergman, *Four Screenplays of Ingmar Bergman* (New York: Simon and Schuster, 1960), xxii.

2 H. L. Mencken, *The Vintage Mencken, Gathered by Alistair Cooke* (New York: Vintage Books, 1955), 146.

3 Antonin Artaud, *The Theater and Its Double* (New York: Grove Press, 1958), 98.

4 *Vintage Mencken*, 2.

5 Suzanne Delehanty, *Paul Thek/Processions* (Philadelphia: Institute of Contemporary Art, University of Pennsylvania, 1977), 3. This catalogue for Thek's only environmental installation in the United States includes the most extensive documentation of the artist's work available. Its meticulous chronology and Ms. Delehanty's insightful analysis of Thek's art were most helpful in the preparation of this article.

6 Robert Pincus-Witten, "Thek's Tomb … Absolute Fetishism," *Artforum* 6, no. 3 (November 1967): 24.

7 Robert Pincus-Witten, "Paul Thek, Stable Gallery," *Artforum* 7, no. 9 (May 1969): 64.

8 Other long-term Thek collaborators include: Robert Beuys, Michele Collison, Wahundra Fitzgerald, Edwin Klein, Lily Malloch, Charles Shuts, and Ildiko Van Viczian.

Sugar and Vice and …
Balthus: A Retrospective

1 Sabine Rewald, *Balthus* (New York: Metropolitan Museum of Art; Harry N. Abrams, 1984), 66.

2 Mary Hassal writing to Aaron Burr, quoted in Hubert Cole, *Christophe: King of Haiti* (New York: Viking Press, 1967), 110.

3 Giovanni Carandente, *Balthus: Drawings and Watercolors* (Boston: New York Graphic Society, 1983), 14.

4 Larry Clark, *Teenage Lust* (New York: self-published, 1984).

5 *Lautréamont's Maldoror*, trans. Alexis Lykiard (New York: Thomas Y. Crowell, 1973), 2.

Down the Airshaft

1 Edith Wharton and Ogden Codman Jr., *The Decoration of Houses* (New York: W. W. Norton, 1978), 17.

2 Henry James, *Roderick Hudson* (Harmondsworth, England: Penguin Classics, 1986), 226.

3 John Gruen, "Paean to Glamour," *Architectural Digest*, September 1987, 103.

4 Christopher Gibbs, "Bennison Style," *House & Garden*, April 1987, 173.

5 Martin Filler, "Le Corbusier's True Colors," *House & Garden*, May 1987, 226.

6 Wharton and Codman, *The Decoration of Houses*, 111.

7 Ibid., 198.

8 Unattributed, "… into the garden," *HG*, June 1988, 108.

9 Ayn Rand, from the screenplay of *The Fountainhead* (1949), directed by King Vidor, produced by Warner Bros., starring Gary Cooper and Patricia Neal.

The Dog and the Suicide

1 Joel E. Siegel, *Val Lewton: The Reality of Terror* (New York: Viking Press, 1973), 113.

2 Manny Farber, *Negative Space* (New York: Praeger, 1971), 49.

3 Lloyd Goodrich, *Albert P. Ryder* (New York: George Braziller, 1959), 13.

4 Siegel, *Reality of Terror*, 126.

Slow. Fade.

1 See pages 15–30 in this volume.

Notes on Digestion and Film:
Matthew Barney

1 Walter Pater, *The Renaissance* (1869; New York: New American Library, 1959), 32.

2 Ibid.

Shadowland

1 Pat Barker, *Regeneration* (New York: Penguin Books, 1993), 184.

2 Claire de Duras, *Ourika*, trans. John Fowles (New York: Modern Language Association of America, 1994), 46.

3 Ibid., 39.

4 Cited in C.L.R. James, *The Black Jacobins: Toussaint L'Ouverture and the San Domingo Revolution* (New York: Random House, 1963), 336.

5 Ibid., 364.

6 Ibid., 334.

7 Cited in Stephen E. Ambrose, *Undaunted Courage: Meriwether Lewis, Thomas Jefferson, and the Opening of the American West* (New York: Simon & Schuster, 1996), 35.

8 Duras, *Ourika*, 23.

9 Ambrose, *Undaunted Courage*, 449.

10 Ibid.

11 Charles Robert Maturin, *Melmoth the Wanderer* (Lincoln: University of Nebraska Press, 1961), 225.

12 Ibid., 123.

13 Cited in Georges Bataille, *Erotism: Death & Sensuality*, trans. Mary Dalwood (San Francisco: City Lights Bookstore, 1986), 194.

14 Ibid., 179.

15 Marquis de Sade, quoted by William F. Axton, "Introduction," in Maturin, *Melmoth the Wanderer*, 15.

16 Bataille, *Erotism*, 174.

17 Ibid., 196.

18 M.L. Rosenthal and A.J.M. Smith, *Exploring Poetry* (New York: Macmillan, 1955), 622.

Curzio Malaparte: Casa Malaparte, 1938

1 Quoted in Marida Talamona, *Casa Malaparte* (New York: Princeton Architectural Press, 1992), 61–62.

2 Ibid., 52.

Douglas Gordon: *24 Hour Psycho*

1 François Truffaut, *Hitchcock* (New York: Simon & Schuster, 1984), 282. First published as: Truffaut, *Le cinéma selon Hitchcock* (Paris: R. Laffont, 1963), trans. François Truffaut.

2 "Hello, It's Me: Douglas Gordon Interviewed by Thomas Lawson," *Frieze*, no. 14 (April 1993): 17.

3 Truffaut, *Hitchcock*, 277.

The Law of Indirections: Robert Gober

1 Walt Whitman, "Laws for Creations," in *The Complete Poems*, ed. Francis Murphy (London: Penguin Books, 1986), 407.

2 Robert Gober, conversation with author, January 23, 1997.

3 Whitman, "My Picture-Gallery," in *Complete Poems*, 421.

4 Edgar Allan Poe, "The Fall of the House of Usher," in *Tales of Mystery and Imagination* (New York: Brentano's, n.d.), 131.

5 Whitman, "Assurances," in *Complete Poems*, 461.

6 Whitman, "Says," in *Complete Poems*, 612.

7 *The Lost Boys* (1987), directed by Joel Schumacher.

8 In February 1990 Gober collaborated on an installation with artist Sherrie Levine at the Hirshhorn Museum in Washington, DC, as part of a larger exhibition titled *Culture and Commentary: An Eighties Perspective*, curated by Kathy Halbreich. The installation included Gober's wallpaper of repeating patterns of a sleeping white man and a lynched black man, which generated responses from some museum employees, who found the imagery offensive and racist. A year later Gober returned to the Hirshhorn to have a conversation about the responses to the work with Teresia Bush, an education officer at the museum, and Ned Rifkin, the chief curator of exhibitions. See "Hanging Man/Sleeping Man: A Conversation between Teresia Bush, Robert Gober, and Ned Rifkin," *Parkett*, no. 27 (March 1991): 90–97.

9 Whitman, "Years of the Modern," in *Complete Poems*, 499.

10 *Robert Gober and Kevin Larmon: An Installation*, Gallery Nature Morte, New York, March 1–28, 1986; *Robert Gober, Nancy Shaver, Alan Turner, Meg Webster*, organized by Robert Gober, Cable Gallery, New York, September 18–October 11, 1986; *Robert Gober and Christopher Wool*, 303 Gallery, New York, April 14–May 8, 1988.

11 Robert Gober, interview with author, in *Robert Gober: Sculpture + Drawing* (Minneapolis: Walker Art Center, 1999), 122; reprinted in the present volume, pages 187–230.

12 Ibid., 123.

13 Kate Chopin, "Désirée's Baby," in *The Awakening and Selected Stories*, ed. Sandra M. Gilbert (New York: Penguin Books, 1984), 194.

14 Gober, interview with author, in *Robert Gober: Sculpture + Drawing*, 124.

15 Poe, "The Masque of the Red Death," in *Tales of Mystery and Imagination*, 268.

16 Gober, interview with author, in *Robert Gober: Sculpture + Drawing*, 134.

17 Whitman, "I Sing the Body Electric," in *Complete Poems*, 135.

18 Linda Nochlin, *The Body in Pieces: The Fragment as a Metaphor of Modernity* (New York: Thames and Hudson, 1994), 38.

19 Gober, interview with author, in *Robert Gober: Sculpture + Drawing*, 126.

20 M.L. Rosenthal and A.J.M. Smith, *Exploring Poetry* (New York: Macmillan, 1959), 668.

21 Whitman, "I Sing the Body Electric," 128.

22 Joan Simon, "Robert Gober and the Extra Ordinary," in *Robert Gober* (Paris: Galerie nationale du Jeu de Paume; Madrid: Museo Nacional Centro de Arte Reina Sofía, 1991), 26.

23 Gober, interview with author, in *Robert Gober: Sculpture + Drawing*, 125.

24 Whitman, "I Sing the Body Electric," 128.

25 Simon, "Robert Gober and the Extra Ordinary," 11.

26 *Parkett*, no. 27 (March 1991).

27 Gober, interview with author, in *Robert Gober: Sculpture + Drawing*, 128.

28 Jean-Paul Sartre, *No Exit and Three Other Plays* (New York: Vintage Books, 1949), 42.

29 Rosenthal and Smith, *Exploring Poetry*, 197.

30 Whitman, "Poets to Come," in *Complete Poems*, 48.

31 *Seven Masterpieces of Gothic Horror*, ed. Robert Donald Spector (New York: Bantam Books, 1963), 2.

32 Ibid., 102.

33 Whitman, "I Sing the Body Electric," 131.

34 Gober, interview with author, in *Robert Gober: Sculpture + Drawing*, 134.

35 Whitman, "Assurances," in *Complete Poems*, 461.

Interview:
Richard Flood and Robert Gober

1 In 1995, for the Carnegie International in Pittsburgh, Gober proposed the idea of creating a work with existing dioramas at the Carnegie Museum of Natural History. Because the dioramas were treated and sealed with arsenic and other chemicals used for preservation, the project was declined by the museum's curators and not realized.

2 Joyce Carol Oates, *Heat*, design and illustrations by Robert Gober (New York: Library Fellows of the Whitney Museum of American Art, 1989).

3 See "The Law of Indirections" in this volume (note 8) for a discussion about the responses generated by the hanging man/sleeping man imagery.

4 *Cindy Sherman*, Metro Pictures, New York, January 6–27, 1990; *Jenny Holzer*, Solomon R. Guggenheim Museum, New York, December 12, 1989–February 25, 1990.

5 "A German student writing his doctoral thesis on my work had a musician play and record the painted music. But it was not really musical, as I took excerpts from the found music and arranged them for visual effect. Musically, it's a bit of garbage." Robert Gober, conversation with author, 1998.

6 The culvert, a pipe typically used for diverting natural streams of water, appeared three-dimensionally for the first time in Gober's oeuvre in three sculptures for the installation at the Museum für Gegenwartskunst, Basel, in 1995: *Chair with Pipe*, 1994–95; *Untitled*, 1994–95 (tissue box); and *Lard Box*, 1994–95. It appeared again two years later at the Museum of Contemporary Art in Los Angeles, where the pipe punctures the statue of the Virgin Mary.

7 Printed Matter is a not-for-profit showcase for artist's books in Manhattan.

8 Robert Gober and Daphne Fitzpatrick, an artist who assisted him in every aspect of both the Dia and MOCA installations.

9 *Robert Gober*, Museum für Gegenwartskunst, Basel, October 27, 1995–April 28, 1996.

10 In 1960 Jasper Johns made *Painted Bronze*, a sculpture of two Ballantine ale cans cast in bronze.

11 The Museum für Gegenwartskunst is located near the Rhine River. A stream coursing to the Rhine is visible from the museum and, at one point, runs beneath it.

12 Richard Prince silkscreened a variety of bait-and-switch jokes. The best known is: A traveling salesman's car broke down one evening on a lonely road and he asked at the only farmhouse in sight, "Can you put me up for the night?" "I reckon I can," said the farmer, "but you'll have to share a room with my young son." "How do you like that," gasped the salesman. "I'm in the wrong joke."

13 *Untitled*, 1980.

14 *Burnt House*, 1980.

15 In *Untitled*, 1993–94 (bronze, wood, brick, aluminum, beeswax, human hair, chrome, pump, water; 56 × 37½ × 34 in.), a male torso lies at the bottom of a well that is capped by a storm drain.

16 While working on the MOCA installation, Gober rented a second studio at 520 West Twenty-First Street in New York City to accommodate the larger scale of the works.

17 *Untitled*, 1994–95; wood, wax, brick, plaster, plastic, leather, iron, charcoal, cotton socks, electric light, motor, 31 × 31 × 30½ in. overall (children's leg limbs gathered in a fireplace).

18 Donald Moffett, artist and partner in the design firm Bureau.

19 Christian Scheidemann is an art conservator in Hamburg.

20 *Untitled*, 1993–94; wood, vinyl, acrylic paint, 80 × 52½ × 24 in.

21 *Last Tango in Paris* (1973), directed by Bernardo Bertolucci. The film's credits are interspersed with Francis Bacon paintings.

22 "These are recollections from early childhood. I haven't verified them or spoken to anyone from that family since I was a child." Robert Gober, in a note to the author, 1998.

23 Zacchini v Scripps-Howard Broadcasting Co., 76–577, Ohio Supreme Court, argued April 25, 1977, decided June 28, 1977.

24 Renny Gleeson was Gober's studio assistant from October 1995 to February 1997.

25 "The sewer drain was also a stand-in for what might be seen as the lower parts of humanity and Mary standing upon it corresponds to my understanding of Jesus's teaching and life. His connection and devotion to the rejected and disenfranchised." Robert Gober, correspondence with author, 1998.

26 Paul Schimmel, chief curator, the Museum of Contemporary Art, Los Angeles.

27 Andres Serrano's *Piss Christ* (1987), a Cibachrome photograph of a plastic crucifix placed in a tank filled with urine, became the focus of a controversy fueled by Senators Jesse Helms and Alphonse M. D'Amato, who condemned Serrano's works as well as Robert Mapplethorpe's as "perverted and deviant." Senators Helms and D'Amato led a public and much-publicized campaign threatening to cancel government funding for arts organizations, including the National Endowment for the Arts (NEA). Ultimately, the NEA received a symbolic cut of $45,000 in operating funds.

28 Jennifer Tipton is a theatrical lighting designer who has designed lighting for works by such choreographers as Jerome Robbins, Mikhail Baryshnikov, Paul Taylor, and Twyla Tharp, and theater companies such as the Wooster Group.

29 *Untitled*, 1991; photolithograph on newsprint with hand-torn edges, printed on both sides and folded three times and hand-colored with coffee by artist; 22⅛ × 13⅞ in.; 75 unique pieces, signed; printed by Maurice Sanchez and Joe Petruzzelli, Derrière L'Etoile Studio, New York. Gober's edition for *Parkett*, no. 27 (March 1991) is a replica of a page from the Metropolitan section of the *New York Times* dated October 4, 1960, complete with wedding announcements, the national weather report, and an article on the drowning death of a six-year-old boy named Robert Gober (the artist was six in 1960) in Wallingford, Connecticut.

30 Roberta Smith, "Religion That's in the Details," *New York Times*, November 18, 1997.

31 Metro Pictures is the gallery that exhibited artists such as Troy Brauntuch, Jack Goldstein, Louise Lawler, Tom Lawson, Sherrie Levine, Richard Prince, and Cindy Sherman.

The Land of the Everlasting Hills
1 David Lowe, *Lost Chicago* (Boston: Houghton Mifflin, 1975), 153.
2 Maurice Maeterlinck, *The Life of the Bee*, trans. Alfred Sutro (New York: Dodd, Mead, 1910), 305, 316, 319.

Gentlemen Callers:
Alice Neel and the Art World
1 Patricia Hills, *Alice Neel* (New York: Harry N. Abrams, 1983), 101.
2 Ibid., 103.
3 See illustrations in Russell Ferguson, *In Memory of My Feelings: Frank O'Hara and American Art* (Los Angeles: Museum of Contemporary Art; Berkeley: University of California Press, 1999), 19–21, 78, 84, 120–21.
4 Hills, *Alice Neel*, 103.
5 Ibid.
6 Ibid.
7 Judith Higgins, "Alice Neel and the Human Comedy," *Art News* 83, no. 8 (October 1984): 77.
8 Hubert Crehan, "Introducing the Portraits of Alice Neel," *Art News* 91, no. 6 (October 1962): 44–47, 68.
9 Hills, *Alice Neel*, 112.
10 David C. Berliner, "Women Artists Today: How Are They Doing Vis-à-Vis the Men," *Cosmopolitan*, October 1973, 219; quoted in Pamela Allara, *Pictures of People: Alice Neel's American Portrait Gallery* (Hanover, NH: Brandeis University Press, 1998), 179.
11 Hills, *Alice Neel*, 138.
12 Barbara Gladstone, conversation with the author; the story was related to her by Robert Mapplethorpe.
13 Hills, *Alice Neel*, 152.
14 Ibid., 142.

Introduction: Zero to Infinity
Unless otherwise noted, all of the quotations that appear in the endnotes are from conversations that took place in 1997.
1 Germano Celant, *Arte Povera/Art Povera* (Milan: Electa, 1985), 31.
2 Francesco Masnata of Galleria La Bertesca in Genoa was the first of the dealers to collide with the historical snowball of Arte Povera. What should be noted is that, while Turin and Rome were the undeniable oases of Arte Povera, Genoa (and, to a lesser degree, Bologna) was also crucial. Genoa was (and remains) Celant's city, and the machinery was in place to initiate his entrepreneurial vision at La Bertesca. Genoa was also so far from the cultural centers that there was nothing to lose through artistic experimentation. It would be an unlikely accident if Emilio Prini—the most combatively anti-materialization, instinctively conceptual artist associated with Arte Povera—was not Genovese. Masnata remarked that "Prini was born with Arte Povera and didn't exist before it." It is an indication of the looseness of the initial situation that, after Masnata introduced Prini to Celant (while the latter was preparing *Arte povera e IM Spazio*), Prini proposed creating "a perimeter of light and sound," and Celant agreed. Writing on the Genovese situation versus that in Turin, Harald Szeemann noted that Prini (as well as Paolo Icaro) benefited because "they know that they are alone" (*Op losse schroeven: Situaties an cryptostructuren* [Amsterdam: Stedelijk Museum, 1969], unpaginated).
3 Germano Celant, "Arte Povera: Appunti per una guerriglia," *Flash Art*, no. 5 (November–December 1967): 3; English translation by Paul Blanchard, in Celant, *Arte Povera/Art Povera*, 35–37; reprinted in *Arte Povera*, ed. Carolyn Christov-Bakargiev (London: Phaidon, 1999), 194.
4 While preparing for this exhibition, we conducted a series of informal interviews with the artists whose work was most consistently exhibited within the context of Arte Povera. One of the questions we

asked each of them concerned the phrase *Arte Povera*: Should it be used in the title of the exhibition we were proposing? The question was posed to twelve artists, and each responded (often with qualifications) that, yes, Arte Povera was essential to the exhibition's title. The artists' unanimity on this point should not be seen as anything more (or less) than a willingness to continue their public association with the phrase. No larger generalization is warranted, but it is an important point that, after more than thirty years, the artists have not dismissed their collective and individual association with Arte Povera.

5 Conversations with the dealers revealed extremely varied impulses and goals. We talked with those who had been there at the very beginning: Tomaso Liverani (La Salita), Gian Enzo Sperone, Fabio Sargentini (L'Attico), and Francesco Masnata (La Bertesca). With the exception of Liverani, all of the dealers were from the same generation as the artists they exhibited. Liverani exhibited the work of Paolini very early and that of Fabro later. Sitting blanketed in his apartment, deep into his retirement, Liverani (who died in 2000) seemed a grandfatherly representative of another time. When asked what he thought of Arte Povera, he chuckled and said, "I thought it was a joke." Yet, in the very conservative (then, as now) art market of Rome, Liverani had made daring choices that raise some fascinating, perhaps unanswerable questions about issues such as the influence of the Dionysian Alberto Burri and the Apollonian Francesco Lo Savio on the generation that followed them.

More provocative, for outsiders, was the Richard Serra question. Serra—who was in Italy while his then-wife, Nancy Graves, studied taxidermy—was referred to in an intentionally provocative, wildly anachronistic exhibition (with, most notoriously, living animals as sculptural materials) at Galleria La Salita in 1966. Who had seen it and who had been changed by it was a sotto voce query running through a number of the inevitably thankless attribution discussions that were part of the planning of the exhibition. (More interesting to Liverani was the notion that Serra had himself been changed after seeing the work of Lo Savio, which is, in the end, a more delicately nuanced matter.)

From his gallery in Turin, Sperone was the first of the dealers to get involved in an international context, a move that he attributes to Pistoletto, who urged him to visit the gallery of Ileana Sonnabend in Paris. Sonnabend went on to become an important client of the Italian artists represented by Sperone as well as a link to other dealers and curators outside Italy. Sperone also noted that when Gilardi returned to Turin after his first visit to the United States in 1967, he brought back a list of artists he thought Sperone should show (Serra, Bruce Nauman, and Keith Sonnier, among others). That year Sperone moved his endeavors into an enormous commercial space, which provided him with "a new way of thinking about how to exhibit work." In Rome, a similar instinct about a new kind of gallery space prompted Fabio Sargentini to physically reinvent his Galleria L'Attico by moving into an underground garage just before Christmas 1968. The formal opening of the radicalized L'Attico took place in January 1969, when Kounellis stabled twelve horses there in a legendary conflation of painting, sculpture, and installation. The following month, Mario Merz drove his Renault from Turin to Rome and into L'Attico (and art history), where the car became another work on the checklist of his exhibition. That year Sargentini also began an aggressively interdisciplinary program when, after his first trip to New York, his friend the choreographer Simone Forti introduced him to Trisha Brown, Steve Paxton, La Monte Young and Marian Zazeela, Terry Riley, and Yvonne Rainer. Sargentini invited them to perform at L'Attico, which they all did in June 1969. Clearly, as Celant was engineering the passage of Italian artists into the international arena, Sargentini was bringing the international arena to Rome.

6 In conversation, especially with those artists based in Turin, there was more than a degree of agreement on what they remembered seeing, what seemed new. It wasn't much: Francis Bacon, Roy Lichtenstein, the Gutai group. The peers they met from abroad, however (Mel Bochner, Jan Dibbets, Sol LeWitt, Richard Long, and Nauman, among many others), summon up much less touristic reminiscences. One begins to understand that, while painting moved a bit to the left and a bit to the right during the 1960s, it was still looking for the inevitable nail in the wall. Sculpture, however, became something entirely new. Surely its makers acknowledged Duchamp, Klein, and Manzoni, but not with nostalgia; their influence was too recent to either mourn or canonize (or demonize).

7 It should be mentioned that the Turinese exhibition did not include Ceroli, Gilardi, Marisa Merz, or Piacentino.

8 Celant, *Arte Povera/Art Povera*, 26.

9 In Christov-Bakargiev, *Arte Povera*, 232.

10 *The Knot: Arte Povera at P.S. 1: Giovanni Anselmo, Alighiero Boetti, Pier Paolo Calzolari, Luciano Fabro, Jannis Kounellis, Mario Merz, Giulio Paolini, Pino Pascali, Giuseppe Penone, Michelangelo Pistoletto, and Gilberto Zorio* (Long Island City, NY: P.S. 1, Institute for Art and Urban Resources; Turin: Umberto Allemandi, 1985), xi.

11 Charles Harrison, "The Late Sixties in London and Elsewhere," in *1965 to 1972: When Attitudes Became Form* (Cambridge, UK: Kettles Yard Gallery, 1984), 13.

12 See Roland Barthes, *Writing Degree Zero*, trans. Annette Lavers and Colin Smith, preface by Susan Sontag (New York: Hill and Wang, 1968).

13 Carolyn Christov-Bakargiev, "Thrust into the Whirlwind: Italian Art before Arte Povera," in *Zero to Infinity: Arte Povera 1962–1972* (Minneapolis: Walker Art Center; London: Tate Modern, 2001), 21–40. —Ed.

14 Corrina Criticos, "Reading Arte Povera," in *Zero to Infinity*, 67–88. —Ed.

15 Masnata suggested a provocative aesthetic alignment between Marisa Merz and Emilio Prini, Arte Povera's other most cryptic participant. "What she does, she is. She was very similar to Prini in this regard, and it is here that they converge in their work. It's less known but very influential. They are the most difficult to include in the cultural industry of the time." Obviously being from Genoa and being a woman (married to an extremely visible artist) are wildly different demographics, but it is tempting to question if being farthest from the geographic and libidinal centers of production resulted in work that challenged by virtue of its sheer elusiveness. Perhaps looking for an easy answer, we asked Merz, "Were you lonely?" Her answer was infinitely larger and lonelier than our question: "You always feel lonely when you say your name; it limits who you are." That limitation might also be seen to lie at the heart of the artists' conflicted relationship with Arte Povera.

Wool Gathering

1 Gregory Corso, *Long Live Man* (New York: New Directions Books, 1959), 67.

2 Allen Ginsberg, *"Howl" and Other Poems* (San Francisco: City Light Books, The Pocket Poets Series, 1956), 22.

3 Gustave Flaubert, *Bouvard and Pécuchet*, trans. A.J. Krailsheimer (1881; London: Penguin Books, 1976), 143.

4 Gustave Flaubert, *Salammbô*, trans. A.J. Krailsheimer (1862; London: Penguin Books, 1977), 107.

5 Kathy Acker, *Implosion* (New York: Wedge Press, 1983), 20.

6 Richard Hell, "Being Christopher Wool," *Whitewall*, no. 3 (Fall 2006): 91.

7 Dave Hickey, "Christopher Wool: Museum of Contemporary Art, Los Angeles," *Artforum* 37, no. 2 (October 1998): 115.

Both of Him

1 Correspondence from Kim Jones to Susan Swenson, April 25, 2005.

Richard Flood is the director of special projects and curator at large at the New Museum, New York. From 2005 to 2010, he served as chief curator. Prior to that, he was the chief curator at the Walker Art Center, Minneapolis. His exhibitions include, among others, *Sigmar Polke: Illumination*; *Brilliant! New Art from London*; *Zero to Infinity: Arte Povera 1962–1972* (with Frances Morris); *Robert Gober: Sculpture + Drawing*; *Matthew Barney, Cremaster 2: The Drones' Exposition*; *Double Album: Daniel Guzman and Steven Shearer*; and *Rivane Neuenschwander: A Day Like Any Other*. Flood was previously managing editor at *Artforum*; curator at P.S. 1, Long Island City, New York; and, for a decade, director of Barbara Gladstone Gallery, New York. He has taught at the Rhode Island School of Design, The Royal College of Art, the National College of Art and Design in Dublin, and CUNY Hunter College in New York.

Published in 2017 by Ridinghouse
46 Lexington Street
London W1F 0LP
United Kingdom
ridinghouse.co.uk

Distributed in the UK and Europe by
Cornerhouse Publications
c/o Home
2 Tony Wilson Place
Manchester M15 4FN
United Kingdom
cornerhousepublications.org

Distributed in the US by
RAM Publications + Distribution, Inc.
2525 Michigan Avenue, Building A2
Santa Monica, CA 90404
United States
rampub.com

This publication was made possible
by Ivor Braka, Thomas Dane, Dimitris
Daskalopoulos, Barbara Gladstone,
and Shaun Caley Regen.

Special thanks are due to
Thomas Dane, Clare Hallin, Ryan Inouye,
Amelia MacKenzie, Michelle Piranio,
Karsten Schubert, Mark Thomson,
and Philippe Vergne.

British Library Cataloguing-in-
    Publication Data
A full catalogue record of this book is
    available from the British Library.

ISBN 978 1 909932 39 5

Copyedited and proofread by
    Michelle Piranio
Picture research by Sophie Kullmann

Designed by Mark Thomson
Set in Haultin (Fred Smeijers)
Printed in Estonia by Tallinna
    Raamatutrükikoja OÜ

Ridinghouse